ABANDONED CENTRAL INDIANA

HIDDEN TREASURES AND UNWONTED SITES

DAVID HUMPHREY AND
W. EVAN HUMPHREY

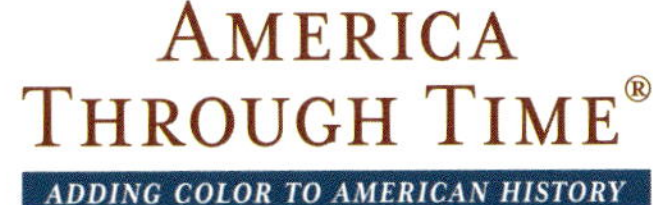

America Through Time is an imprint of Fonthill Media LLC
www.through-time.com
office@through-time.com

Published by Arcadia Publishing by arrangement with Fonthill Media LLC
For all general information, please contact Arcadia Publishing:
Telephone: 843-853-2070
Fax: 843-853-0044
E-mail: sales@arcadiapublishing.com
For customer service and orders:
Toll-Free 1-888-313-2665

www.arcadiapublishing.com

First published 2023

ISBN 978-1-63499-446-0

Typeset in Trade Gothic
Printed and bound in England

CONTENTS

ABOUT THE AUTHORS

David Humphrey is the author of *Abandoned Madison County, Indianapolis: The City Known as Naptown, He Never Complained,* and *Indiana's Lost National Road.* The award-winning photographer is the recipient of the 2005 Kodak Gallery Award for Portrait Photography, 2005 Gordon Parks International Photography Merit Award, and Best of Show at the 1999 Indiana State Fair. He resides in Pendleton, Indiana.

Walker Humphrey is an award-winning musician and composer. Humphrey co-authored *He Never Complained,* his first published book. He earned a Bachelor of Arts in English Literature from Ball State University in 2022 and aspires to write novels. He resides in Muncie, Indiana.

INTRODUCTION

In 1825, Indianapolis became the capital of Indiana and remains the epicenter of the Hoosier state. The Circle City is home to the Indiana Pacers, Indianapolis Colts, and the world-renowned Indianapolis 500. As of July of 2019, Indianapolis had an estimated 14,000 abandoned homes and buildings in and around the city, some of which are historic sites that might possibly face demolition.

Indiana Landmarks is a non-profit organization that helps people restore and repurpose historic buildings. Over the past sixty years, Indiana Landmarks has saved dozens of historic sites in central Indiana including Bush Stadium in Indianapolis, and the Oasis Diner in nearby Plainfield. In 2021, Indiana Landmarks placed the Church of the Holy Cross in Indianapolis on its Ten Most Endangered List. Built in 1921, the church is one of the city's most exquisite examples of Italian Renaissance Revival architecture. But in recent years, the church congregation began to lessen, making it more problematic for parishioners to sustain the building. In 2015, the temple's arched portico collapsed, forcing the Church of the Holy Cross to permanently close.

In the realm of entertainment, The Ritz Theatre has been abandoned for nearly fifty years. The 1,400-seat theatre located near downtown Indianapolis opened in 1927 and went through many stages until it shut down in late 1972. Today, with its marquee gone and boarded-up windows, the Ritz is a stark reminder of early day theatres longing for rejuvenation.

Forty miles northeast of Indianapolis is Muncie, a city that many love to hate. It is easy to compare Muncie to Anderson since both communities once relied on factories to keep the cities alive. During the Gas Boom of the late 1800s, 162 factories came to Anderson, Kokomo, Marion, New Castle, and Muncie—a quintuplet of major factory cities. In the early 1900s, the emergence of the automobile industry brought even more factories to central Indiana, including General Motors in Kokomo and

Anderson, Chrysler in New Castle, and Chevrolet and Borg Warner in Muncie. But by the end of the twentieth century, industrialization came to an abrupt halt in these factory towns. In the 1970s, more than twenty percent of Muncie's population had been employed by factories. That number dropped to a staggering seven percent in the year 2000. The effects of deindustrialization, globalization, and dismantling of unions in the 1980s were felt all across the country, not just in central Indiana. Since 1980, an estimated 7.5 million Americans have lost their jobs due to the closing of factories. Employment in manufacturing is lower now than it has been in many years, and the country continues to drift away from the industry-driven economy it once was.

For decades, the economy in central Indiana was heavily based on the automobile industry. But there were also manufacturing plants in the area not affiliated with automobiles. RCA (Radio Corporation of America) had factories in Indianapolis, Marion, and the bougie college town of Bloomington. During its heyday, the RCA plant in Marion employed over 4,000 people and produced millions of televisions a year. When the plant closed in 2004, the remaining 990 employees were handed pink slips. Bridgestone Firestone was the biggest employer in Hamilton County for over seventy years. Located in the heart of Noblesville, Firestone closed in 2009 and moved its operation to Mexico. Over 300 workers lost their jobs when the air-spring manufacturing plant shut down production. To avoid paying taxes, Firestone removed the walls and ceilings of the factory, leaving only the concrete floors and slabs. However, before relocating, the company buried burned trash, sulfuric acid, rubber, limestone, and cyanide at the 70-acre site. In order for a new business to build on the property, the city of Noblesville had to clean and remove the contamination. This issue is not unique to Noblesville, as many former facility sites remain polluted to this day. The Borg Warner plant in Muncie sits as rubble in a vast lot contained by a barbed wire fence. This empty space cannot currently be used, as it is considered polluted brownfield land. In decades past, the residents of Bloomington in particular struggled with the dumping of PCB toxins originating from the manufacture of electrical capacitors that poisoned farmland and rivers. Some areas of the city are still considered dangerously polluted.

During the mid-1900s, Armour Meats had the dog kids love to bite. Kahns boasted of having the wiener the world awaited. And all kids wanted to be an Oscar Meyer wiener so everyone would be in love with them. Emge Packing Company and Marhoefer Packing Company in Indiana had catchy slogans and jingles to help better sales. "Gimme Emge Gimme Protein!" was heard on Anderson's WHUT Radio and shown as a commercial on WTTV in Indianapolis. The truth of the matter is that Emge lunch meat and hot dogs contained everything but protein. The phrase "mystery meat" comes to mind, and consumers were either ignorant to the meat industry's issues or tried to not think too hard about what was really ground up and packed in those sausage casings. Marhoefer in Muncie was considered one of the top twelve meat packing companies in the nation. Maybe it was the company jingle that made Marhoefer so successful:

I'm a mealtime joy for a girl or boy
The kids all think I'm keener
And the grown-ups too cause I'm good for you
I'm a Marhoefer Happy Wiener!

Unfortunately, not all of the jingles and advertising in the world could save the Emge and Marhoefer packing companies. On March 15, 1978, Marhoefer began phasing out its 800 employees. After several failed attempts to find a buyer, Marhoefer Packing Company filed for bankruptcy on June 2, 1978. Emge Packing Company in Anderson closed in 1990, with over 900 employees losing their jobs. The Emge packing plant was razed in 2017, but the abandoned Marhoefer building still stands, surrounded by a barbed wire fence.

As populations grow older, the number of former schools decreases. Older schools are either demolished, merged, or simply abandoned. Sometimes, this is for safety reasons; the former Pendleton Middle School was torn down due to asbestos in the walls. Other schools are merged or changed from their original designations. In the 1960s, the former Markleville High School and Pendleton High School merged to create the current school: Pendleton Heights High School. Farther north, in Anderson, Highland High School and Anderson High School were similarly consolidated in the early 2010s, using the building of Madison Heights High School. The former Highland High School building is now used as the area's middle school. Perhaps the worst fate of the Anderson high schools belongs to the original Anderson High School building, which burned to the ground on June 25, 1999. Fortunately, its historic Wigwam gymnasium still stands. Similarly, the nearly century-old Muncie Fieldhouse, which, at its construction, had more seats than the biggest universities in the state, is still used by the much more modern Muncie Central High School. In June of 2014, Muncie Southside High School closed, leaving Muncie Central as the city's lone high school. The number of people who must regrettably say that their old schools are gone in one way or another grows by the day. The decline of factories led to a lack of jobs, which led to people moving away, which led to fewer students, which brings us back to the disuse of these both personally and historically significant buildings.

The common link between all these places is that they are now abandoned or otherwise changed from their former selves. Once proud buildings now stand rusty, filthy, and caved-in. Though these sites may be common in day-to-day life, it is rare that they receive the honor of being intentionally photographed, let alone published. This photographic anthology explores some of the derelict locations throughout central Indiana. From movie theaters to farmland, presented here is road trip through forgotten places from a bygone era.

1

I AM A TOWN

Ashes to ashes, dust to dust. This somber saying describes an inevitable existential truth: everything must one day cease and fade away. The same is true, of course, for businesses. In today's highly efficient and corporate-driven world, dominated by sprawling supermarkets and online shopping, it can be easy to forget that at one time, small businesses were practically the only businesses, save for the woefully disappearing department stores. A stroll downtown could take shoppers past a multitude of family-owned businesses: barber shops, grocery stores, pharmacies, service stations, record shops, bookstores, restaurants ... the list goes on.

Sadly, many of these businesses have long since gone under, whether it be competition from corporations, nobody willing to take the reins, or simply providing an obsolete service. As the world started moving faster and faster, there was no need for businesses that could not offer their products as quickly, cheaply, or efficiently as their rapidly growing corporate competitors. While the businesses themselves are long gone, many buildings remain. With boarded-up windows, unkempt facades, and sun-bleached signs with decades of peeling paint, these buildings serve as a reminder of the small-town America that once was.

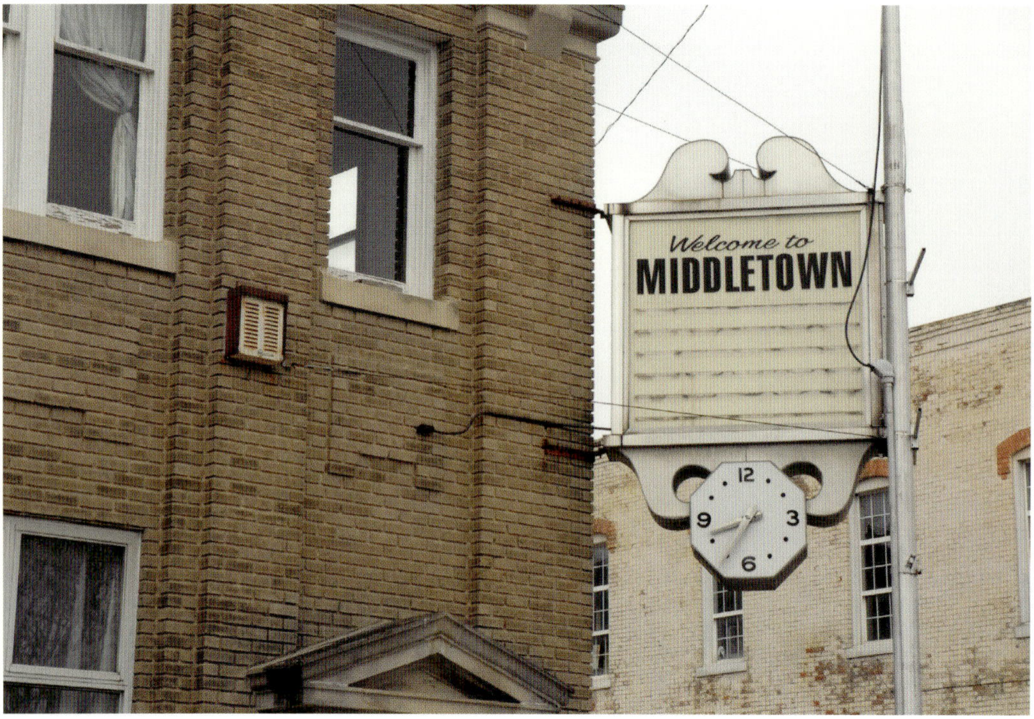

A clock suspended in time hangs on the exterior wall of a closed business in downtown Middletown.

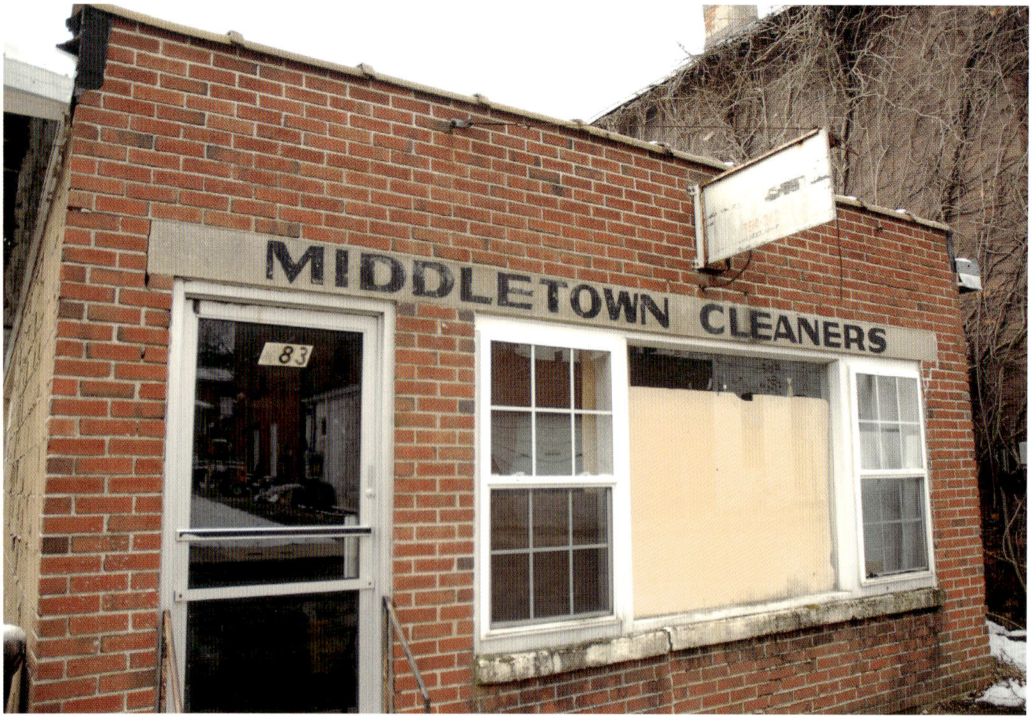

This vacated building once housed the Middletown Cleaners on Locust Street.

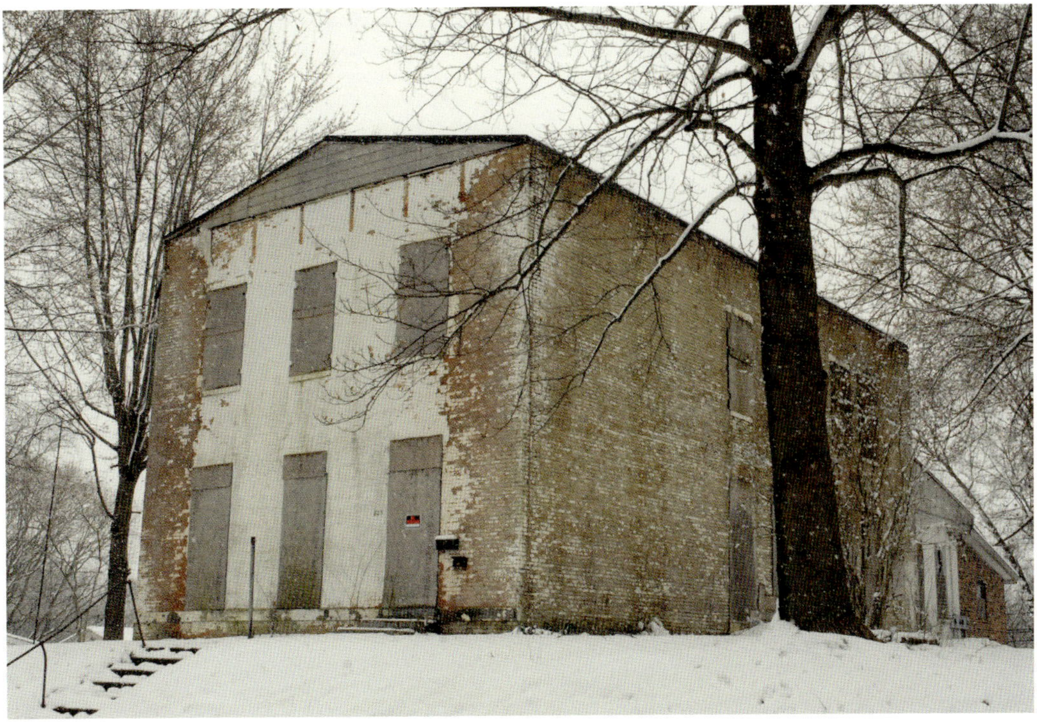

An abandoned home sits on a snow-covered hillside in Middletown.

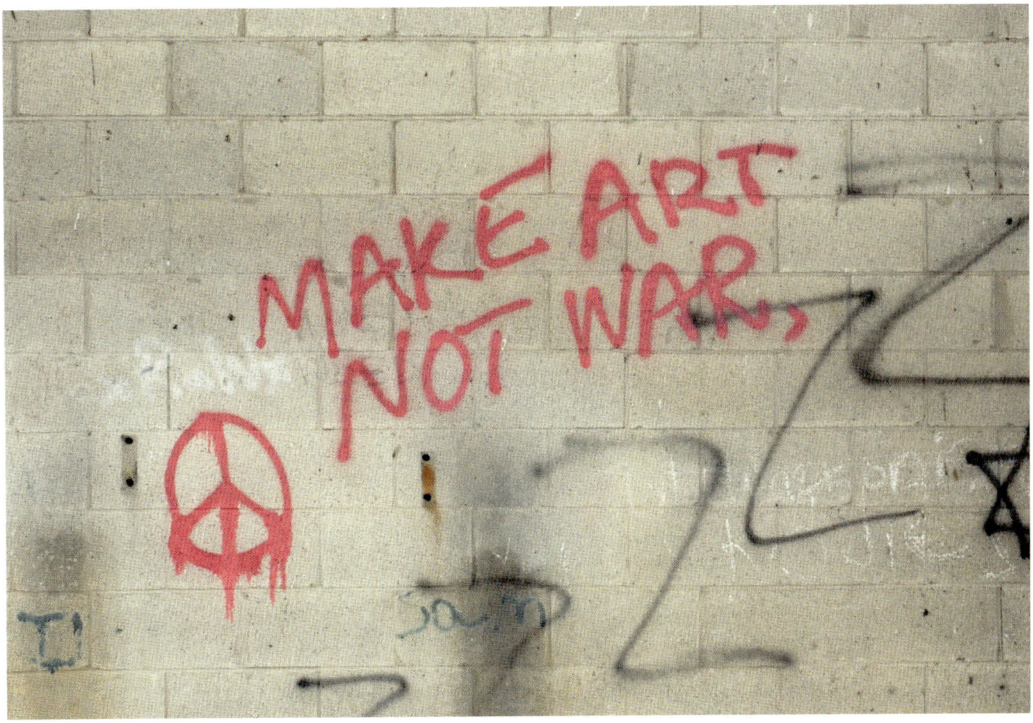

A closed car wash in Middletown allows graffiti artists to express themselves.

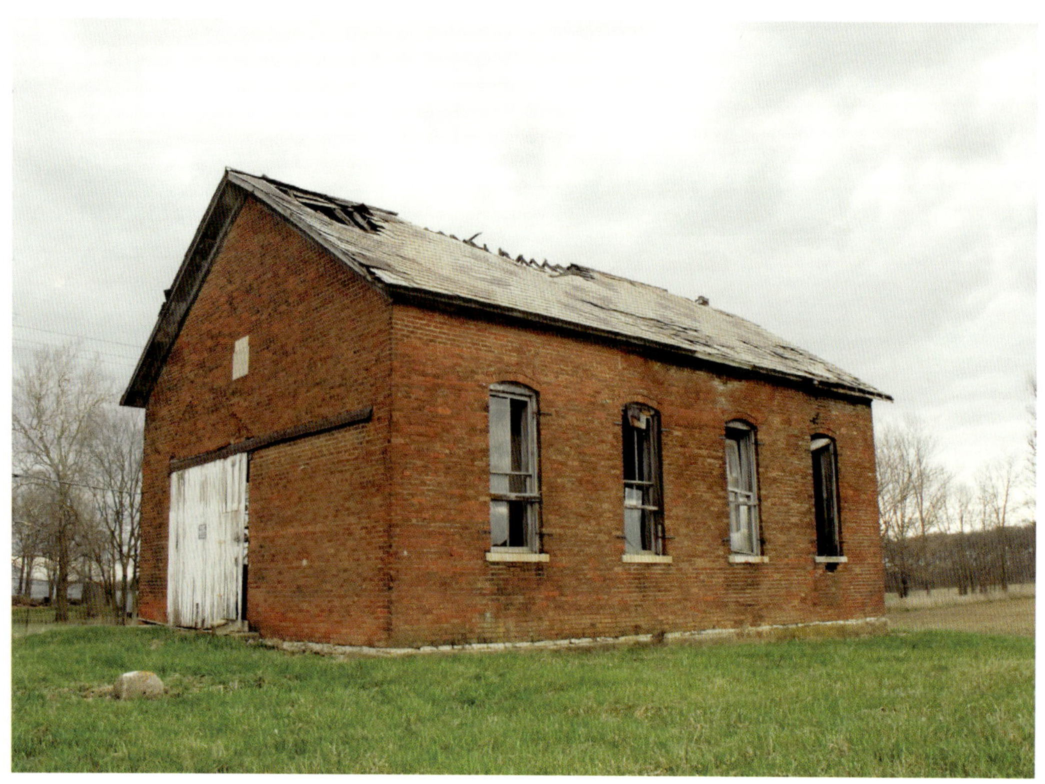

On the outskirts of Middletown is the old District No. 5 School House. The structure was built by A. B. Hopper in 1883.

Opposite: This grain elevator in Farmland has been empty and not used by local farmers for many years.

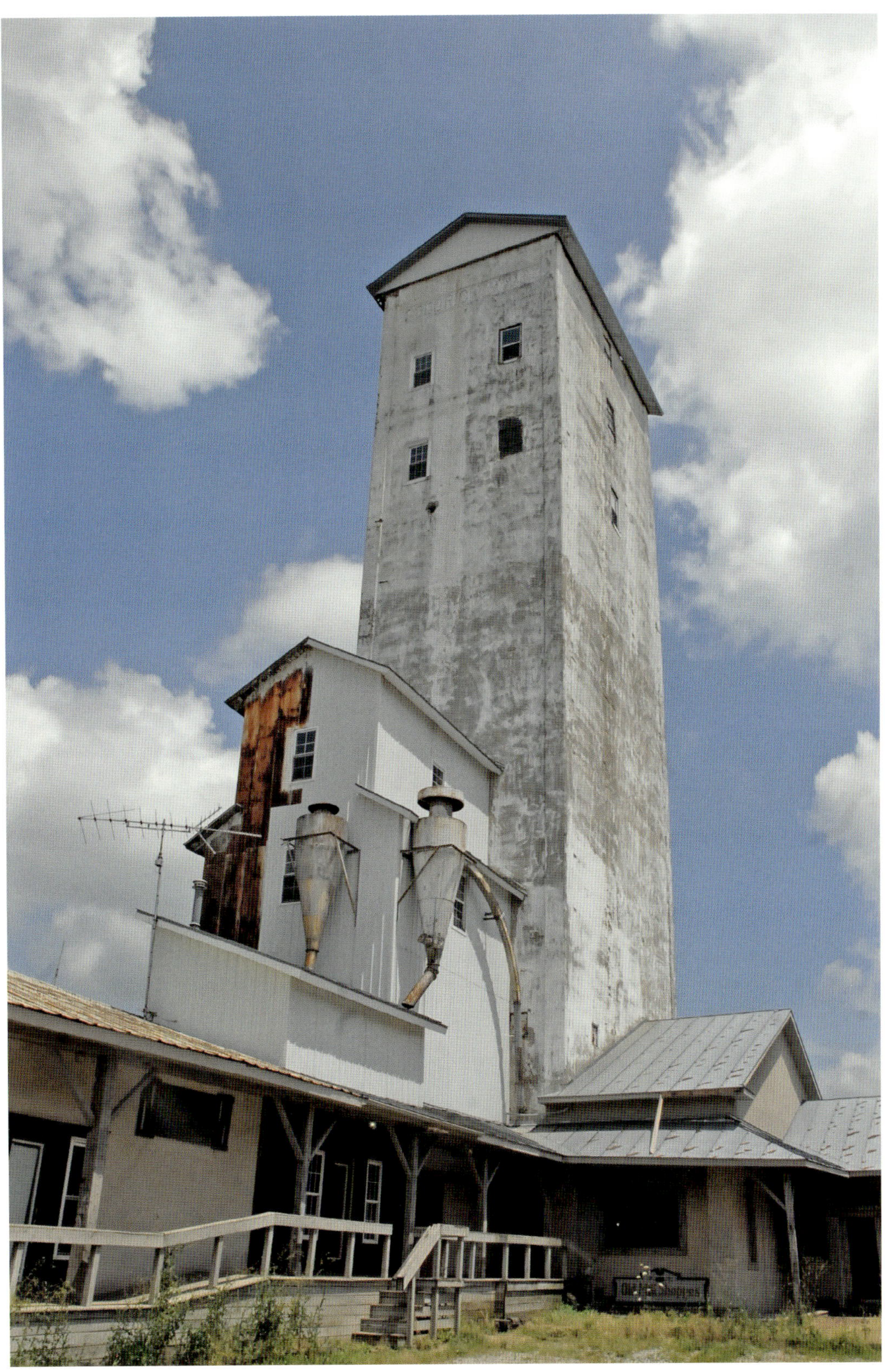

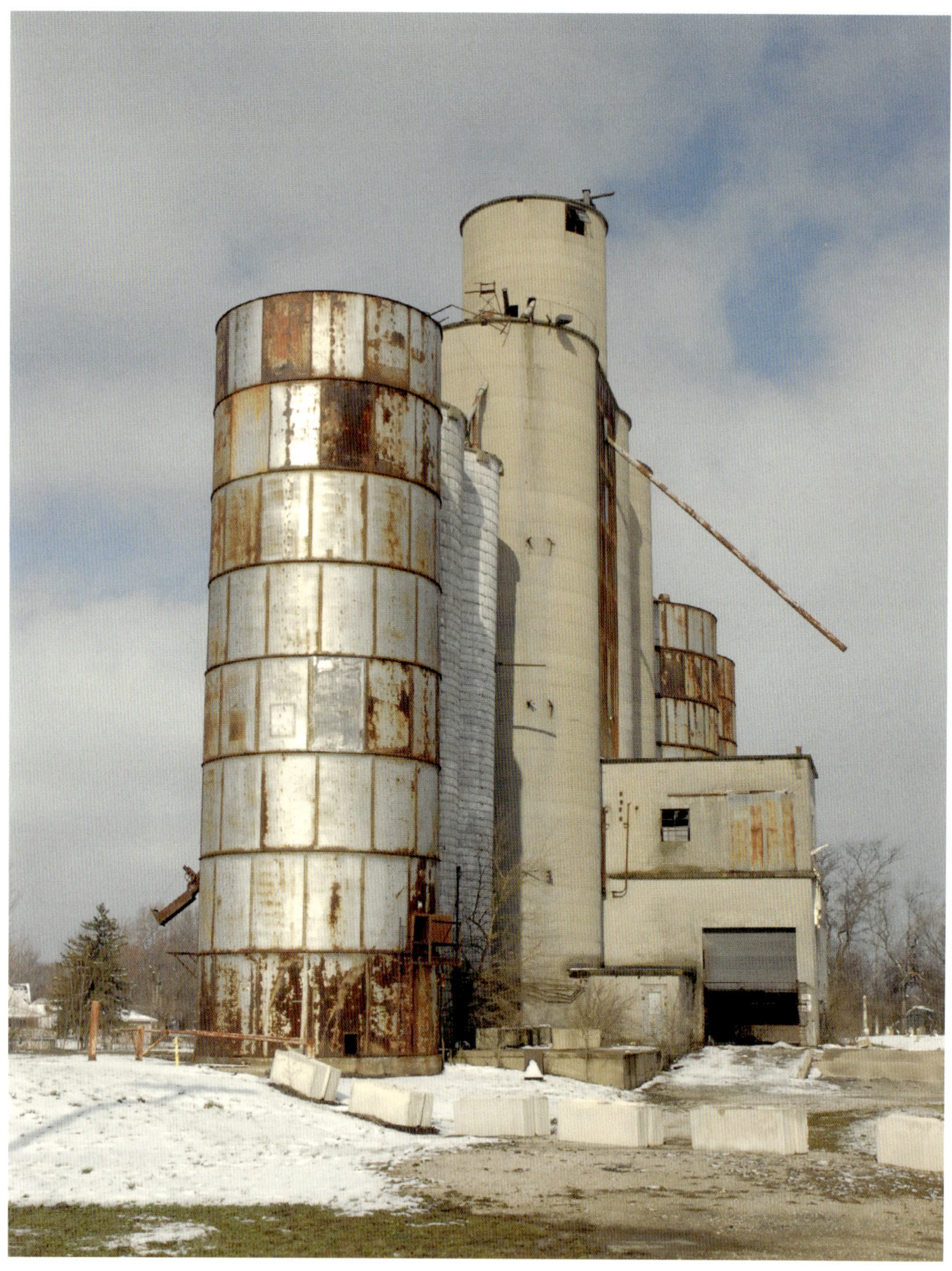

Situated off US 36 in Sulphur Springs is this abandoned grain elevator and silo. There are roughly 300 grain elevators still in operation in Indiana, but they are quickly disappearing from the landscape.

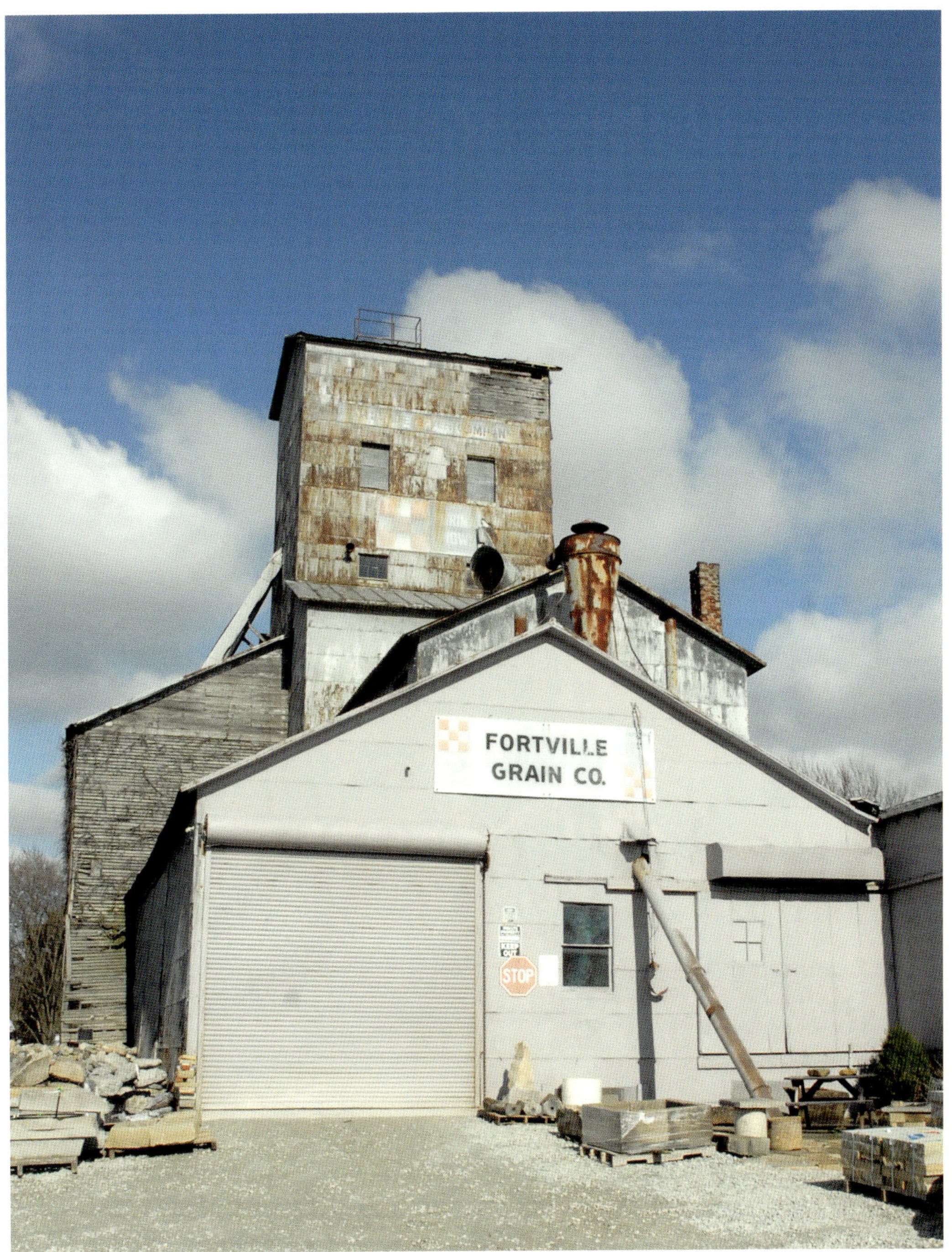

In downtown Fortville is this grain elevator once owned and operated by the Fortville Grain Company. Watercolor artist Cathleen Huffman included a painting of the Fortville grain elevator in her Bicentennial Legacy Project.

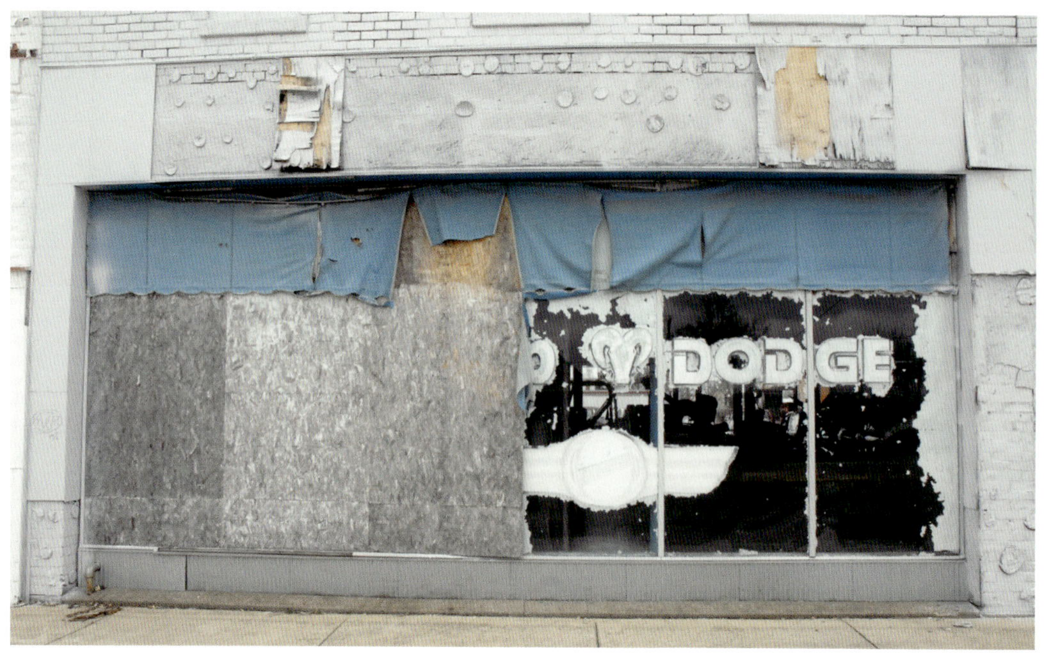

Boarded-up building in Farmland that once was a Dodge automobile dealership.

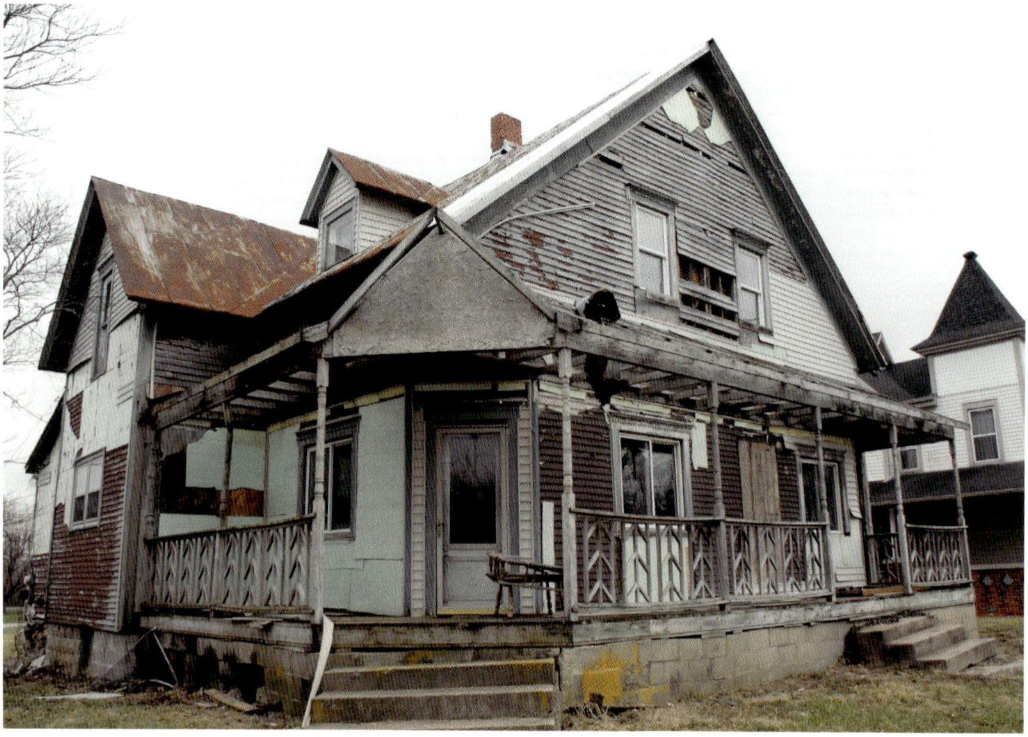

Vacated properties in downtown Farmland are unusual to find in the small Randolph County town. Farmland was listed on the National Register of Historic Places in 1994. One of the more popular sites in Farmland is the Chocolate Moose, a throwback to old soda fountain shops.

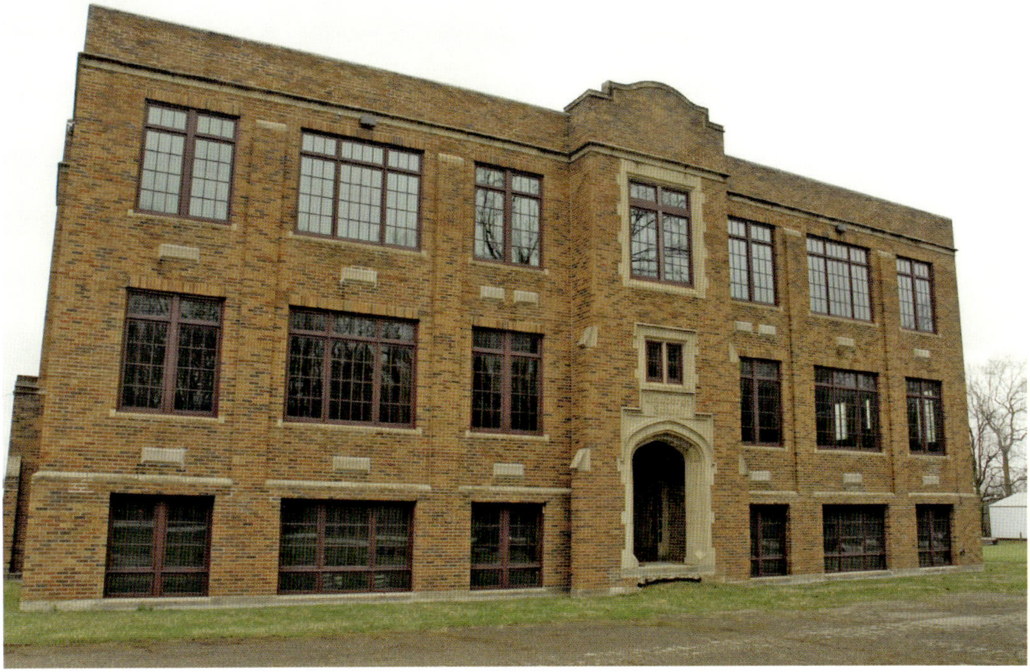

Above: Lindbergh School is located on State Road 32, just outside the Lebanon city limits. The school opened in 1927 and is named after Charles Lindbergh. In its early years, Lindbergh was part of the Central Township school organization, and served grades 1-8. In the late 1960s, Lindbergh merged with Lebanon schools. The school closed in May of 1971 and was sold in 1978. It later became the site of a museum until closing in 1988. Lindbergh School is currently empty and for sale.

Right: Front entrance to Lindbergh School near Lebanon in Boone County.

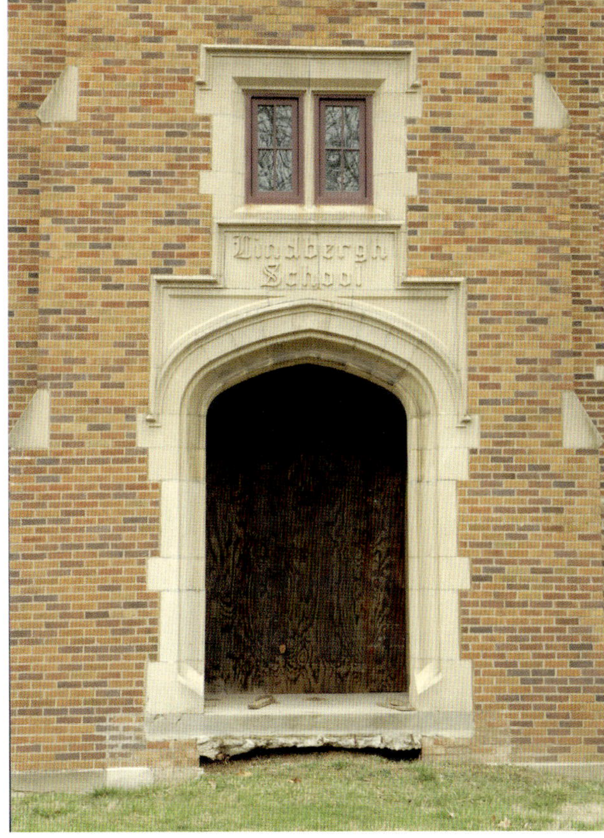

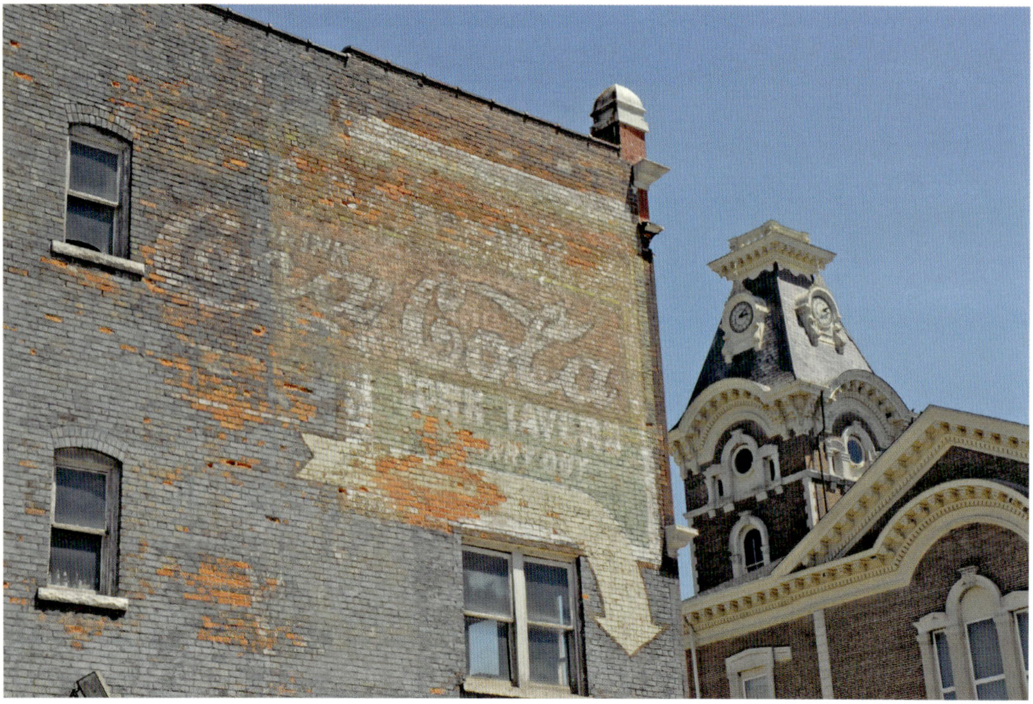

A faded Coca-Cola advertisement is barely visible on this building in downtown New Castle. Looming in the background is the New Castle Courthouse.

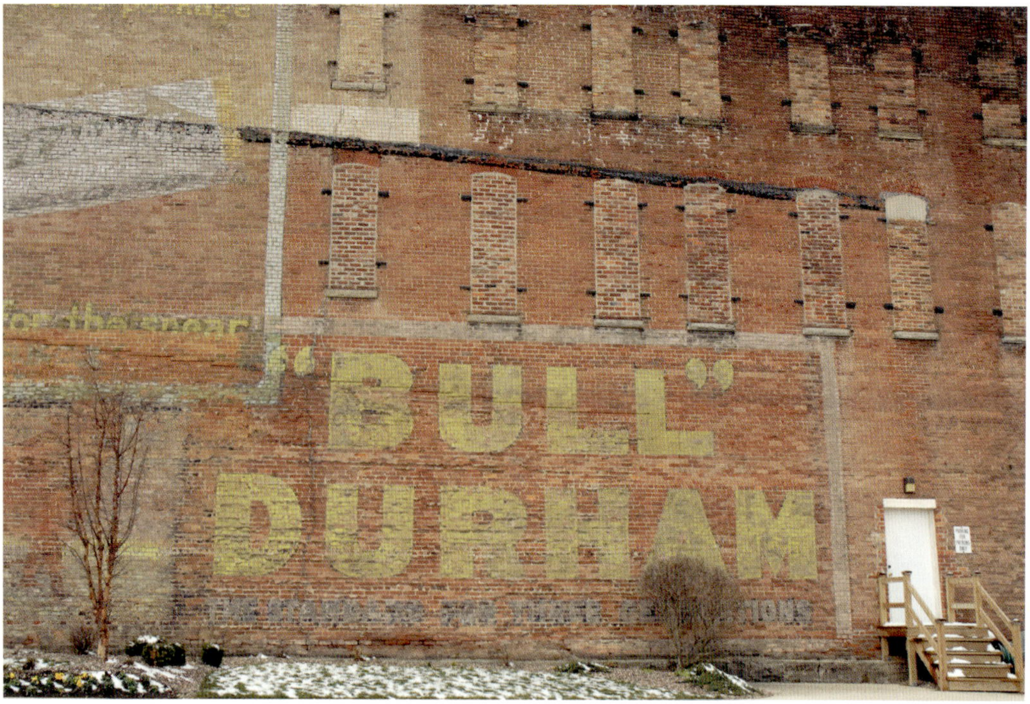

Painted advertisement for Bull Durham tobacco on a building in New Castle. Bull Durham tobacco originated in the 1850s and remained in production until 1988.

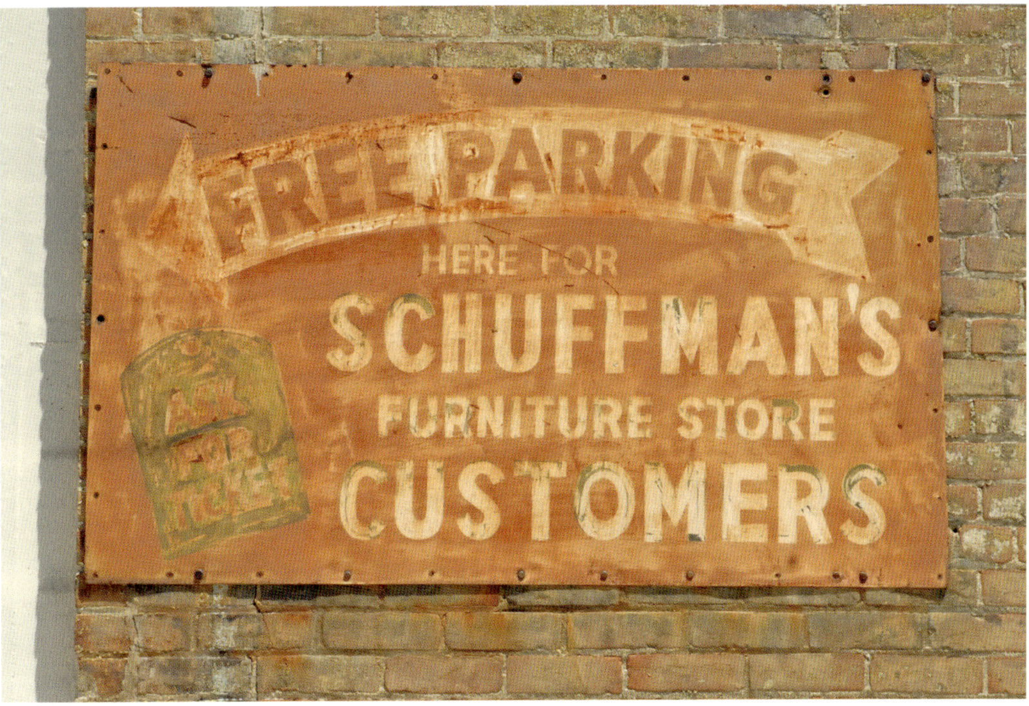

Abraham Schuffman founded Schuffman's Furniture Store in the late 1920s. Schuffman operated his New Castle store at 15th and Broad Streets with additional businesses in Muncie and Marion. This rusted sign still hangs on the building where the New Castle furniture store once operated.

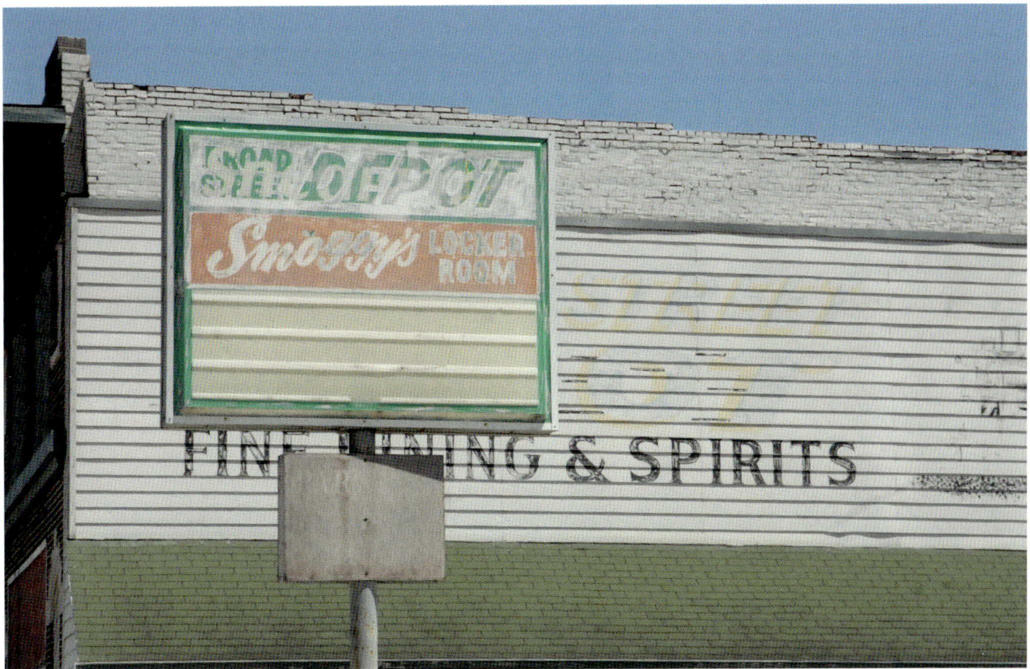

No longer in business is Smoggy's Locker Room Fine Dining and Spirits in New Castle.

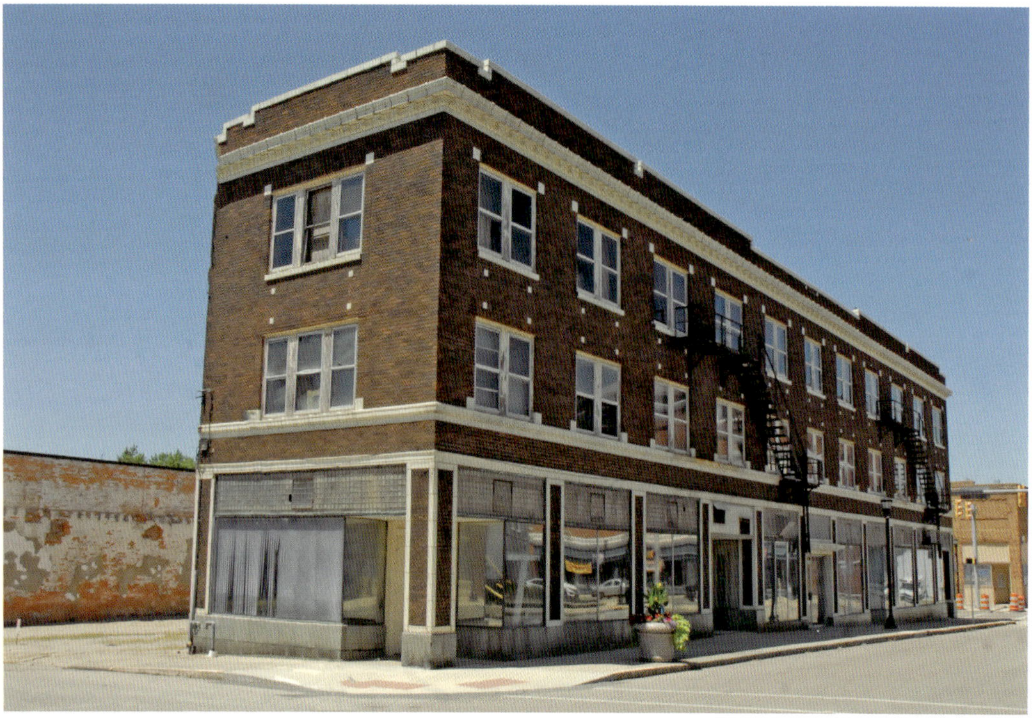

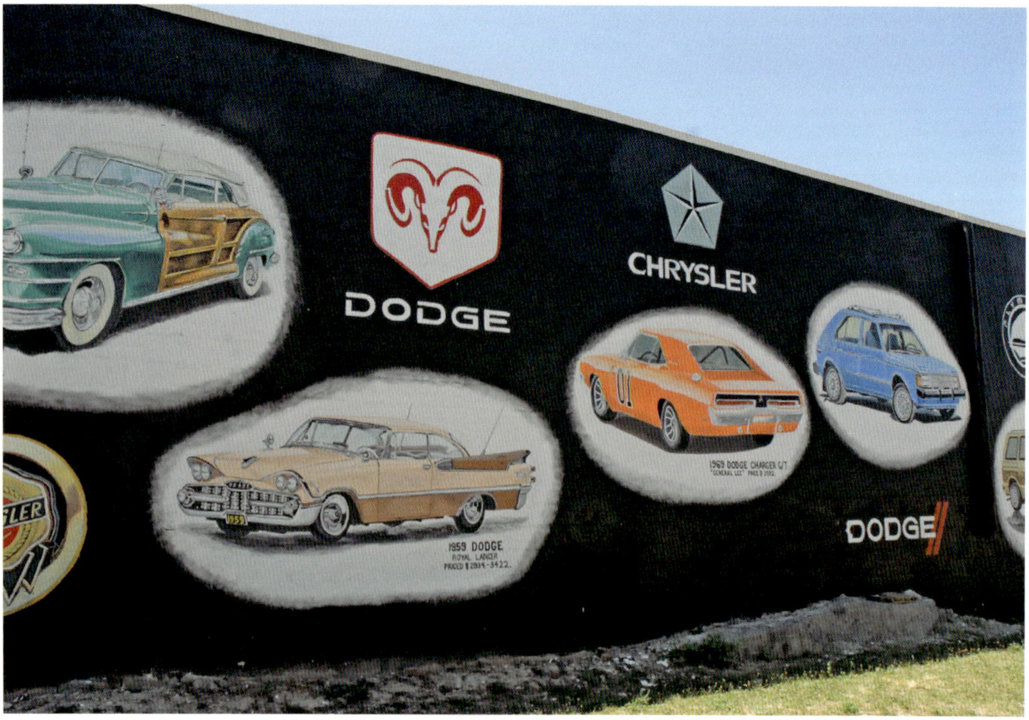

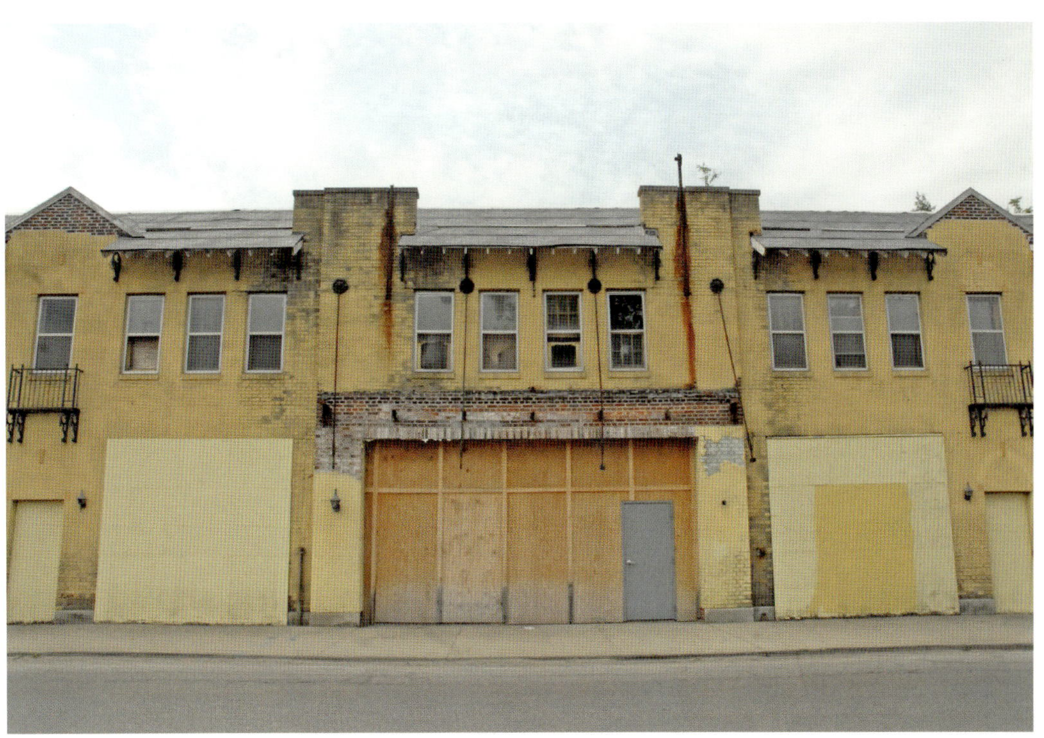

The Rivoli Theatre in Indianapolis opened in 1927 and closed in 1992. Located on East 10th Street, the theatre has gone through many changes and owners through the years, but remains one of the city's most treasured landmarks. During the 1970s, the Rivoli hosted concerts featuring popular bands from the era including Golden Earring, Lynard Skynard, and Kansas. Legendary screen actress Gloria Swanson appeared at the Rivoli in 1974, to discuss her sixty-year film career.

Opposite above: Indiana Landmarks has placed the Courthouse Annex in New Castle on its 10 Most Endangered List. The building has been empty for over twenty years and used primarily to store county records. The Courthouse Annex is listed on the National Register of Historic Places, as part of New Castle's Historic District.

Opposite below: A new mural nicknamed "Chrysler Through the Decades" has been painted on the east wall of the Hope Building in downtown New Castle. The mural is in honor of the Chrysler Plant that once operated in New Castle. In 1934, the Chrysler plant employed 6,700 people. Chrysler in New Castle ceased operation in 2009.

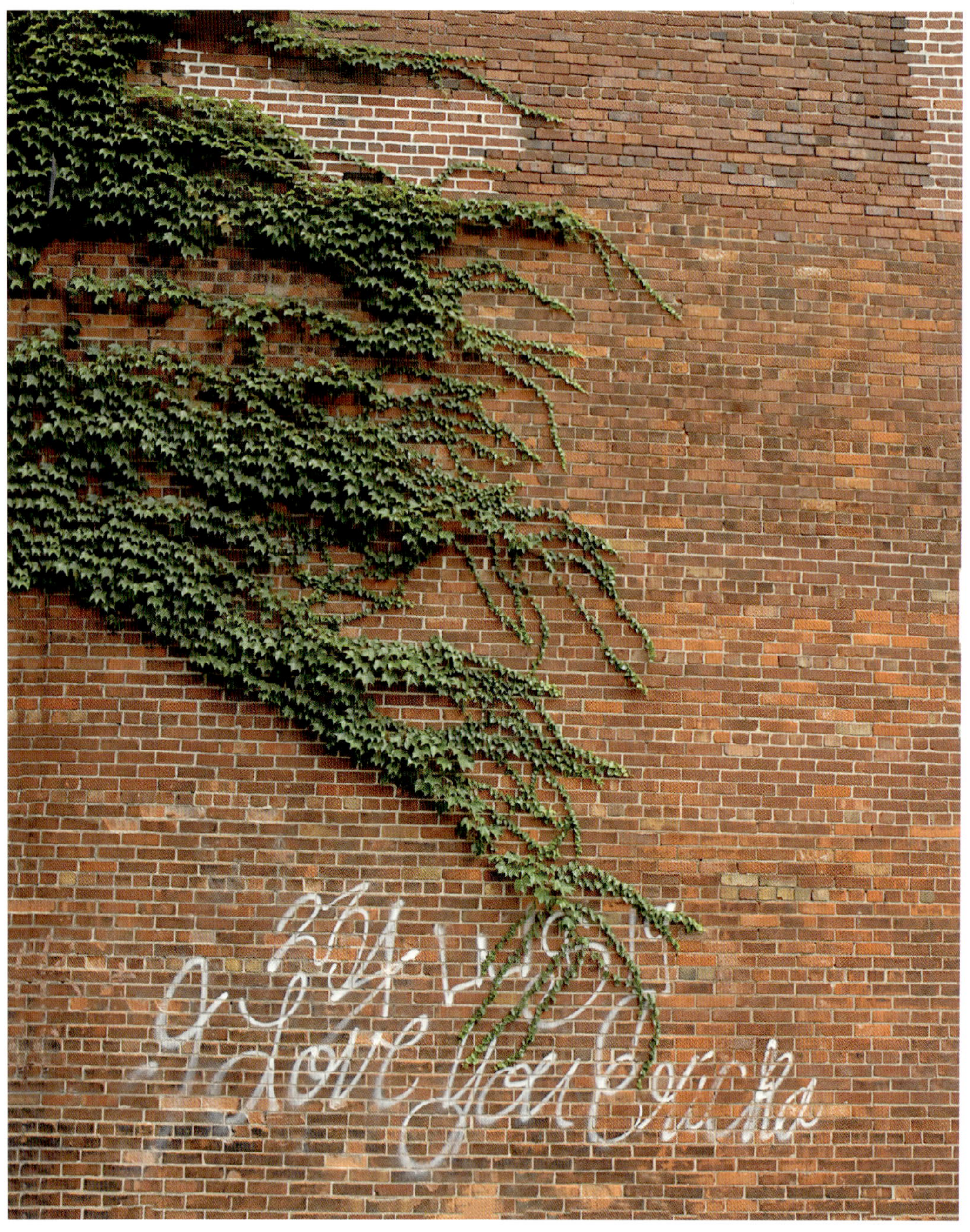

Vines grow on the south wall of the Rivoli, with the message "I Love You Ericka" written on the bricks.

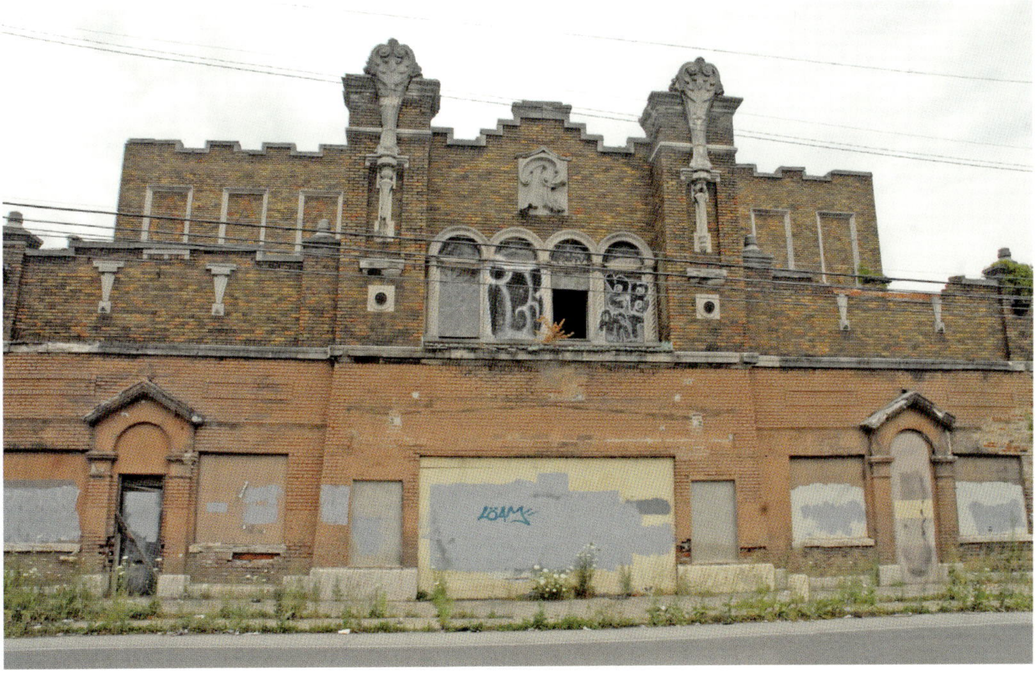

The Ritz Theatre is located in the 3400 block of North Illinois in Indianapolis. The Ritz opened in 1927 and remained open until 1972. In the years before the theatre closed, its name was changed to Middle Earth and became a rock concert venue. Frank Zappa, Richie Havens, Alice Cooper, and Country Joe McDonald were a few of the acts to perform there. The Ritz is currently for sale with an asking price of $759,500.

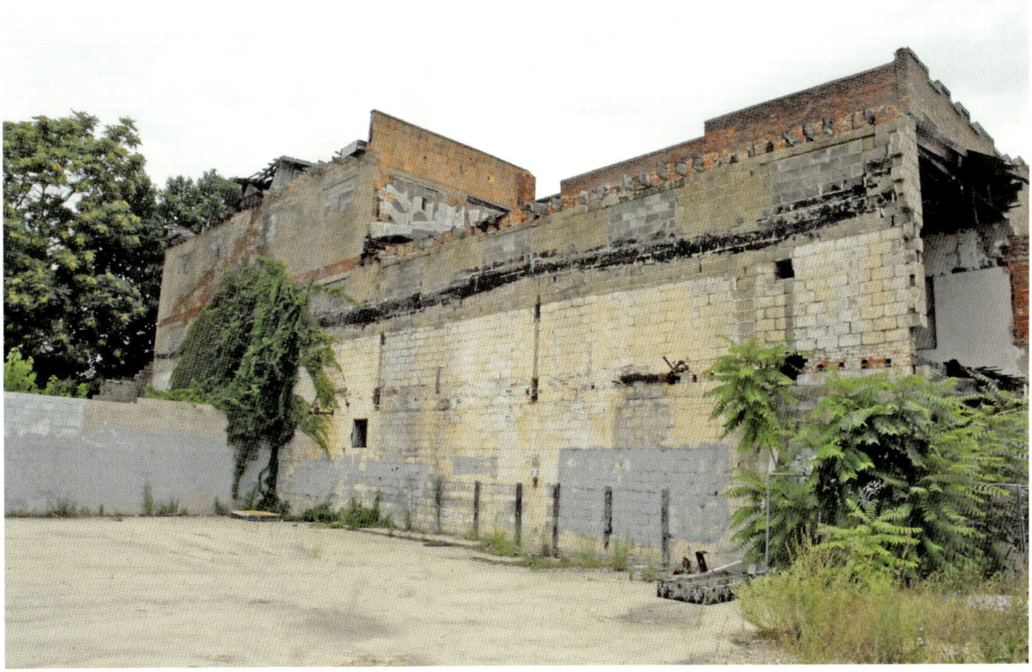

Photo of the south wall of the Ritz shows damage done to its exterior. Floors and walls inside the building have caved in. The marquee was removed many years ago.

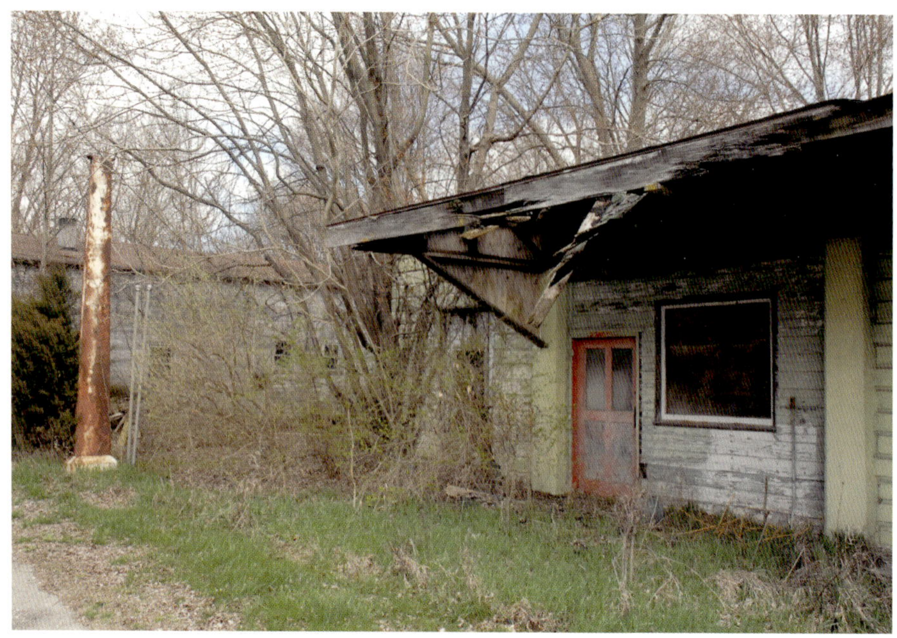

These vacated buildings in Mechanicsburg are visible from the road while travelling on US 36. Mechanicsburg was founded in 1858 and is located in Henry County. It is believed that the town earned its name from the high number of settlers who earned a living as mechanics.

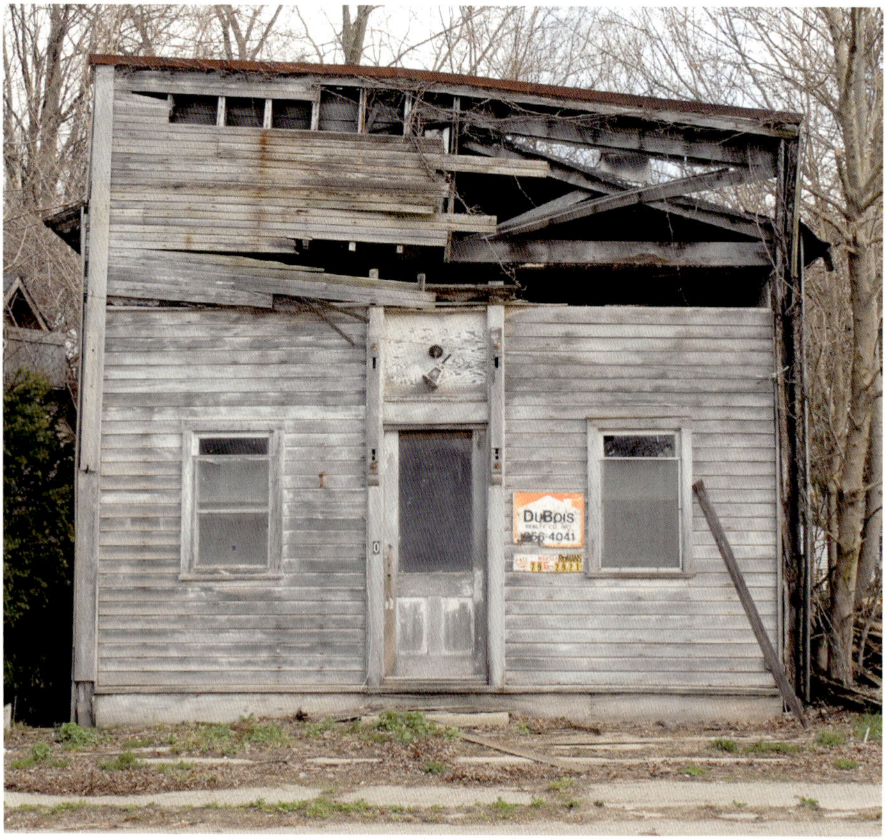

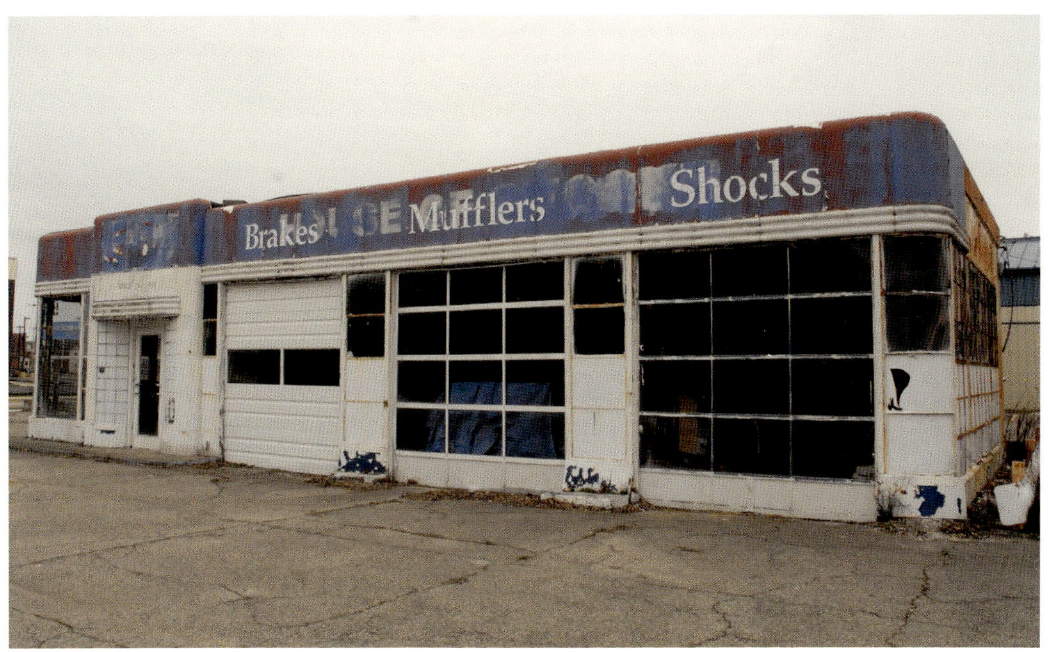

There was a time when full-service filling stations had onsite mechanics to work on automobiles. Customers were greeted by service stations attendants with the words "Fill 'er up?", who also cleaned windshields and checked your automobile's oil level free of charge. If waiting on an oil change or repairs on your automobile, a customer could enjoy a cold bottle of pop from a Coke or Pepsi machine. These closed filling stations are located in the cities of Muncie and New Castle.

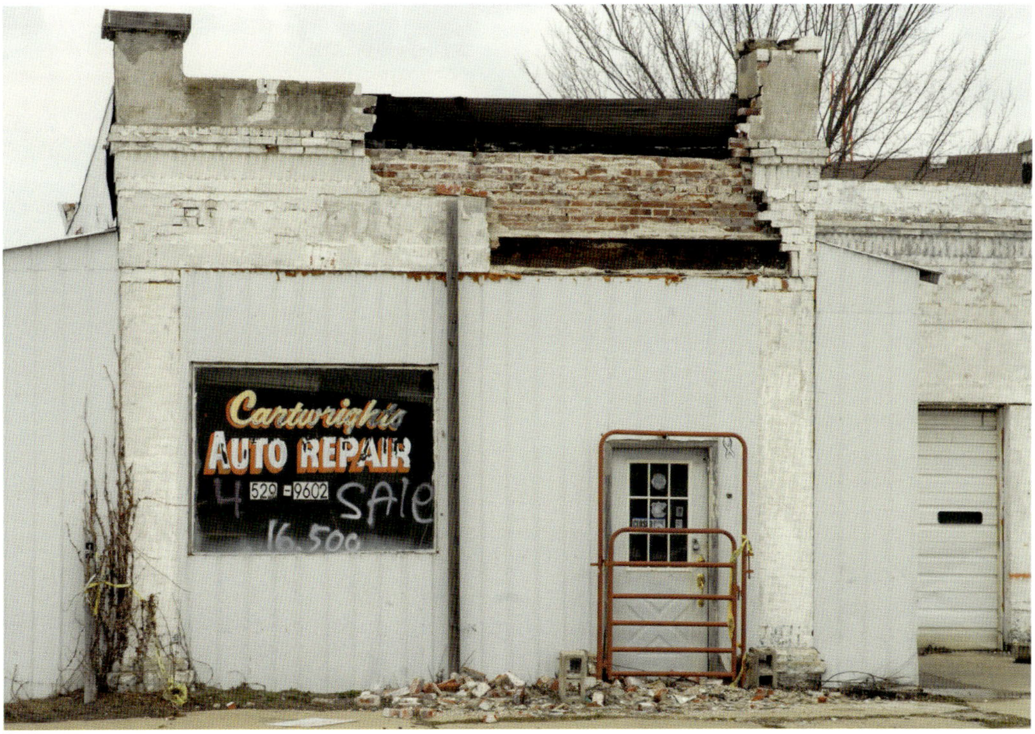

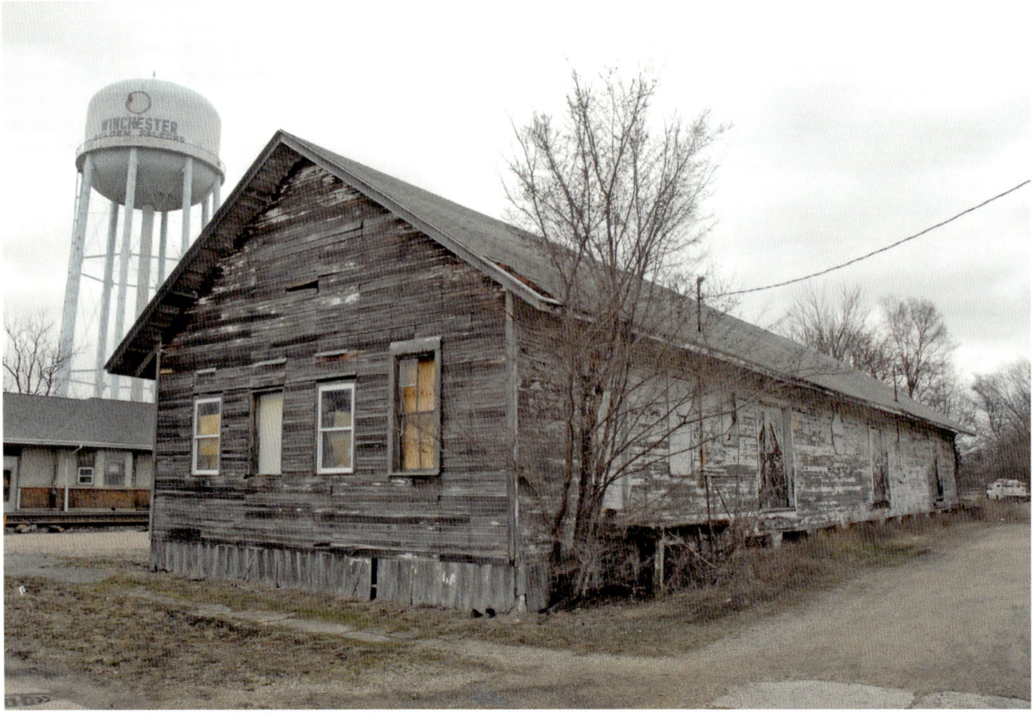

The Winchester feed mill has stood empty for many years. In the background is the Winchester water tower and the old Winchester Train Depot. The depot is currently being used by CSX Transportation.

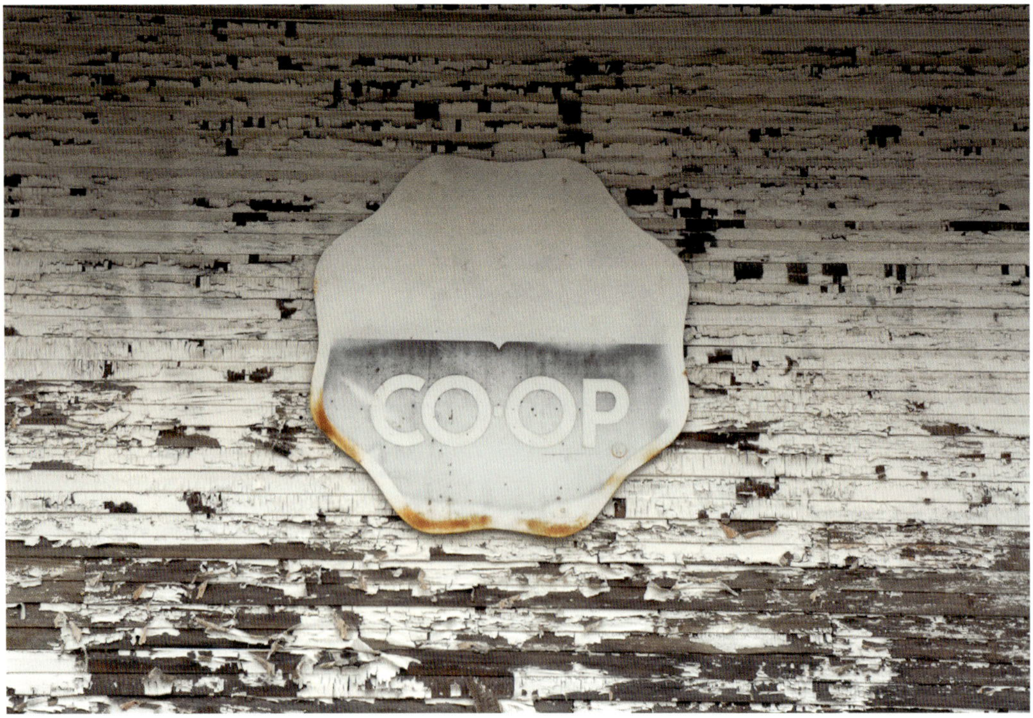

A faded Co-Op sign on the exterior of the old Winchester feed mill.

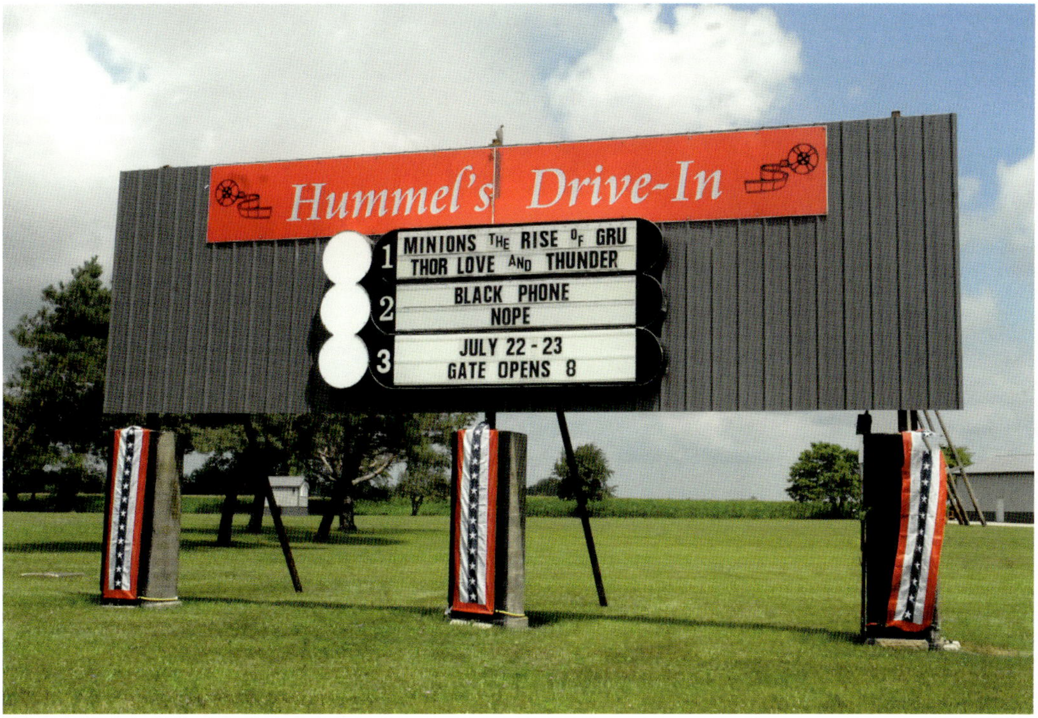

Though it was closed for a few years, the Hummel Drive-In has since reopened. Located on State Road 32 just east of Winchester, Hummel's is one of twenty drive-in movie theatres still in operation in Indiana.

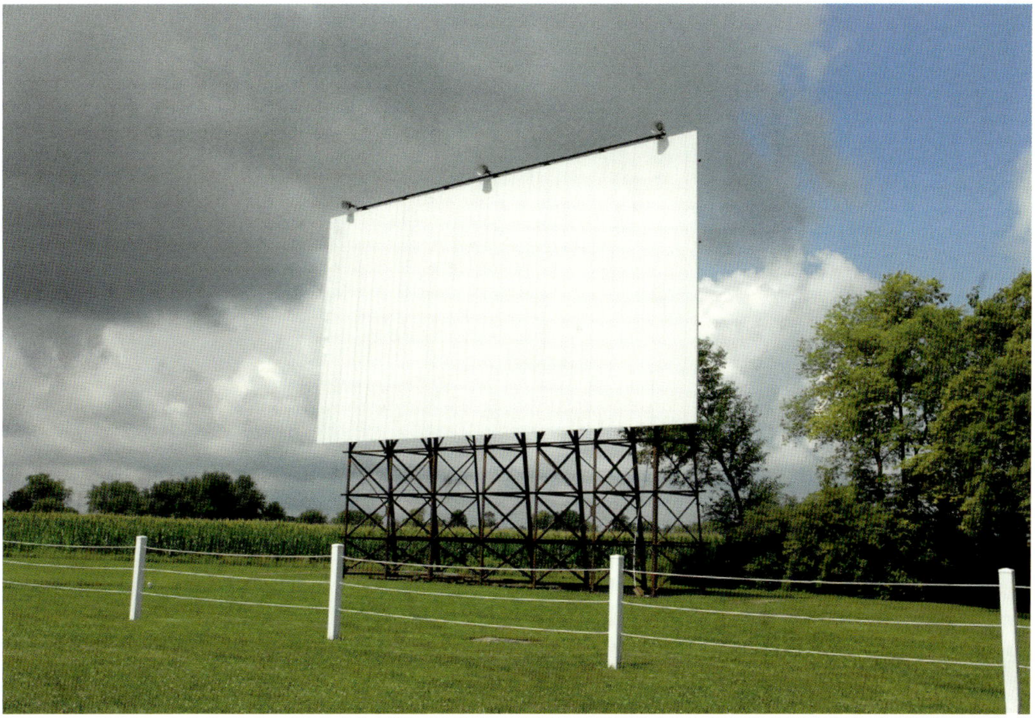

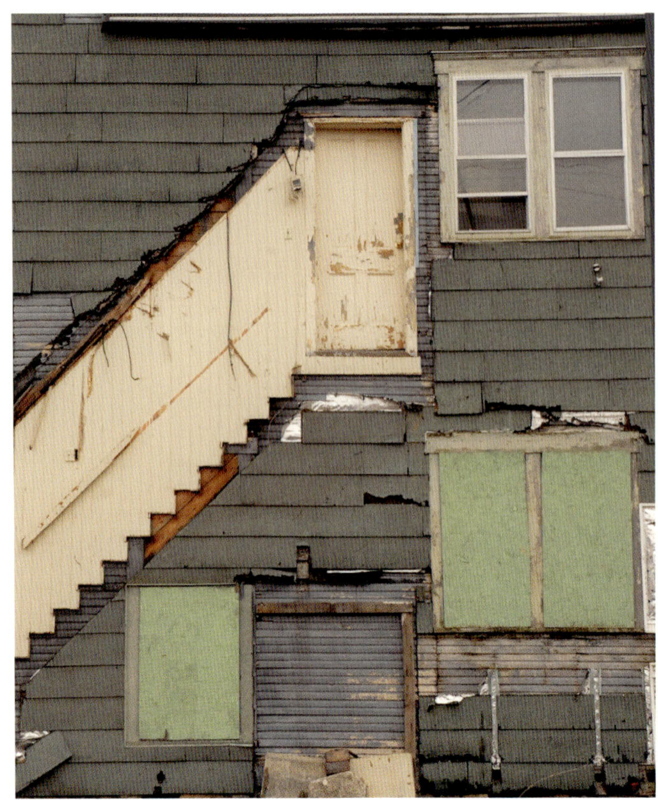

Left: Missing from this abandoned apartment building in Muncie are the outside stairs leading to the second floor.

Below: A vacant apartment building with boarded-up windows on Jackson Street in downtown Muncie.

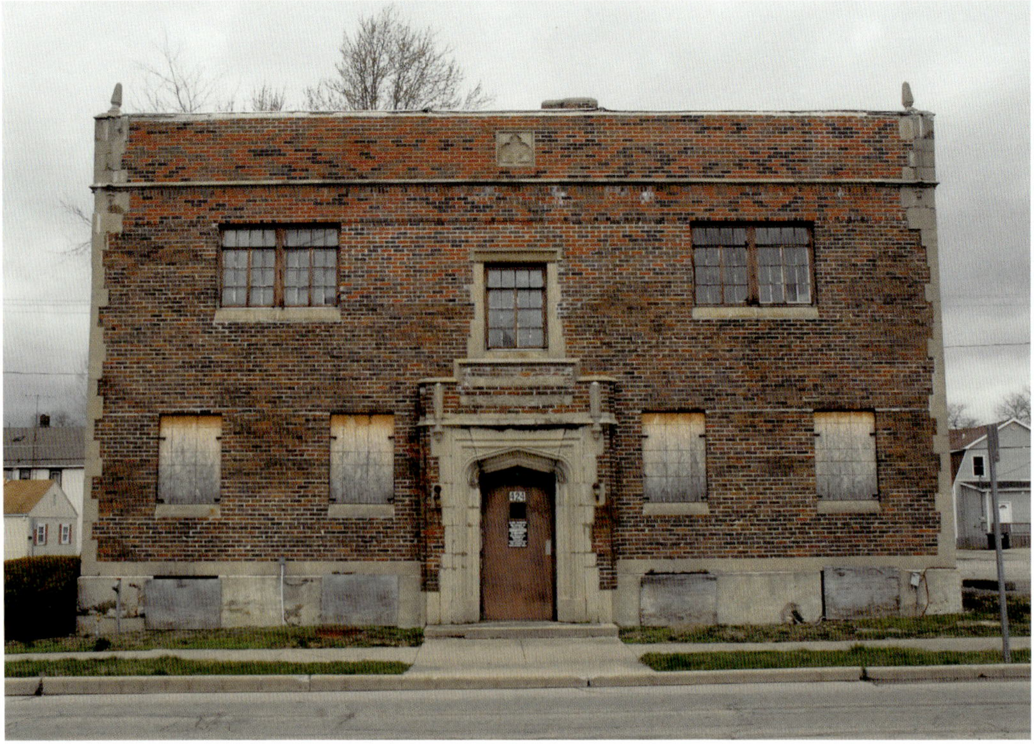

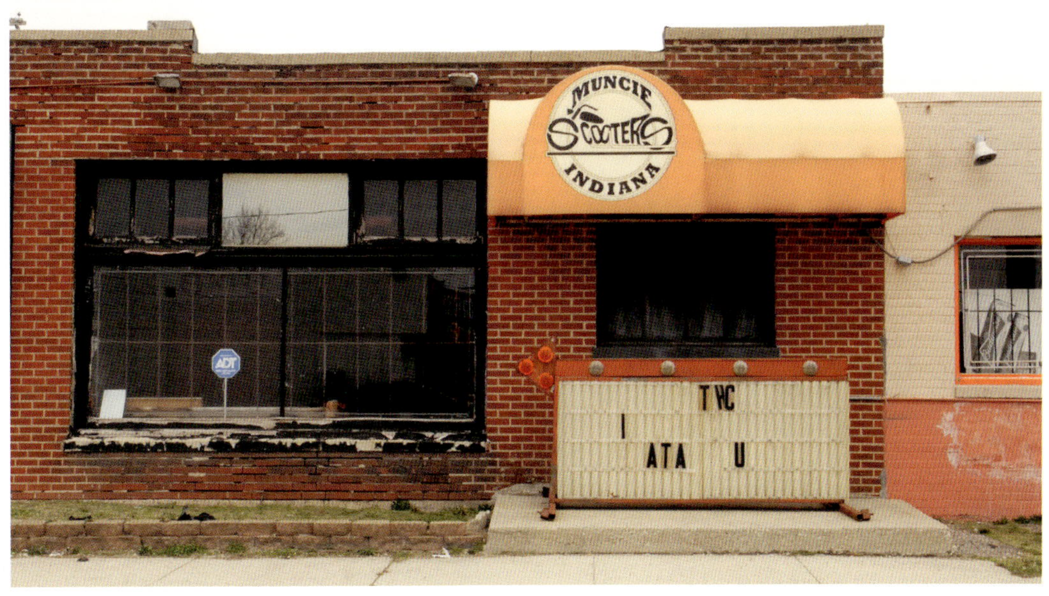

Muncie Scooters and Madison Street Liquor once operated from the same property on Muncie's south side but are now closed.

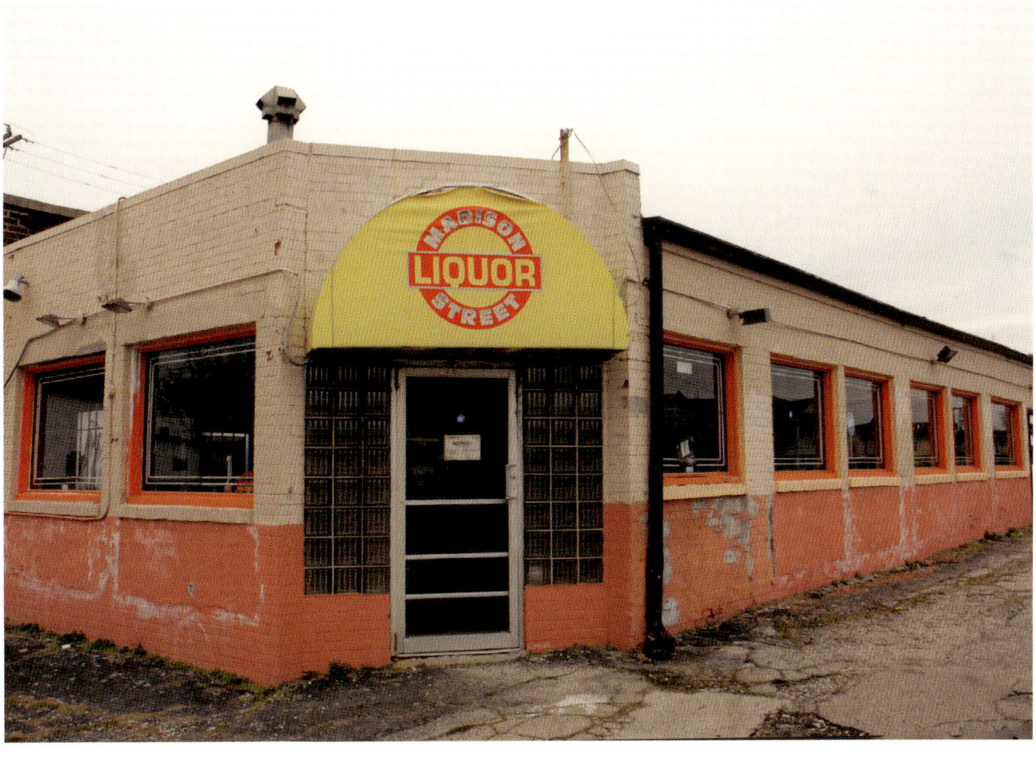

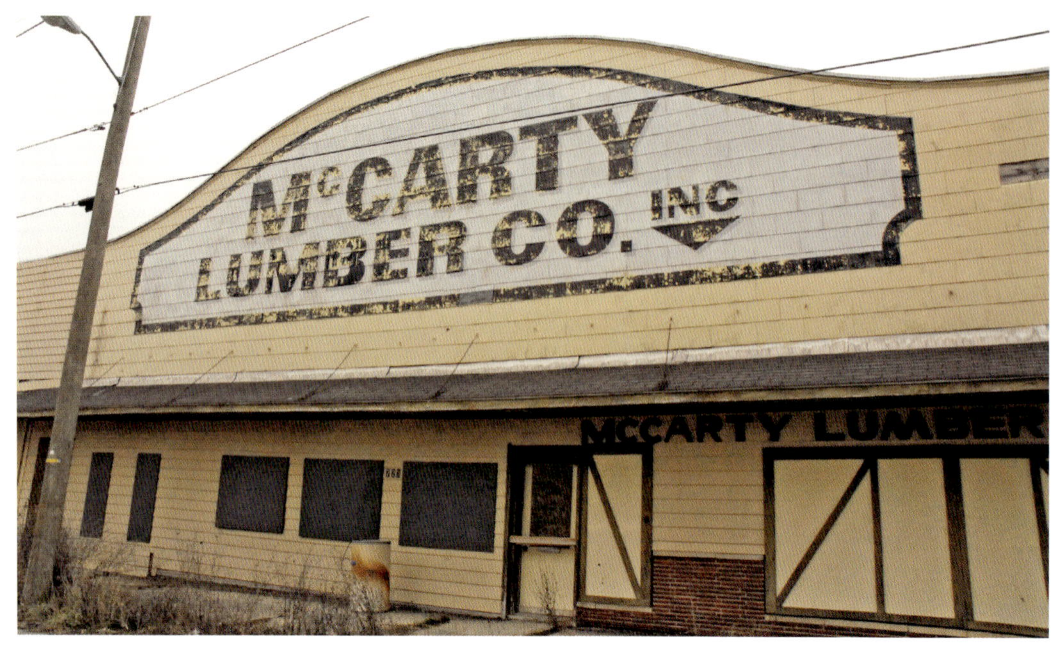

McCarty Lumber Company was founded in 1945 by Tom McCarty and Marvin Nichols. After Nichols passed away in 1952, McCarty became sole owner, after purchasing his deceased partner's share of the company. In 1964, the lumber company suffered a devastating financial loss after a fire destroyed the company stockyard. The company managed to rebuild and bought out the Delaware Lumber Company in 1972, making them one of the largest lumber wholesale companies in Muncie. Large chain stores took business away from McCarty Lumber Company, forcing it to close in October of 2012.

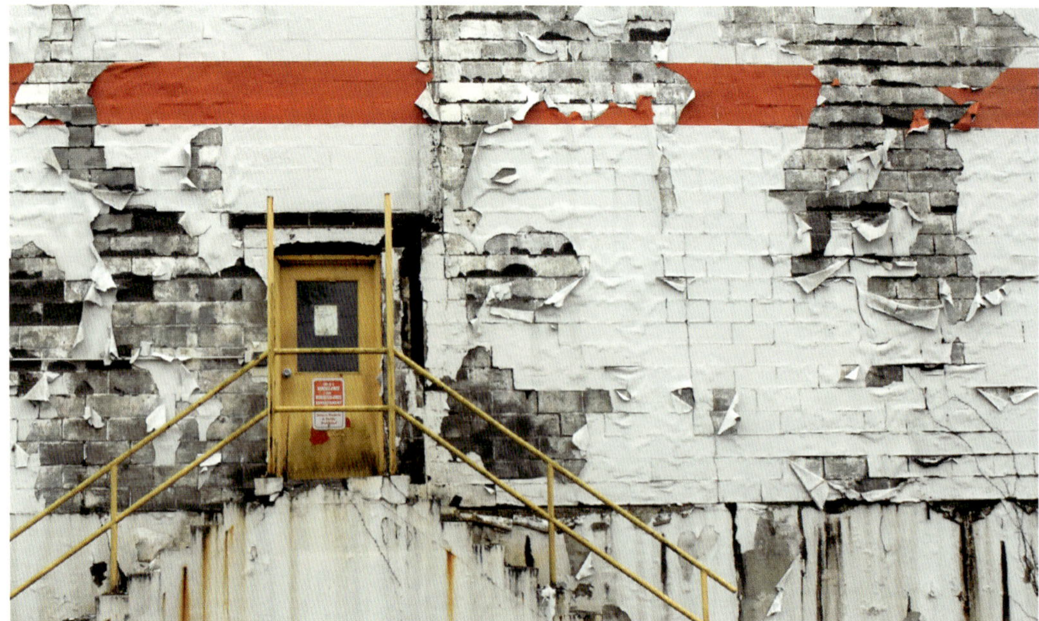

The Marsh Supermarkets Warehouse in Yorktown closed in 2016, leaving seventy-two people out of work. Marsh Supermarkets was a retail food chain headquartered in Indianapolis with stores primarily located in central Indiana. The company filed for bankruptcy in May of 2017, with all supermarkets closing by July of that year.

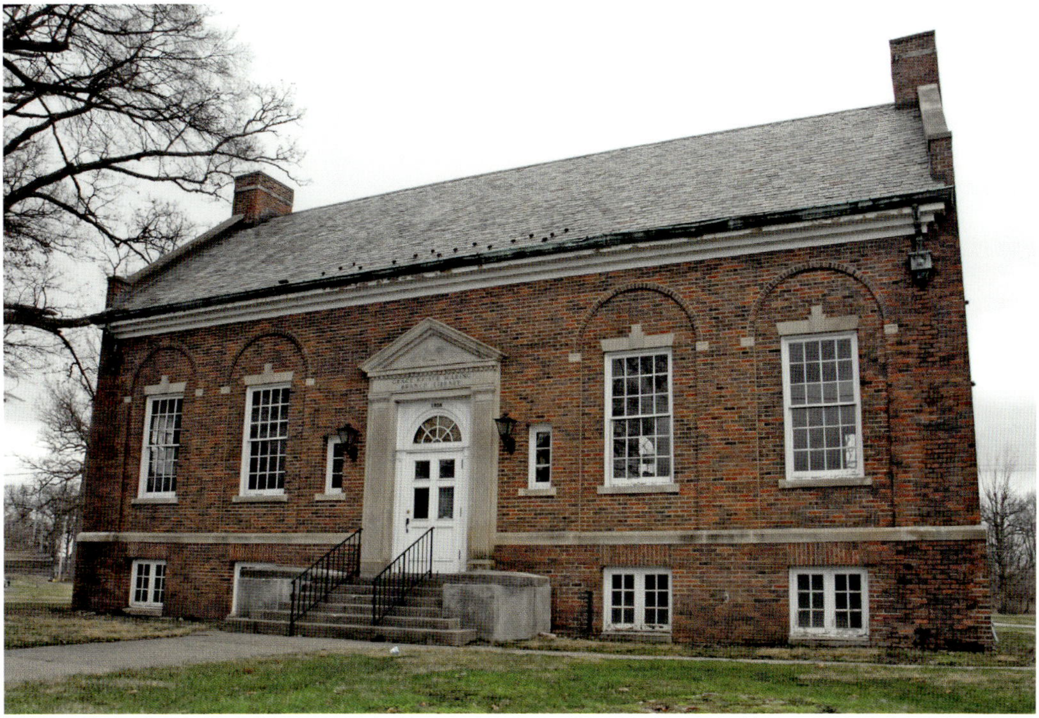

The Grace Keiser Maring Library opened in 1930 and was the first branch library in the city of Muncie. Grace Maring was a philanthropist and advocate for education. She was married to Joel Maring, founder of glass factories in Muncie. The library is listed on the National Register of Historic Places and has been vacant since 1999.

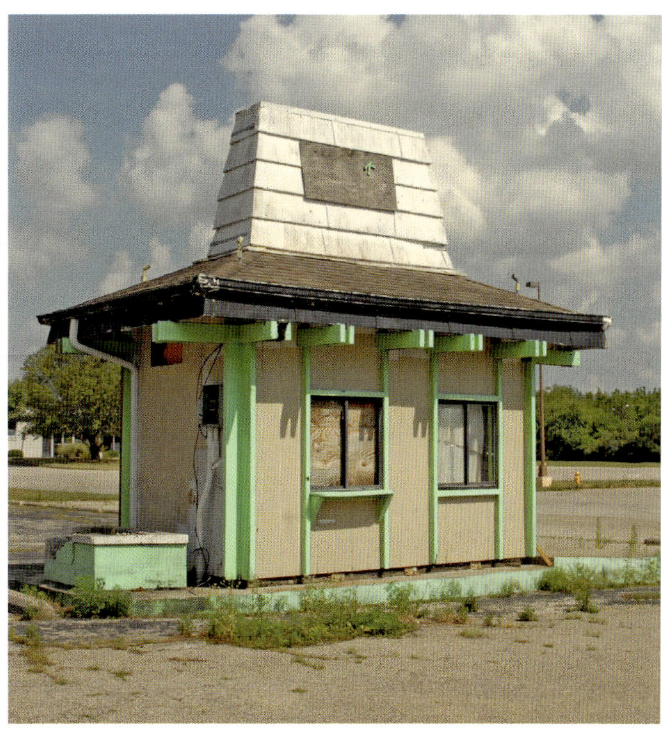

During the 1970s and 1980s, Fotomat stores were popular throughout the United States. Charles Brown came up with the idea of the Fotomat, with the first store opening in Pinellas, Florida, in 1965. Fotomat employees would greet customers at a drive-up window, and have their film developed and printed in twenty-four hours. On the south side of Muncie is this structure that served as a Fotomat store during its heyday.

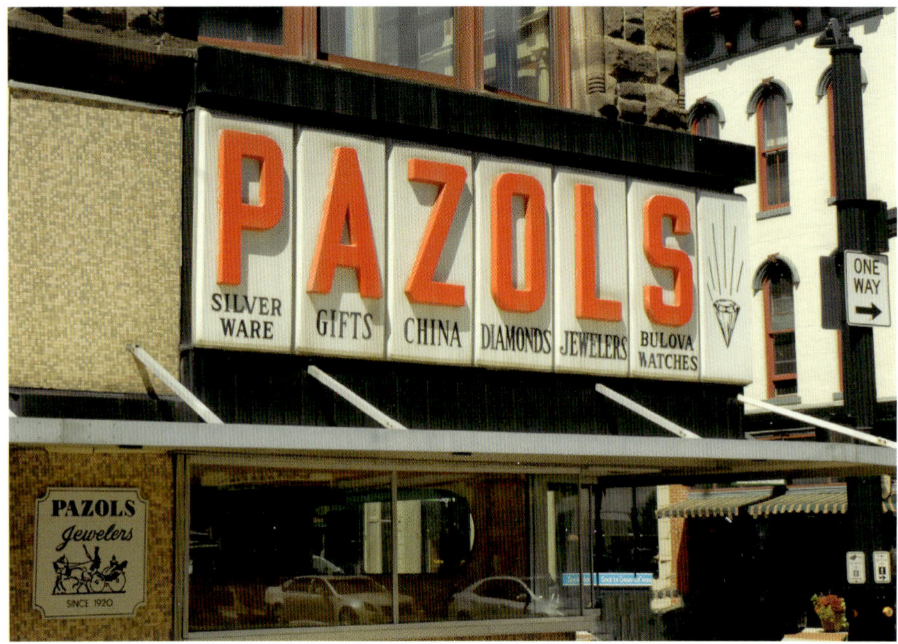

Pazols Jewelers was founded in 1920 by Harry Pazol. Located in downtown Muncie since 1941, the store celebrated 100 years in business before closing in the spring of 2021. Penny Prow took over ownership of the jewelry store in 1980 and remained manager until the store closed.

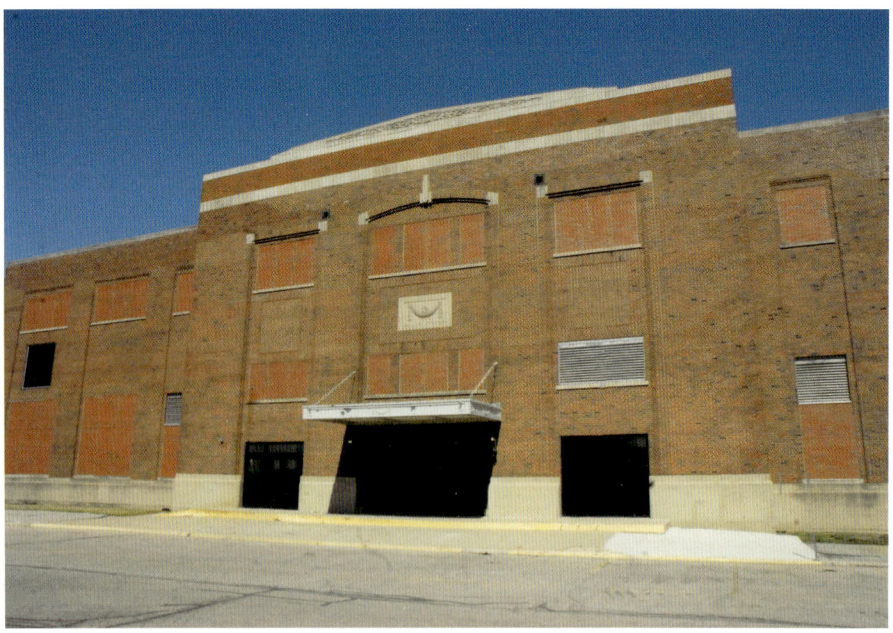

The Muncie Fieldhouse opened in 1928 and built at a cost of $407,000. Since then, the Muncie Fieldhouse has produced eight state boys' basketball titles. It is home to the Muncie Bearcats of Muncie Central High School. The gymnasium has gone through three renovations, with the latest being in 2017. The first basketball game at the newly constructed gymnasium was attended by 7,600, who watched the Muncie Bearcats defeat the Anderson Indians 35-24.

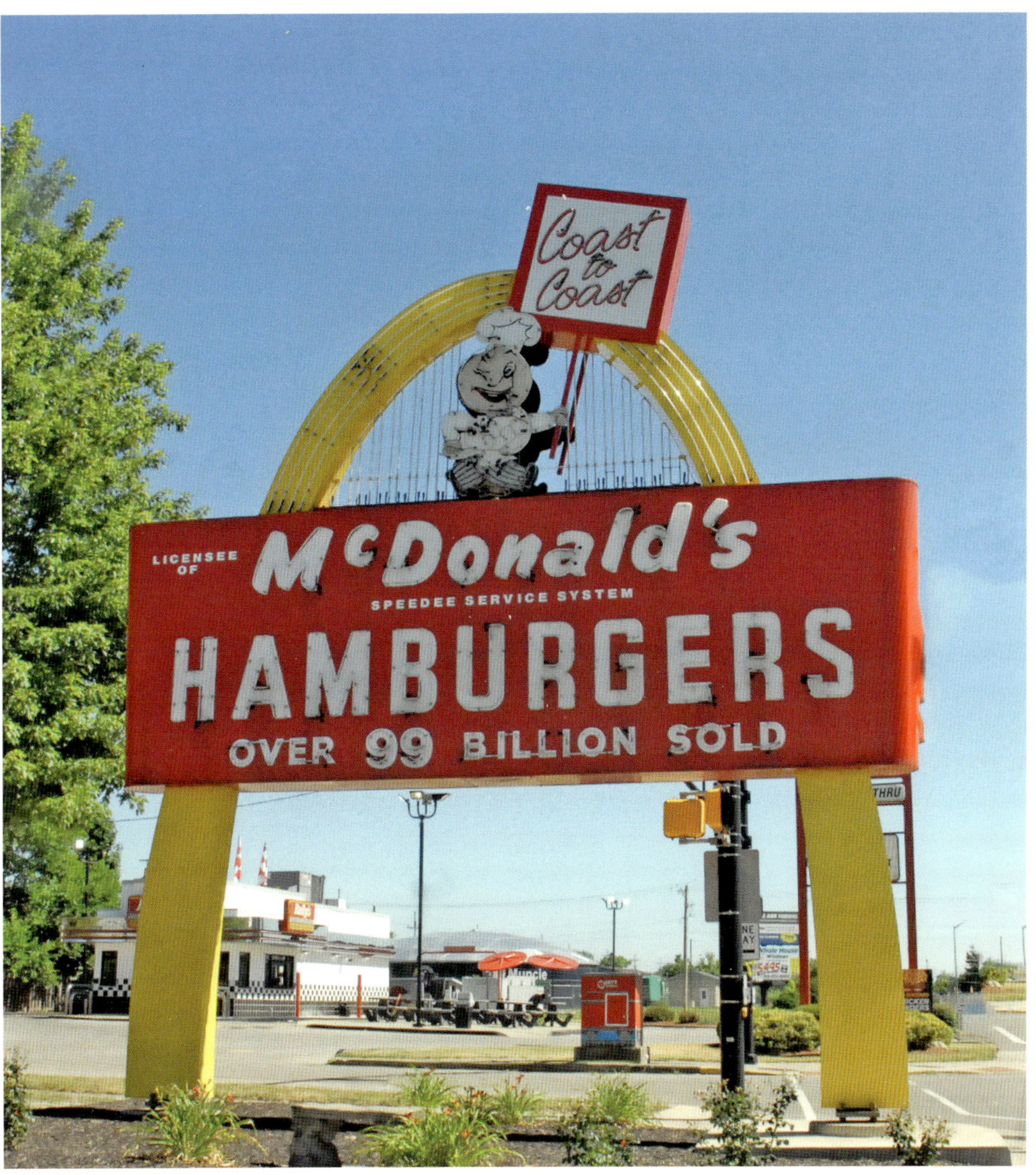

The McDonald's Restaurant on East Charles Street in Muncie opened in 1958. It is one of three McDonald's restaurants in the country with the original single-arch design. Through the years the restaurant has gone through renovations, but the historic sign remains untouched.

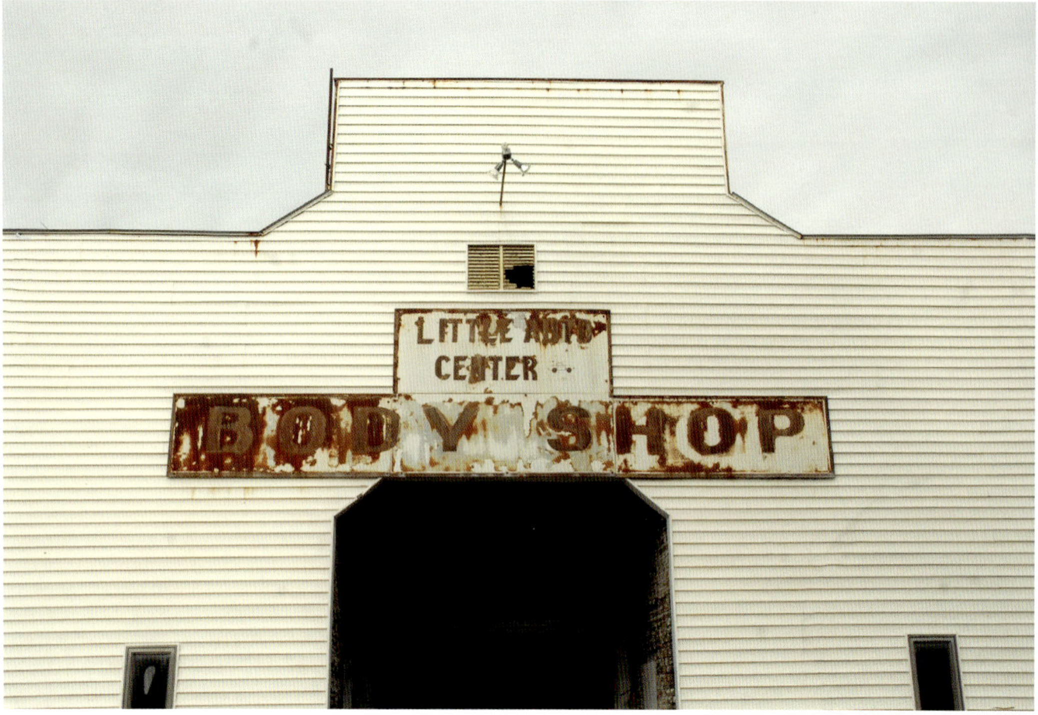

A rusted sign hangs on the exterior of the now closed Little Auto Center Body Shop in Fairmount.

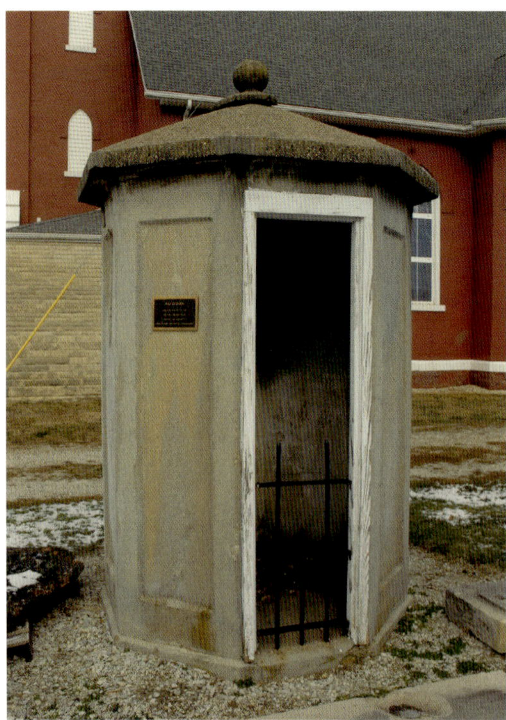

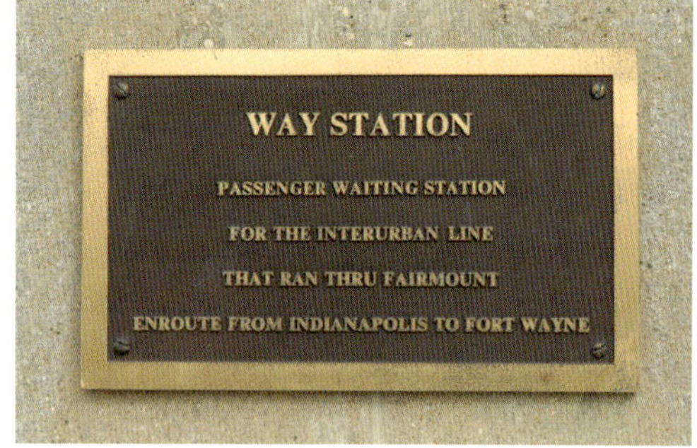

A way station still stands on Walnut Street in downtown Fairmount, just north of East Washington Streets. The way station served as a passenger waiting station for the Interurban Line that ran through Fairmount enroute from Indianapolis to Fort Wayne.

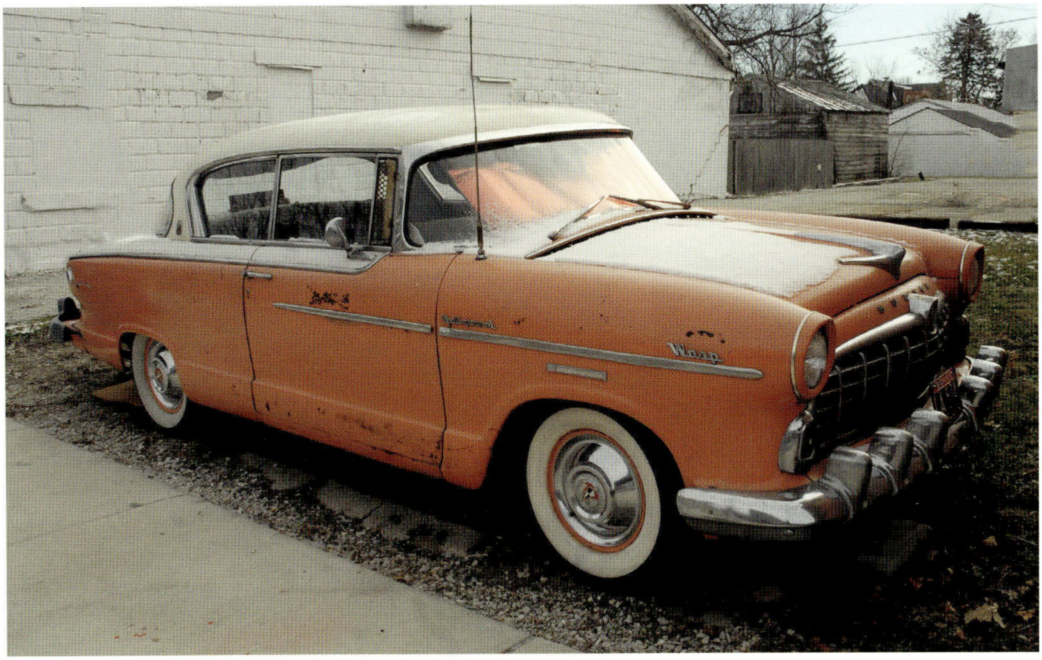

A 1955 Hudson Hornet Wasp sits in the parking lot of a closed tavern in Fairmount. The classic automobile was originally owned by George V. Koehler.

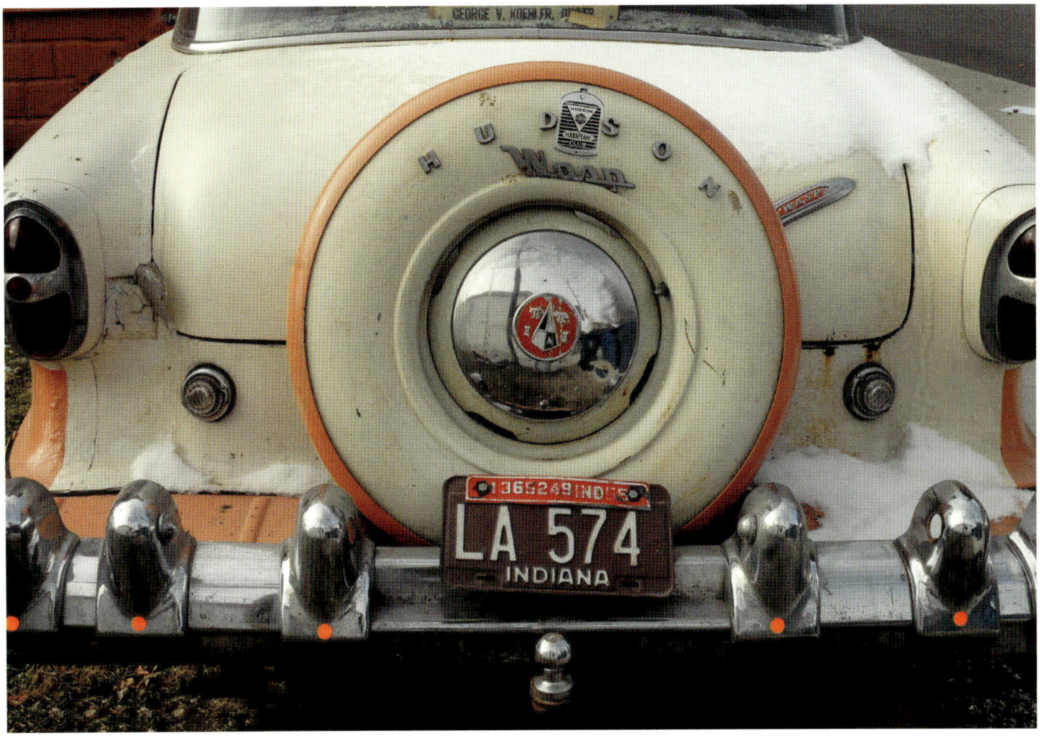

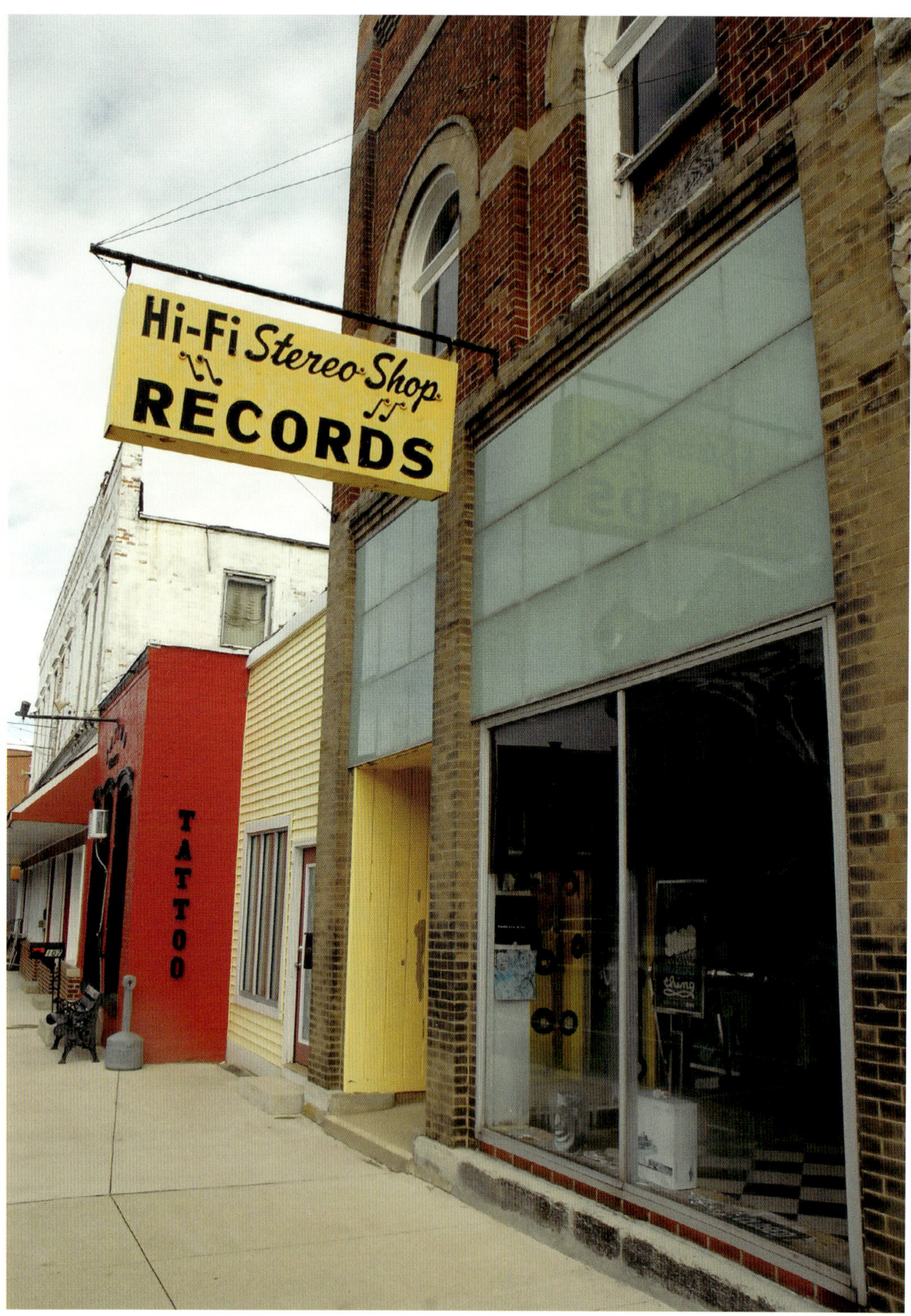

The Hi-Fi Stereo Shop in Fairmount was Indiana's oldest record store. Helen Broyles opened the record store in 1960 and remained its owner until the shop closed in 2016. Broyles passed away in 2018 at the age of ninety-four.

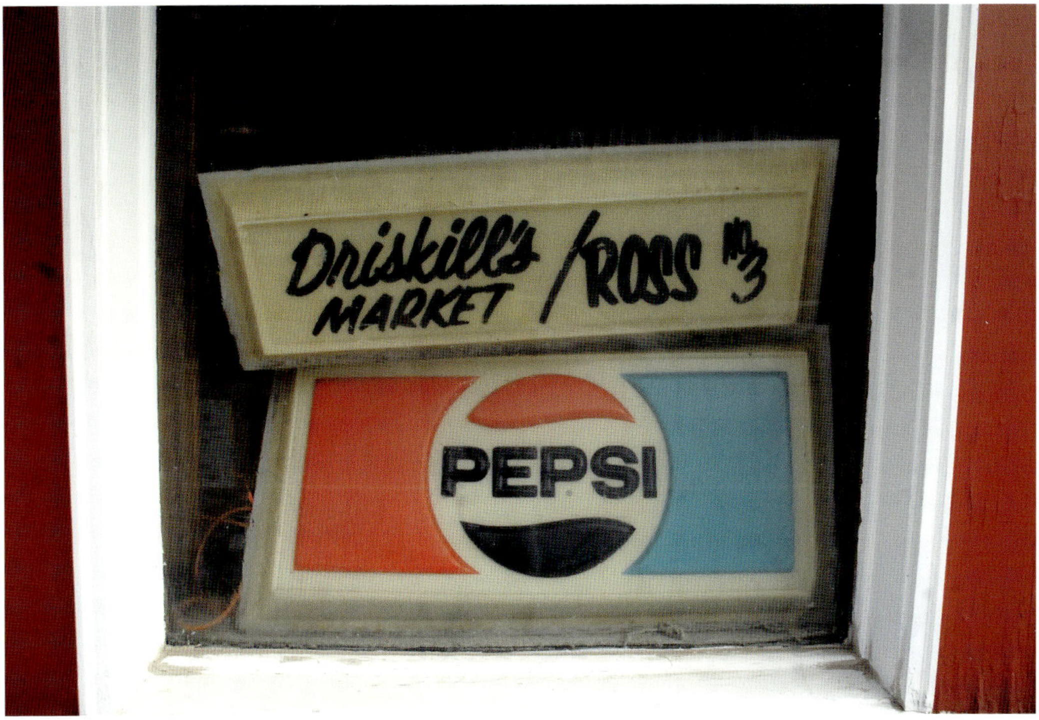

Old Pepsi sign once displayed in Driskill's Market located in Fairmount. Driskill's Market is now known as Horner's Market with locations in Fairmount, Alexandria, and Marion.

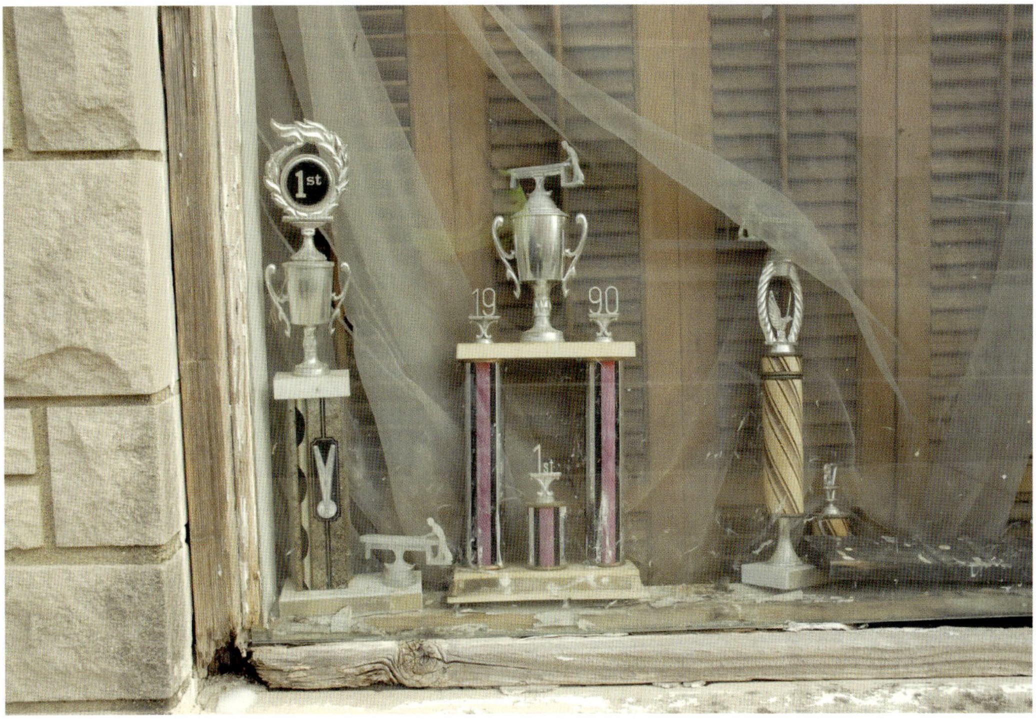

Old trophies sit in the window of an empty building in Fairmount, previous site of an arcade repair shop.

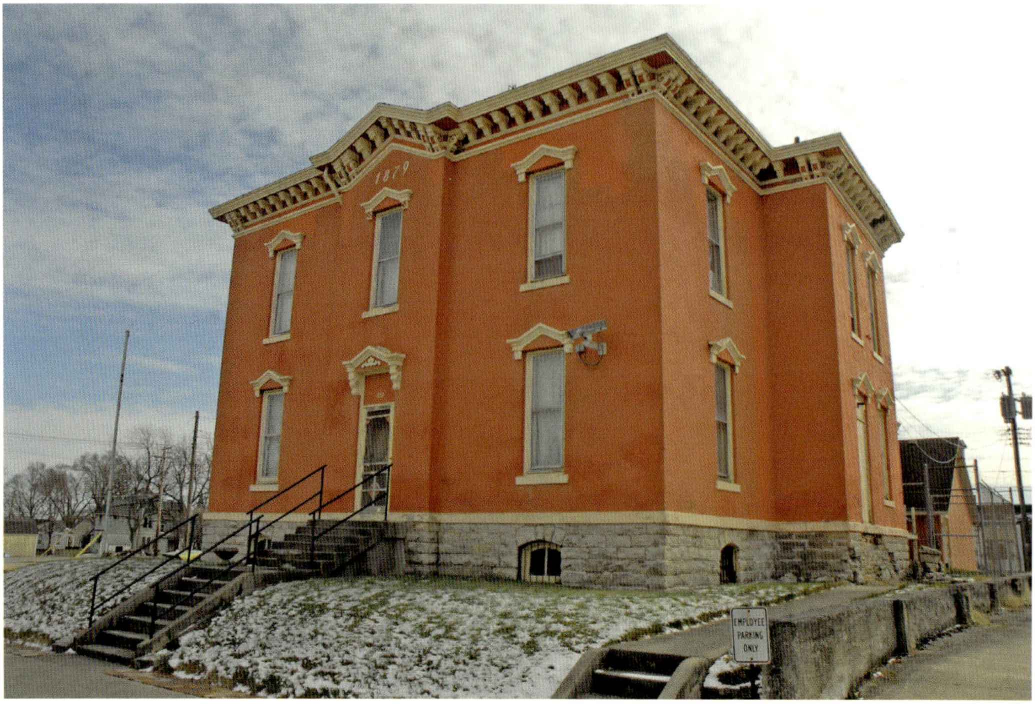

The old Blackford County Jail is located in downtown Hartford City. The jail was established in 1879 and housed prisoners until 1995. During his reign as Public Enemy Number One, Indiana born John Dillinger was once held prisoner at the Blackford County Jail.

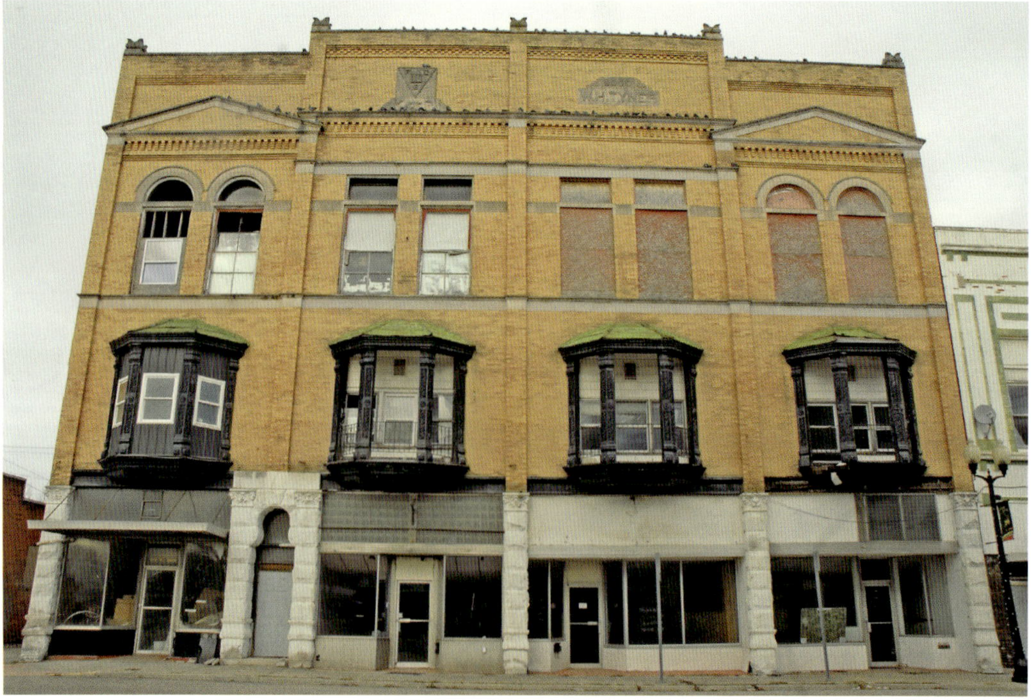

A vacated building has become home to pigeons in the downtown Hartford City business district.

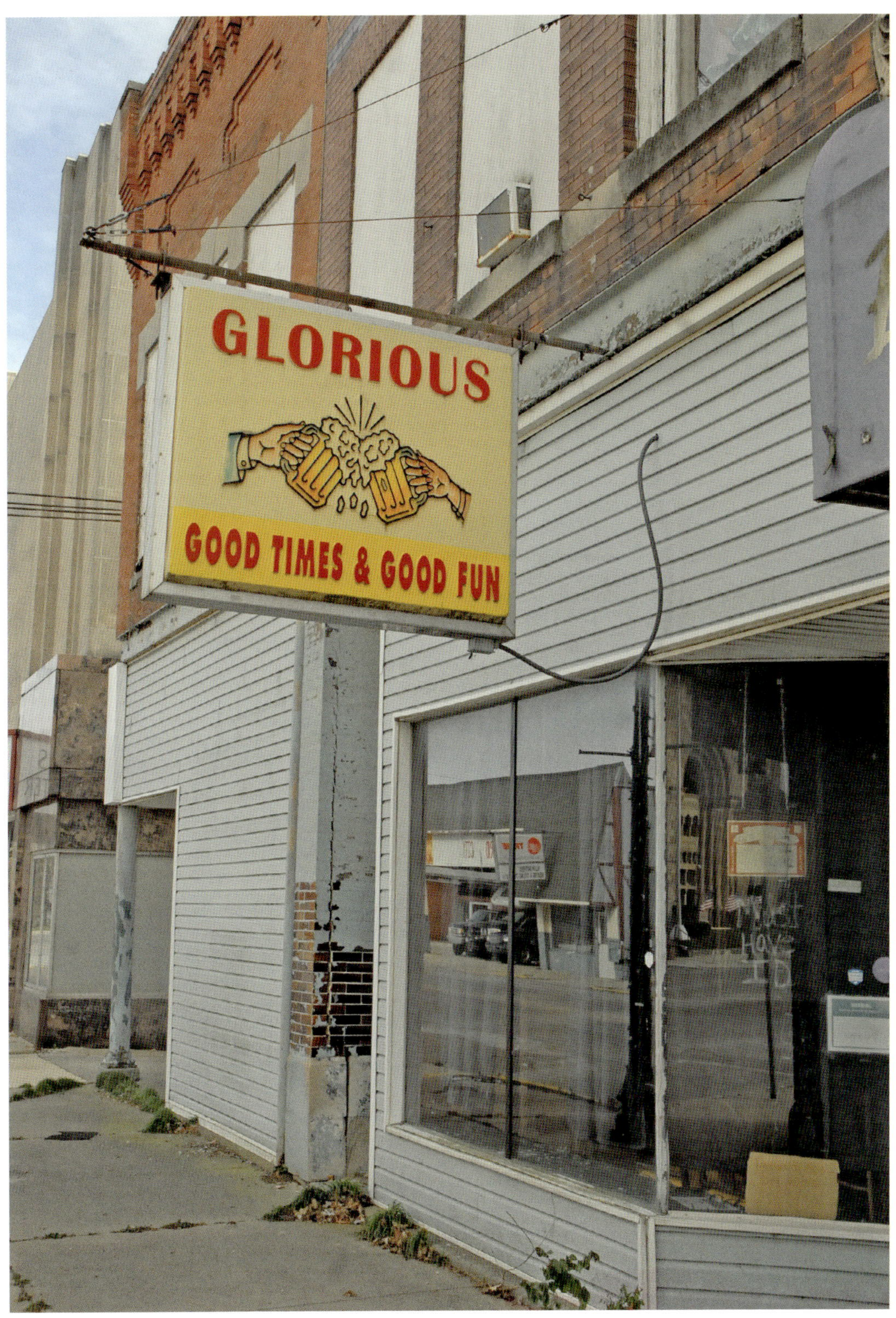

The Glorious Good Times and Good Fun tavern in downtown Hartford City is no longer a watering hole for the town's residents.

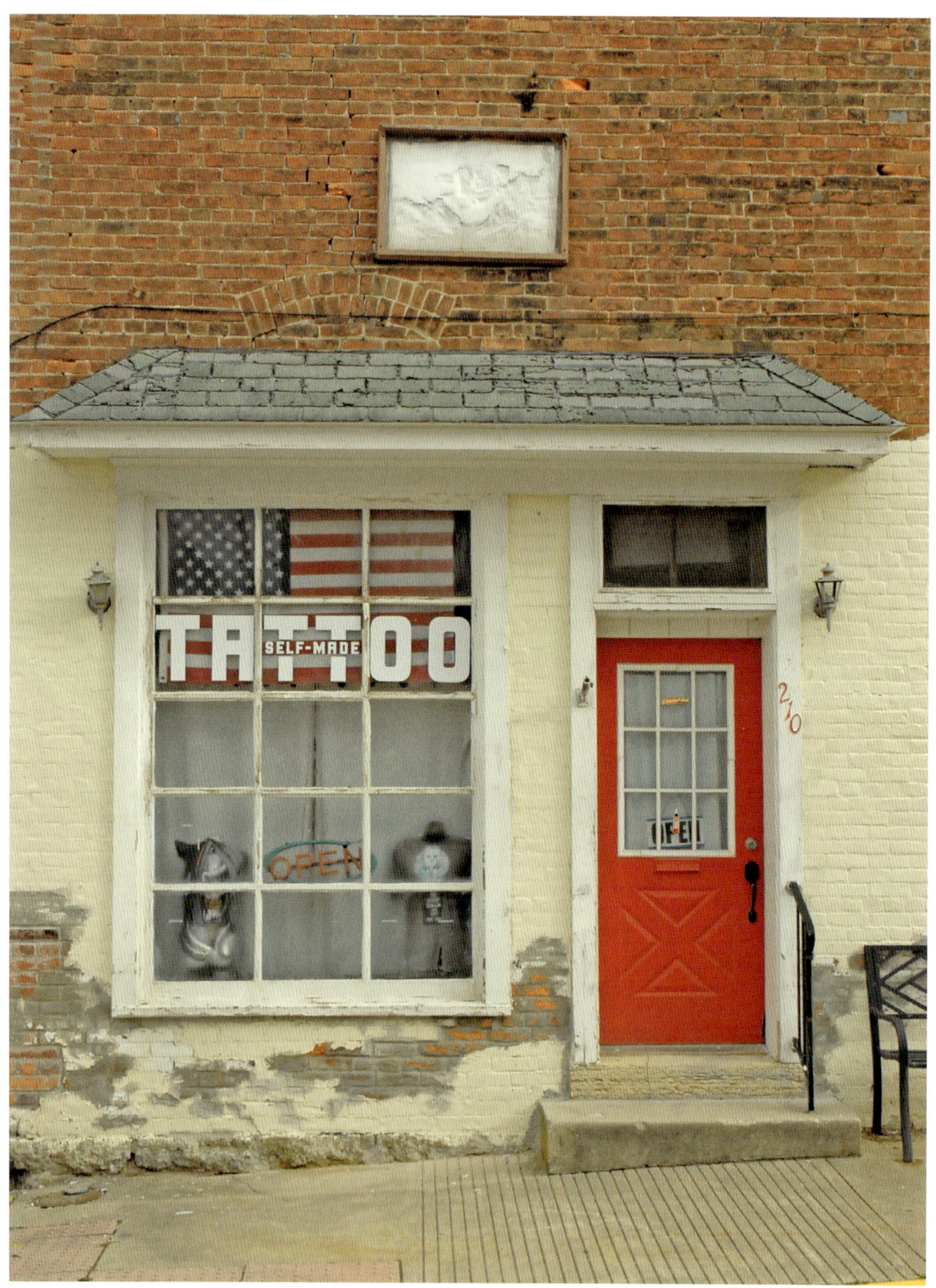

An American flag hangs in the window of the closed Self Made Tattoo Shop in Hartford City.

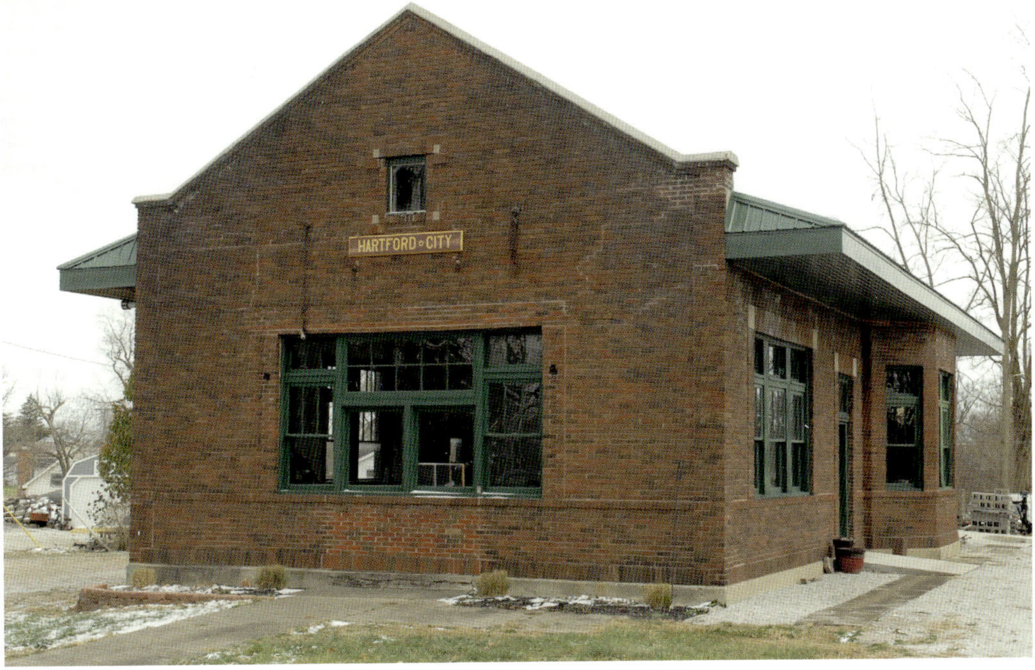

The Hartford City Train Depot was in operation from 1928 to 1958. Built at a cost of $30,000, the train depot was dedicated on August 28, 1928. Over 1,000 people attended the ceremony, where guests were treated to ice cream, lemonade, and cigars.

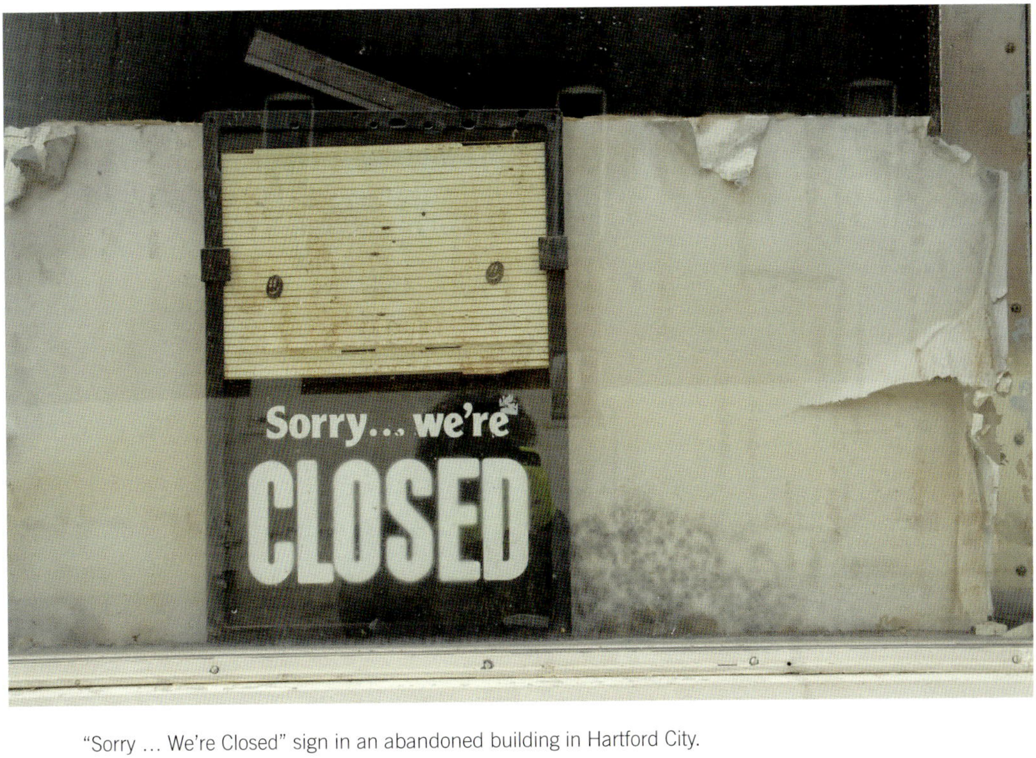

"Sorry ... We're Closed" sign in an abandoned building in Hartford City.

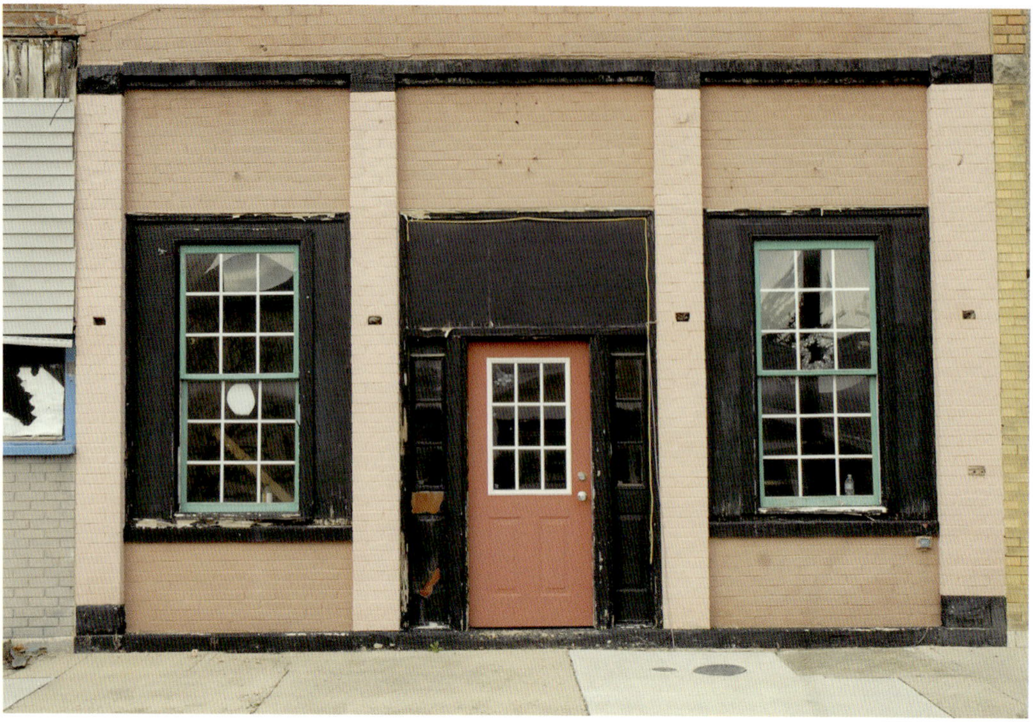

This vacated building was once a thriving business in the small town of Eaton, located in northern Delaware County.

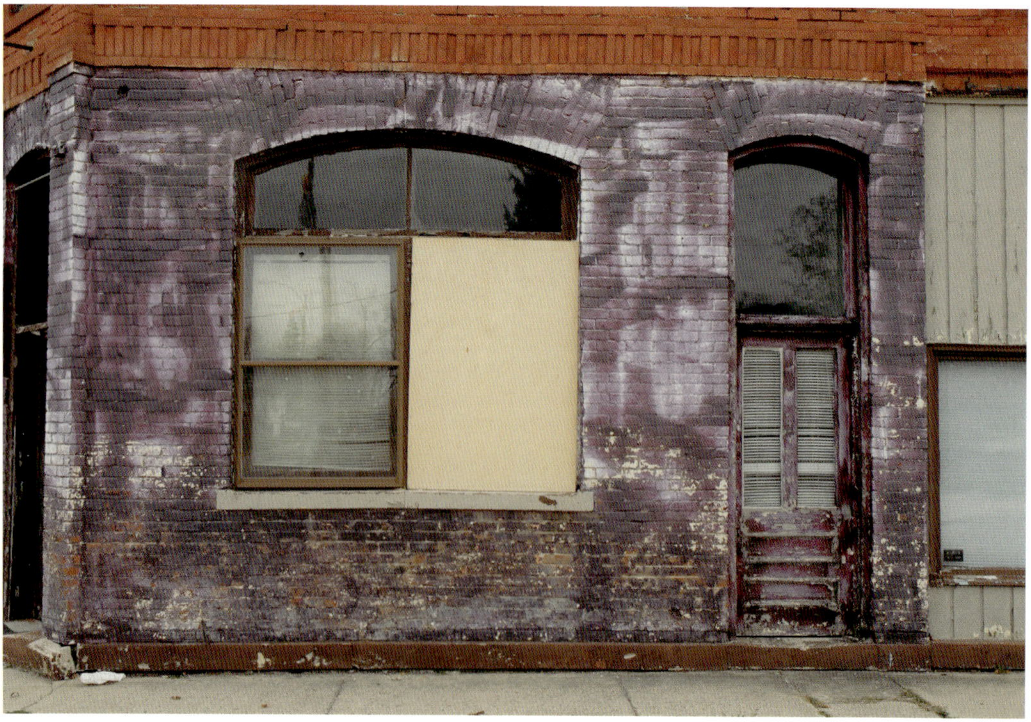

Situated on the main street that runs through Eaton is this empty purple painted building.

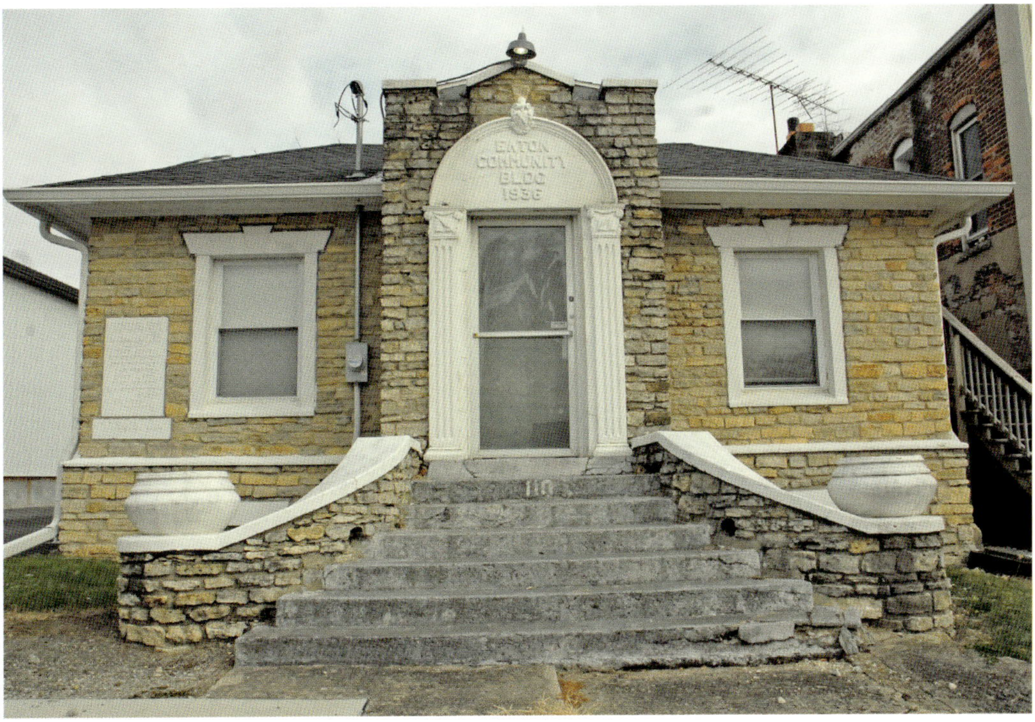

The empty Eaton Community Building was built in 1936, as part of President Franklin Roosevelt's WPA Project. A plaque on the exterior wall of the community center lists the names of the building's designer and town board members.

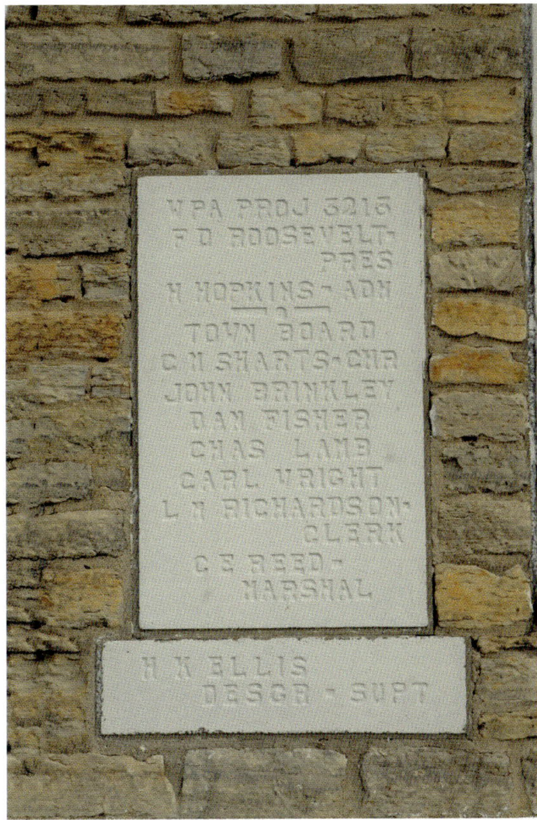

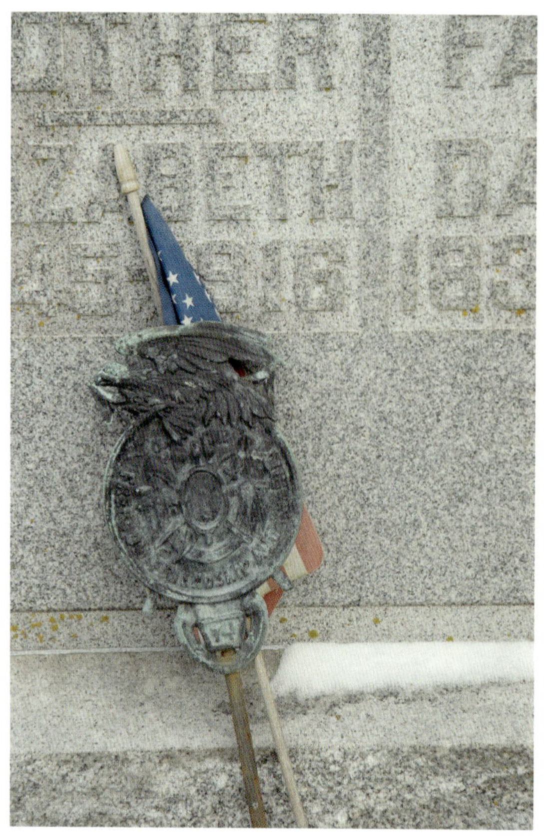

Left: Eaton Cemetery is located just north of Indiana Avenue and not visible from the road. The property is surrounded by a wire fence and littered with fallen trees and branches. Many of the early inhabitants of Eaton are buried at the cemetery. Pictured here is the headstone for Charles and Elizabeth Babb. Charles was a member of Co. A, 8th Regiment of the Indiana Infantry. He fought in the Civil War from September 5, 1861, to January 17, 1863. Charles was born on November 1, 1836, and died on February 27, 1918. Elizabeth lived from 1845 to 1916.

Below: A bench near the graves of John and Elizabeth Hoffman. John fought for the Union Army during the Civil War and served as a private in Company G, 78th Pennsylvania Infantry. Private Hoffman was discharged on September 11, 1865. John and Elizabeth married on September 25, 1873, and had one son named Ralph.

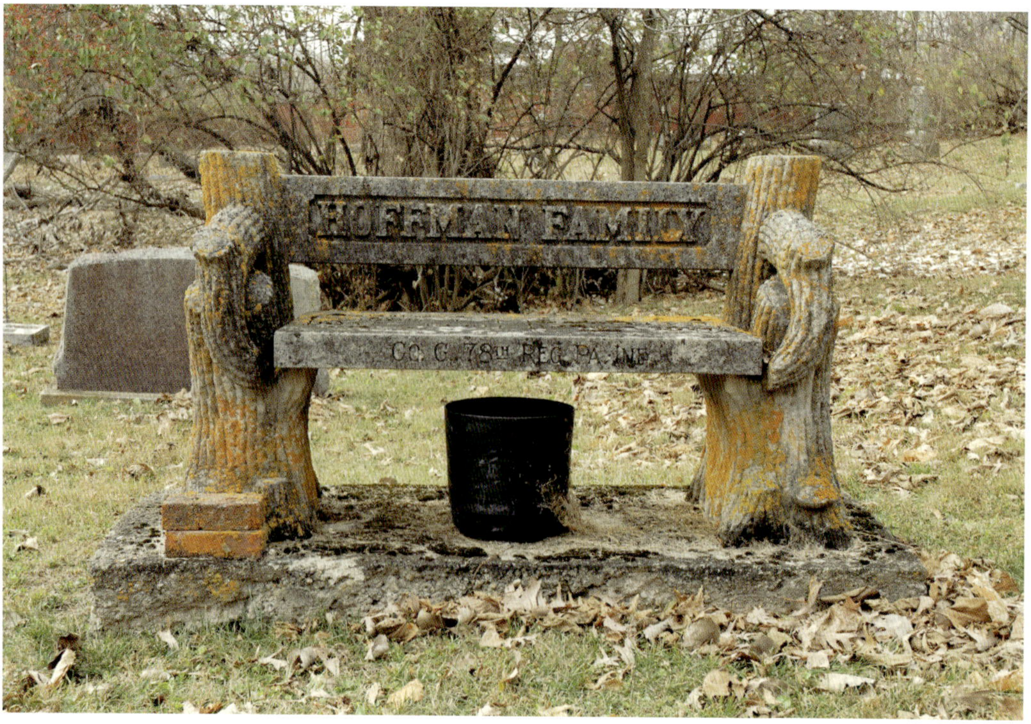

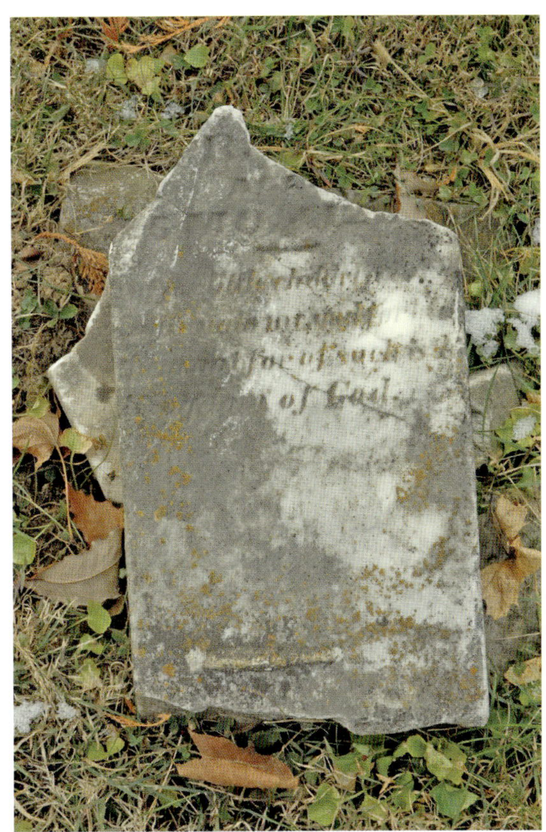

Right: Unearthed grave marker with scripture from the Bible.

Below: Moss covered tombstone of John A. Younce who was born on September 7, 1838, and died on December 28, 1900.

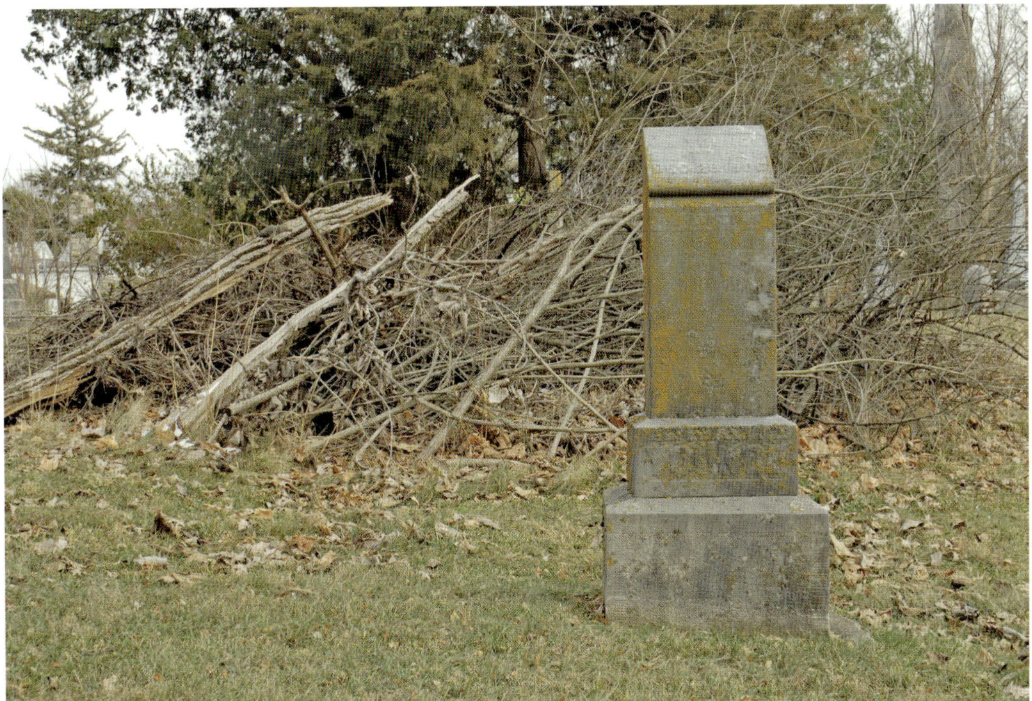

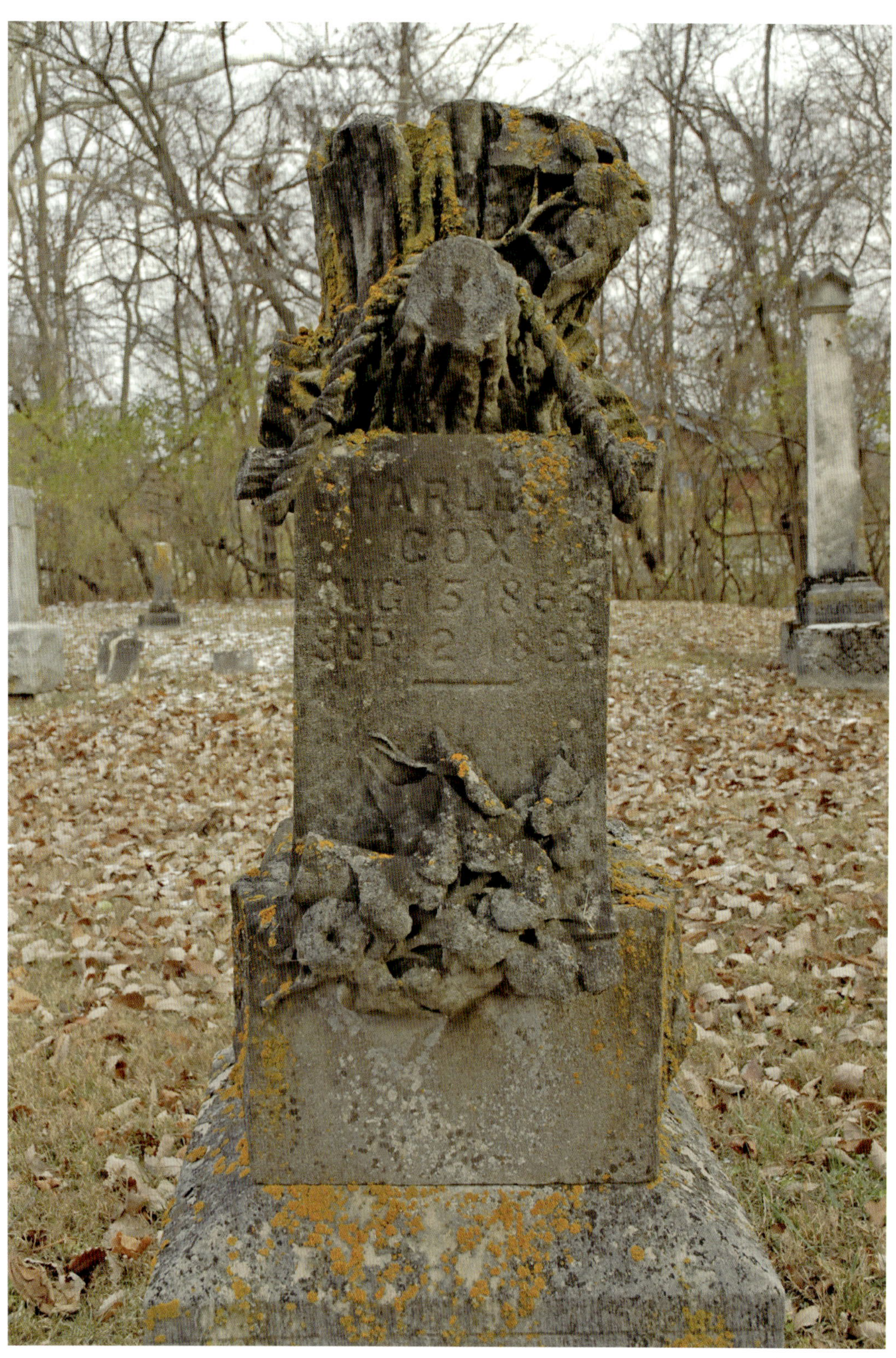

Tombstone for Charles Cox. Born on August 15, 1865, and died on September 12, 1895.

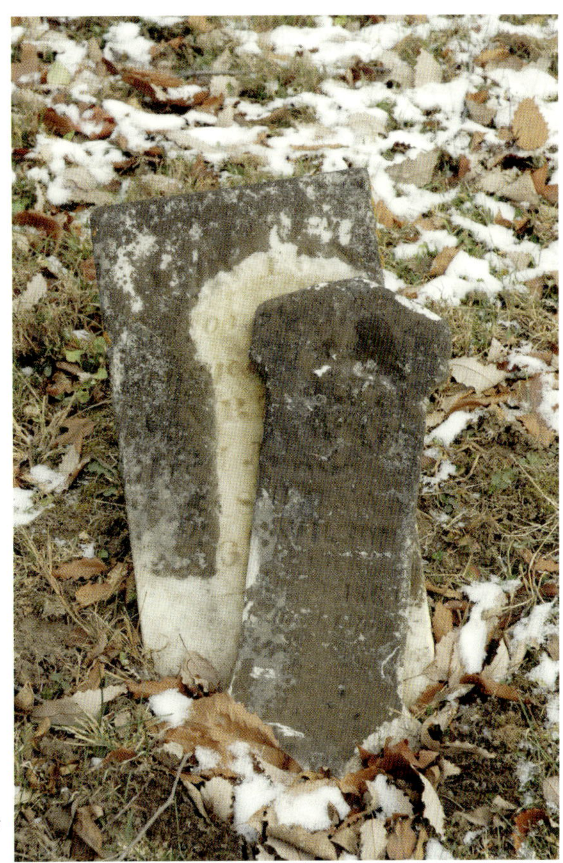

Right: Snow covered headstones at Eaton Cemetery.

Below: Tombstone for James Hummer born on January 31, 1845, and died on December 12, 1887.

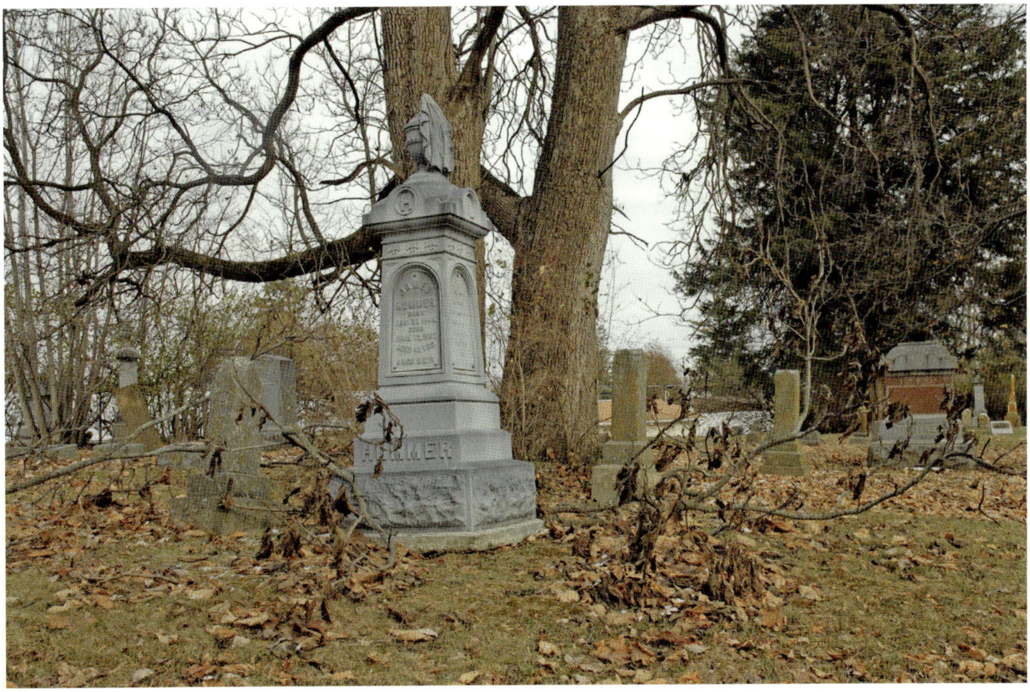

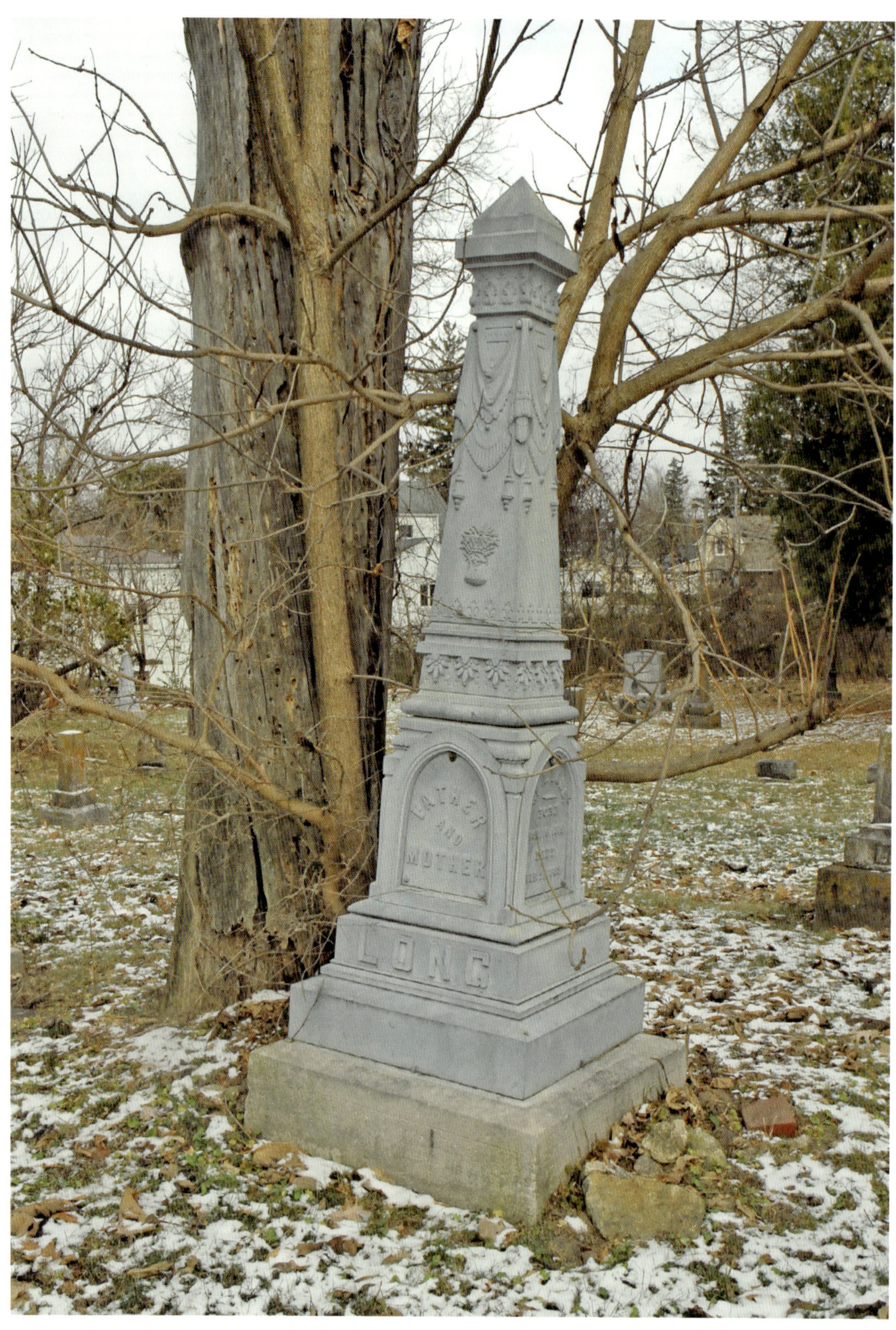

Time has taken its toll on the tombstone of William and Anna Long. William and Anna passed away in 1884 and 1864, respectively.

2

RAIL TRAVEL OF YESTERYEAR

Trains have fascinated people for decades. Countless children have been enthralled by toy trains, ranging from electric locomotives zipping around looped layouts to linkable wooden tracks. A common saying goes something along the lines of, "Boys never grow up; their toys just get bigger and more expensive." The vastly popular hobby of model railroading seems to agree. It is safe to assume that trains are ingrained in our culture. The reason, to quote a beloved children's series about trains, is because they are "really useful."

Most trains seen nowadays in America are freight trains. Many large cities have subways or perhaps street trolleys, but the widespread use of passenger trains is now scarce. In the past, cross-country passenger train routes stretched across the continental United States. Following World War II, improved interstate highways and the rapidly growing airline industry pushed the railways to the side. Like many things that had a heyday in the past, all that remains today are abandoned relics of a bygone era. Formerly bustling train stations lay dormant, and depots lay empty. Abandoned train cars sit quiet and still on defunct rail lines. Not even these behemoth vehicular symbols of travel are safe from being discarded.

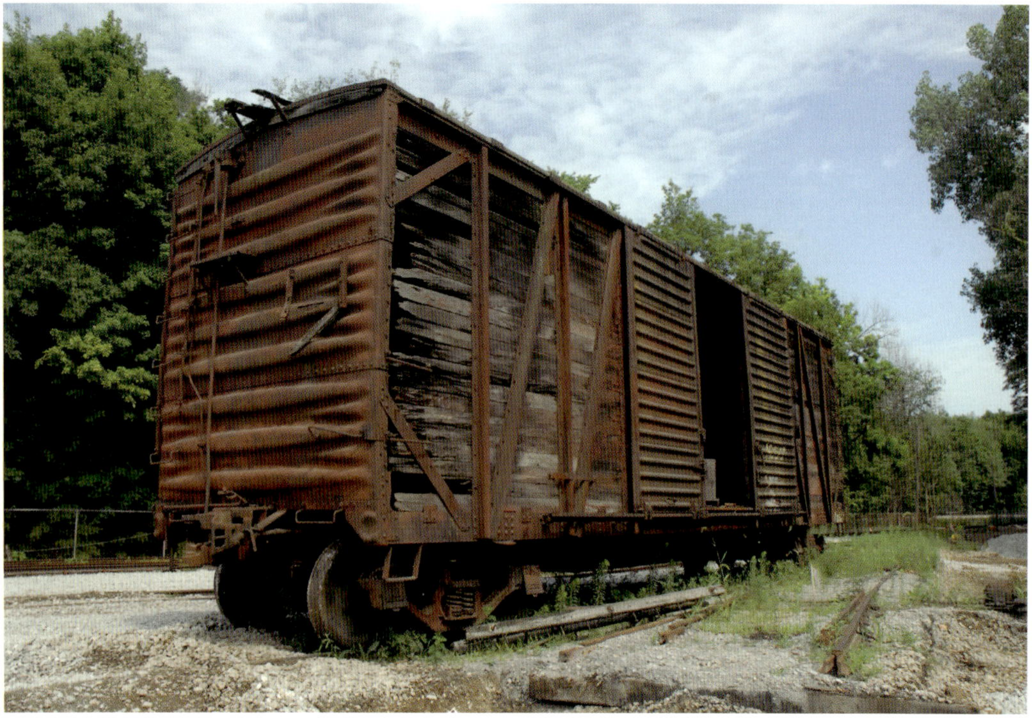

A graveyard of old trains at Forest Park on the east side of Noblesville includes this 1920s boxcar with wood sides.

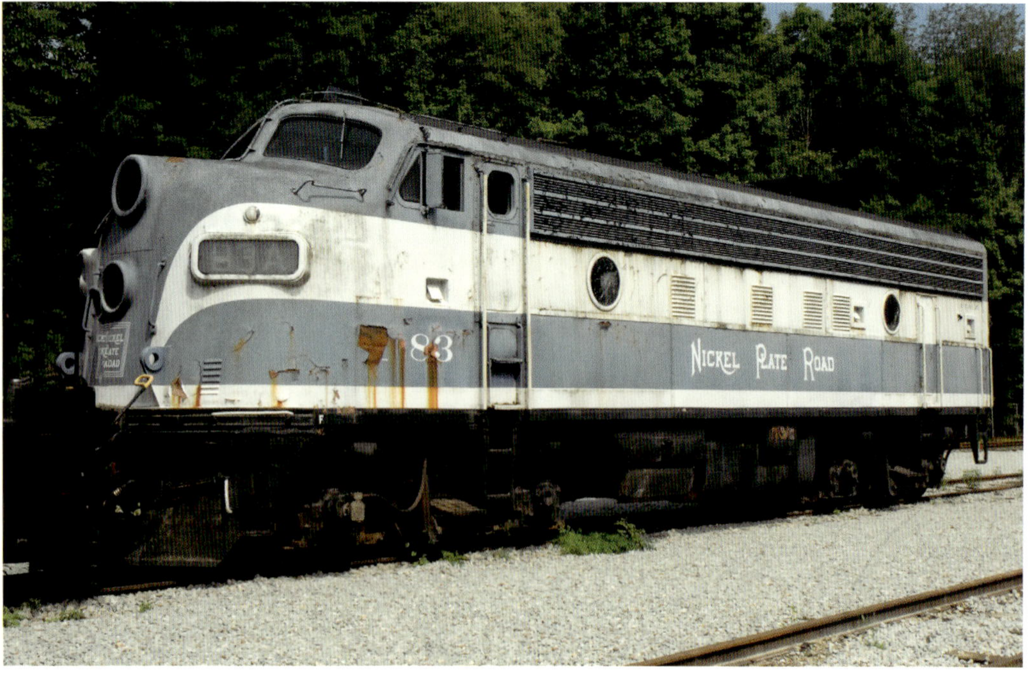

The NKP FA Unit was a diesel-electric locomotive built to haul passenger trains. General Electric and the American Locomotive Company built the locomotive between the years of 1946-1953. It operated on sixteen cylinders with a maximum speed of 117 mph.

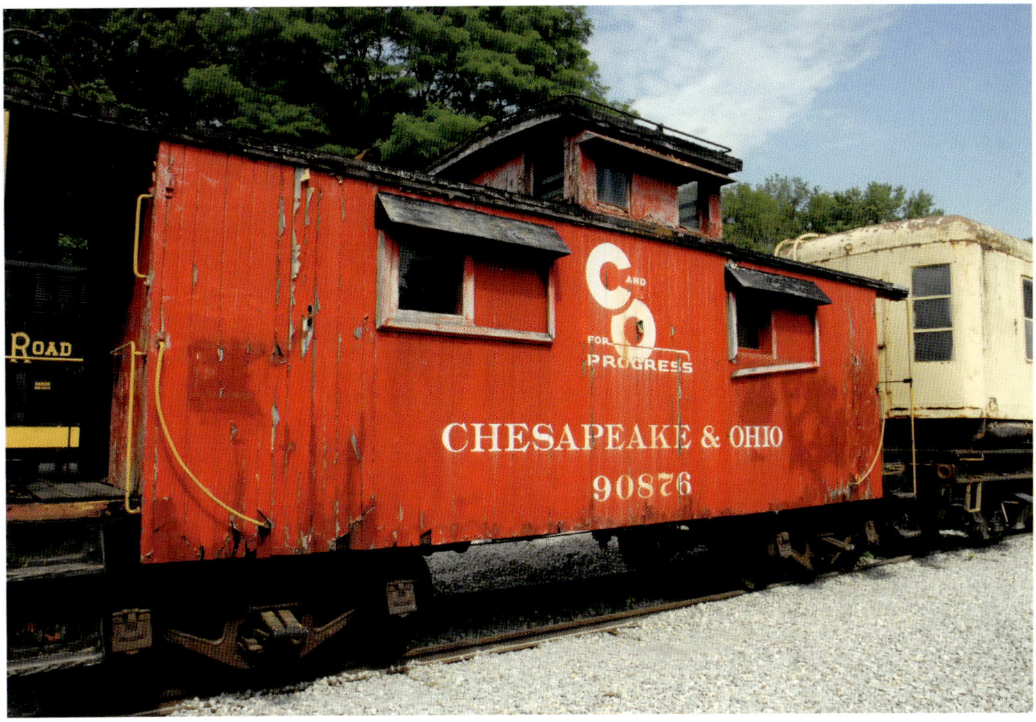

Pictured here is a caboose from the Chesapeake and Ohio Railroad. The caboose was first developed around the 1840s and continued to be used by some railroads until the 1980s. The crummy, shack, shanty and cabin car were a few of the slang names given to the caboose.

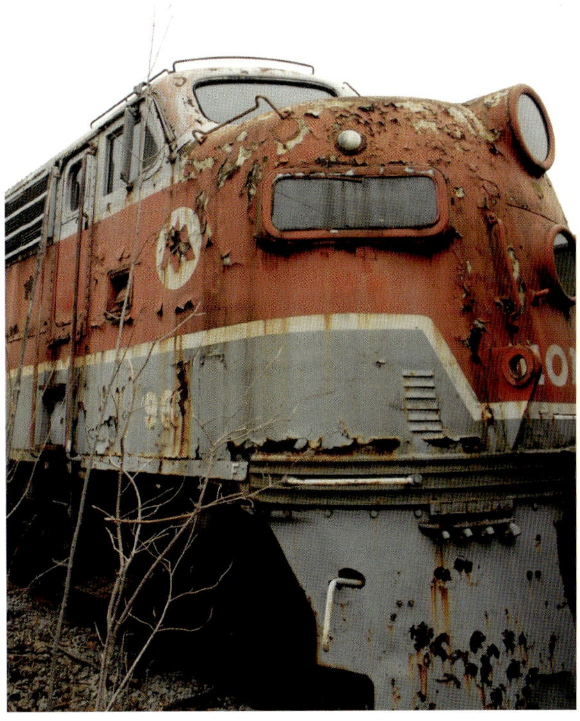

Front view of the MONON FA Unit. At one time the Chicago, Indianapolis, and Louisville Railroad was known as the MONON. *Monon* was a Potawatomie Indian word meaning "swift running." In the 1880s, the Chicago, Indianapolis, and Louisville Railroad began printing "THE MONON ROUTE" on company maps, and later named itself "MONON-The Hoosier Line" on letterheads. The MONON merged into the Louisville and Nashville Railroad in 1971. To many Hoosiers, the MONON will always be remembered as Indiana's railroad.

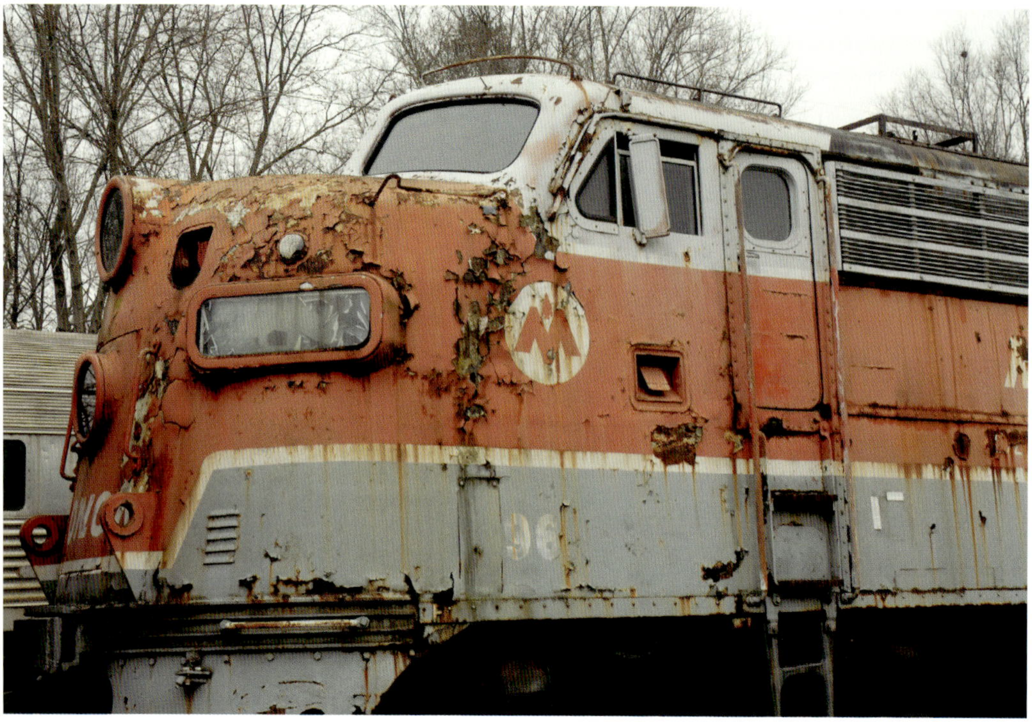

Side view of the MONON FA Unit.

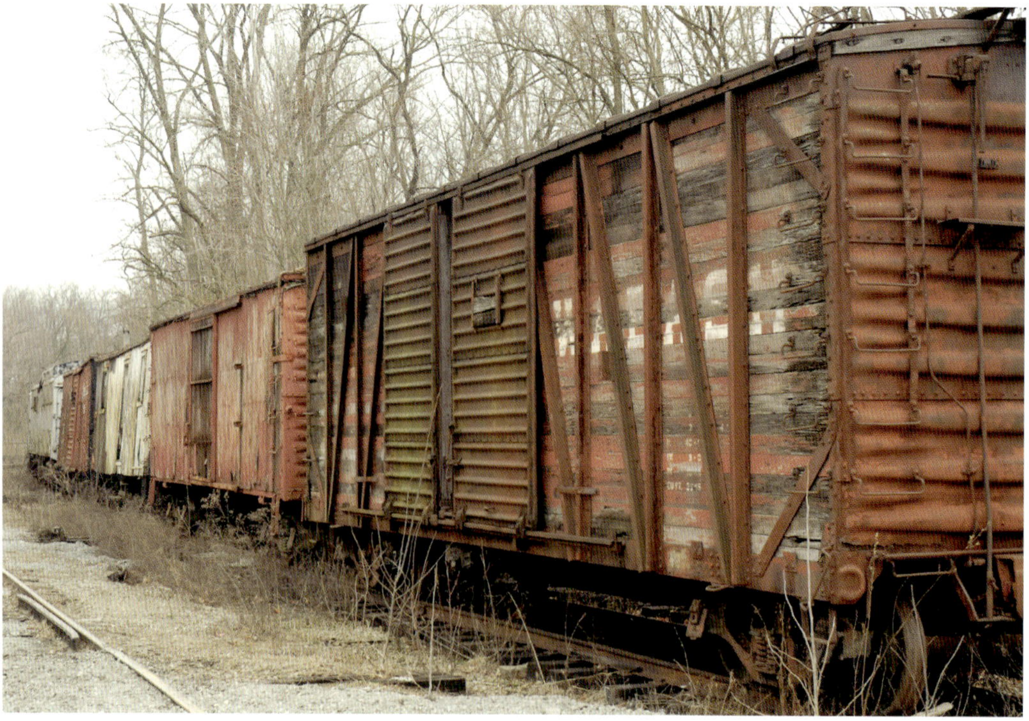

Photo of four boxcars with a caboose at the end and a Wabash in the lead.

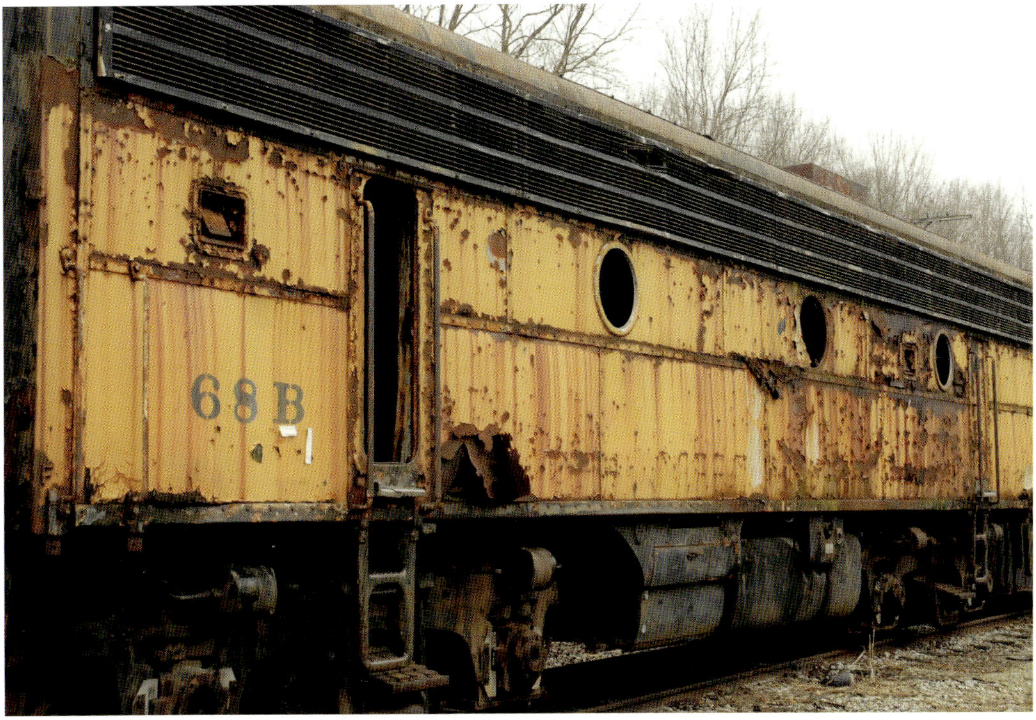

FB Power Unit designed to haul freight trains. This particular model was built from 1946-1959, with over 1,500 produced.

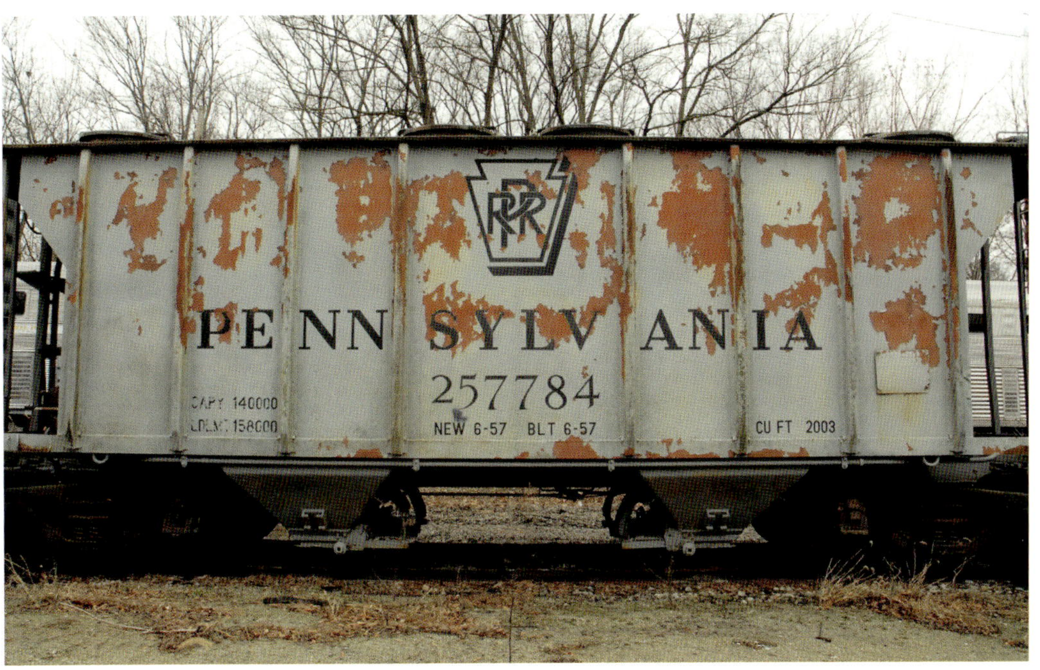

Pennsylvania Railroad hopper car once used to transport coal, grain, and ore.

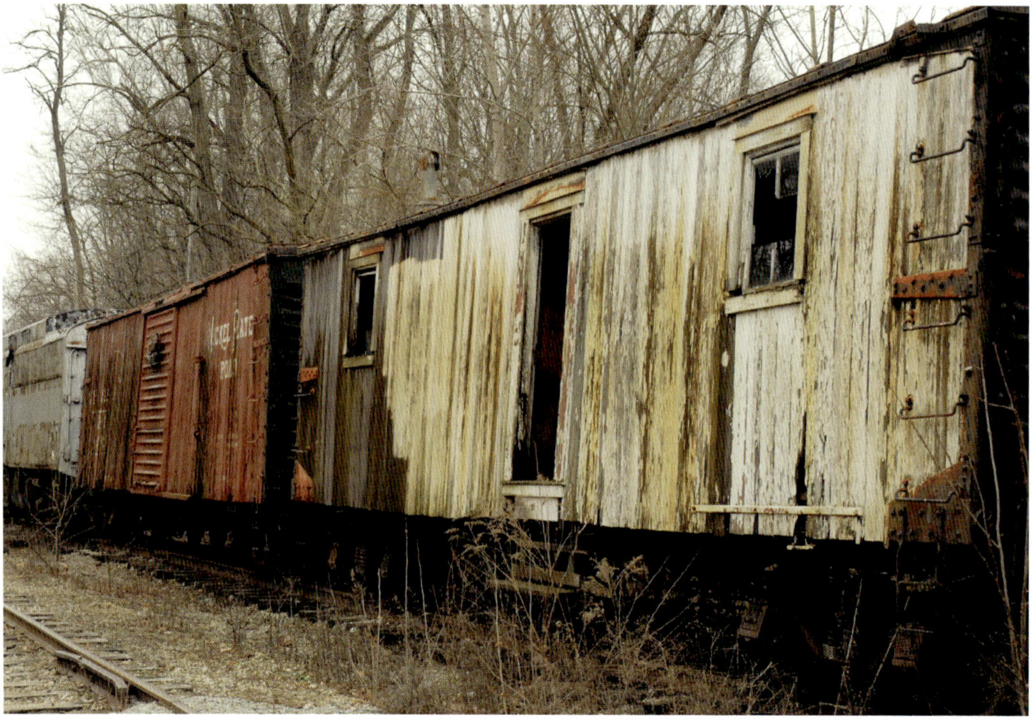

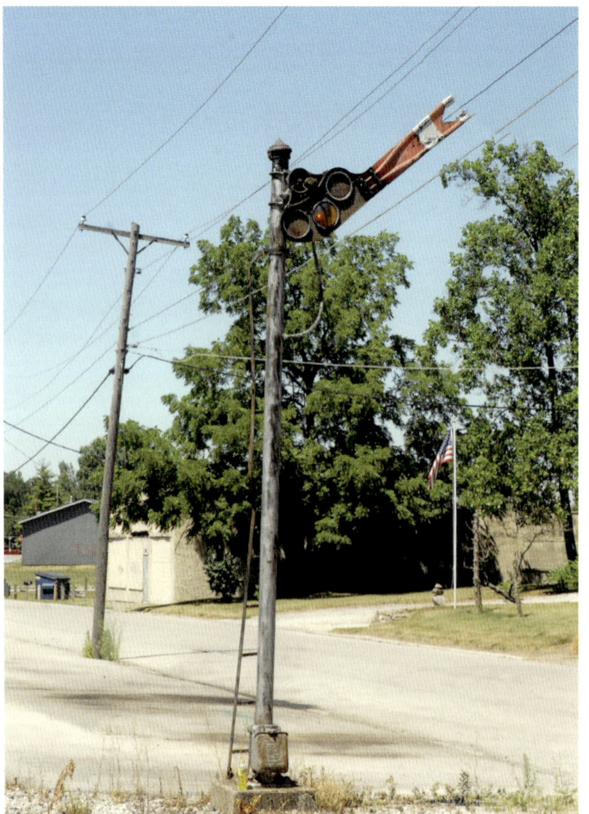

Above: Work car with wood sides leading a boxcar and the caboose.

Left: Signal set for telling trains to slow ahead.

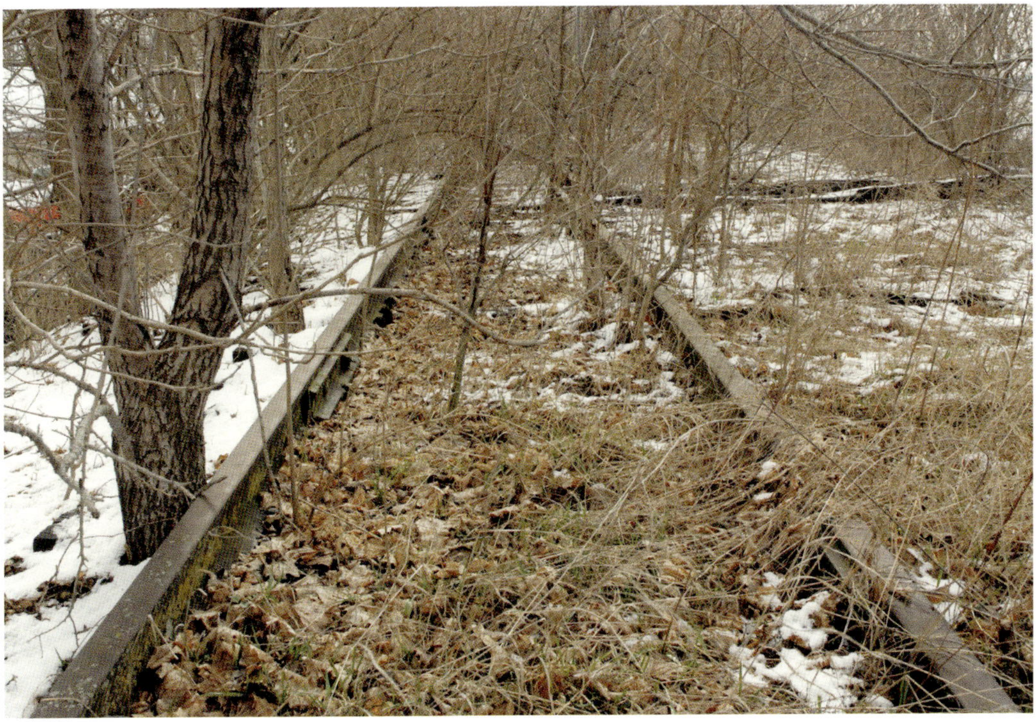

Abandoned railroad tracks near Sulphur Springs in Henry County.

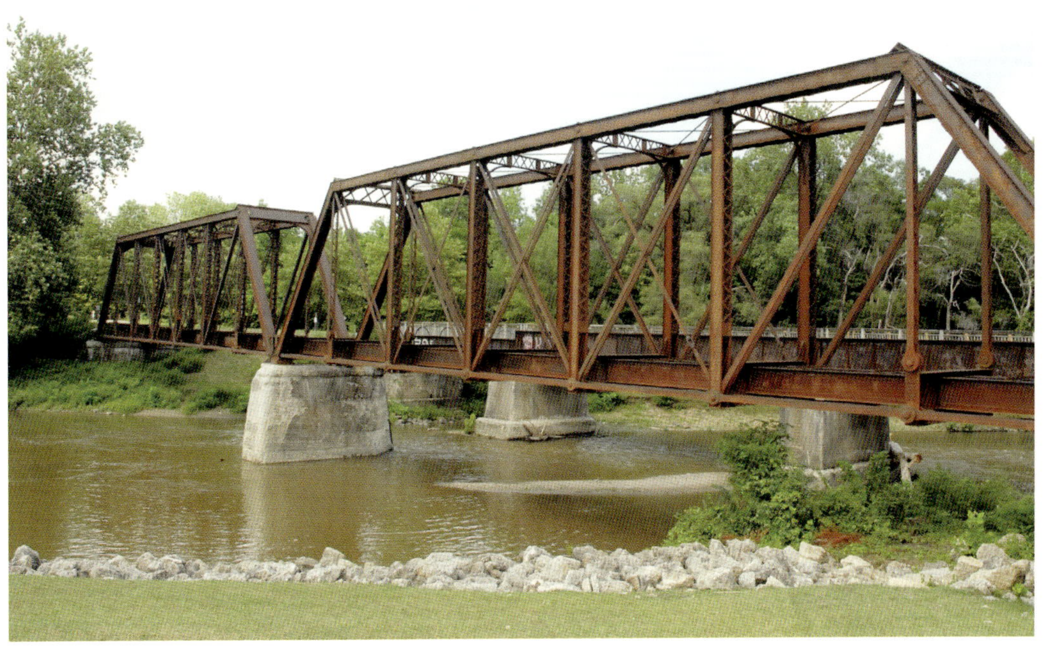

This abandoned bridge once used by the Pennsylvania Railroad can be found near McCullough Park in Muncie. The bridge was built in 1855 and spans over White River.

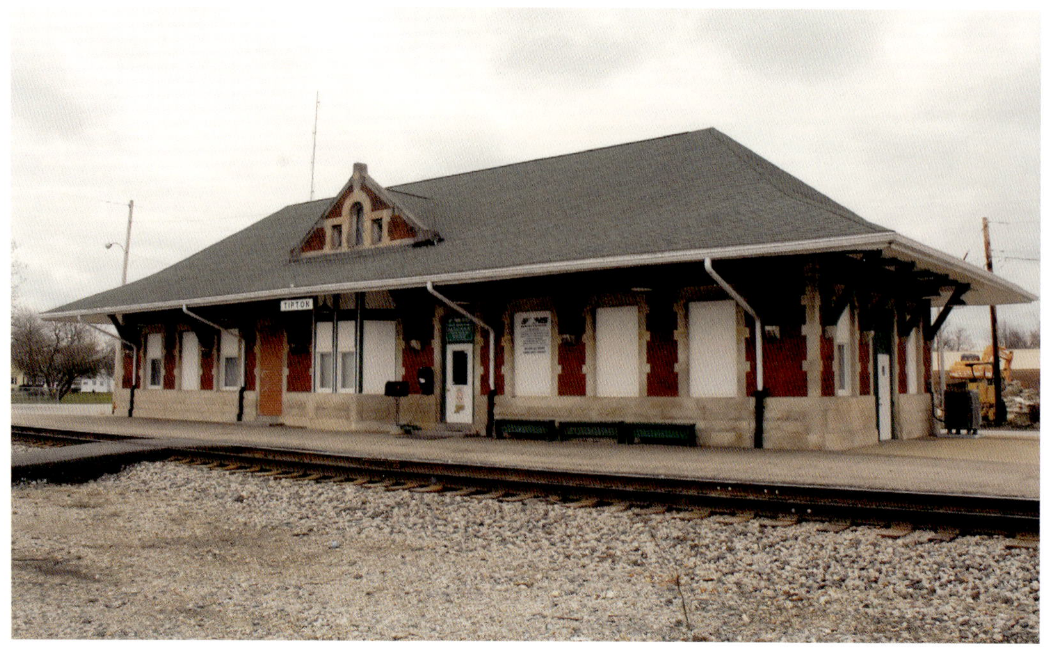

Still standing is the passenger train depot in Tipton. The train depot was built by the Lake Erie & Western Railroad and is now owned by Norfolk Southern.

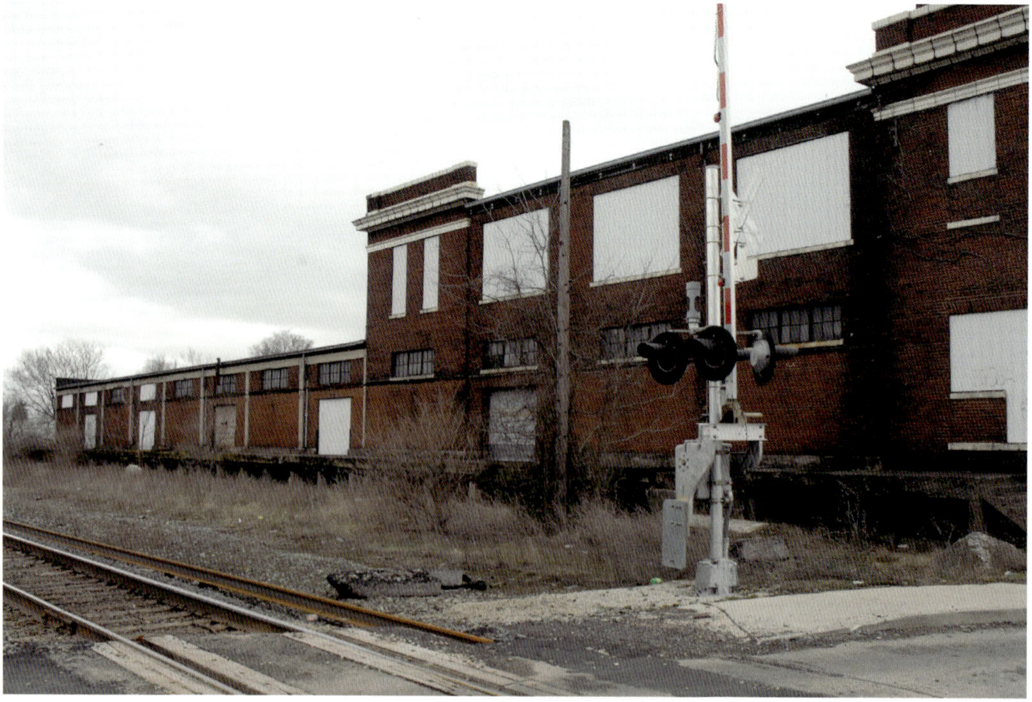

In 1920, the Cleveland, Cincinnati, Chicago, and St. Louis Railroad Company built a freight agency office and an attached freight building on South Liberty Street in Muncie. After New York Central stopped handling their own small shipments, freight forwarding companies operated in the Muncie freight house. The C.C.C. & St. L. R. R. building still stands and is currently for sale.

3

RURAL SCENES

Perhaps the most famous attribute of the Midwest is its connection to agriculture. Any Midwesterner, save for those in truly urban areas, is well-acquainted with the sight of farmland. In the oft-nicknamed "Breadbasket" or "Corn Belt," fields of corn and soybeans stretch as far as the eye can see. Traveling on the highways, the only view out the car window is often corn, silos, corn, a barn, soybeans, a quaint little farmhouse, more corn.

Such a crop yield requires significant agricultural infrastructure. In modern times, tractors towing planters sow millions of seeds in neat rows, and massive combine harvesters reap bushels and bushels months later. While the core concept of agriculture has changed little in millennia, the equipment certainly has. It was truly not that long ago that ox-drawn plows tilled the land to be sewn by hand. Fortunately, sophisticated machinery was eventually built to assist farmers.

The image of an early-twentieth century tractor is iconic. Equally iconic is the picturesque big red barn with white painted accents and a silo companion. Unfortunately, tractors rust away, and barns rot, leaning precariously on the verge of collapse. These agricultural necessities, once so many families' ways of life, are fading into obscurity.

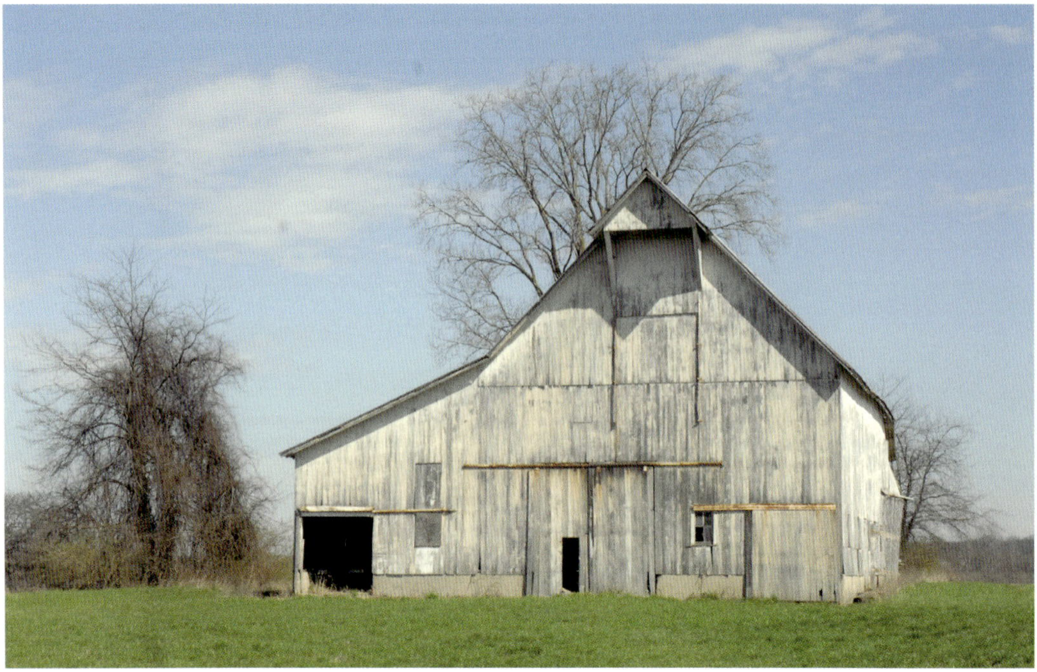

This dilapidated barn stands off State Road 32 in Hamilton County. Old-fashioned barns that speckle our landscape are vanishing. Some barns are demolished, while others, weak with years, simply crumple.

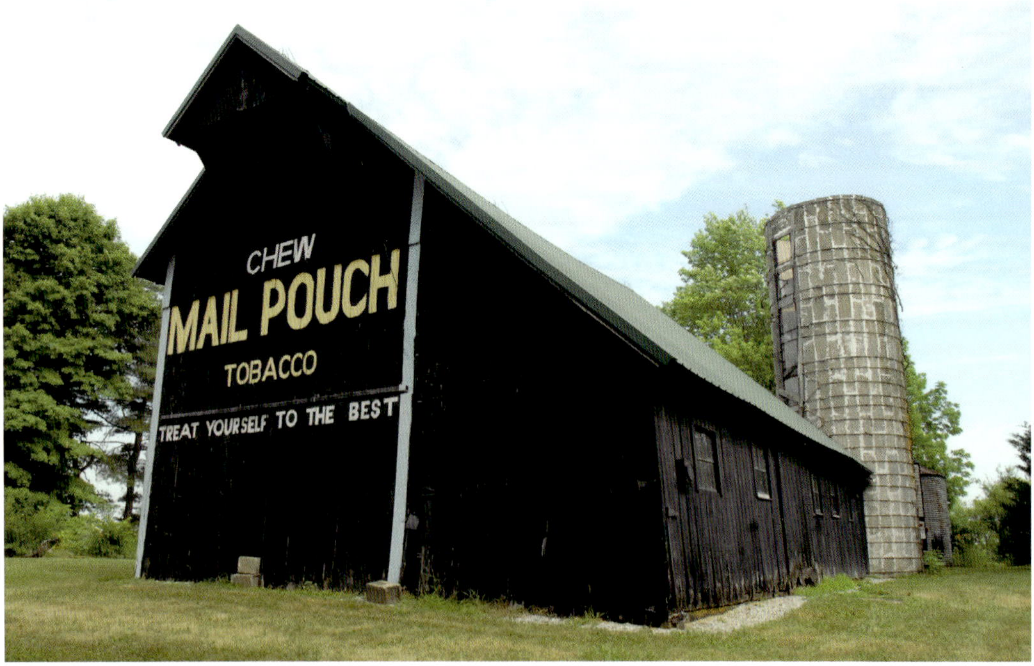

A Mail Pouch Tobacco barn located north of Noblesville was recently revived with a fresh coat of paint. In the early 1960s, there were over 20,000 Mail Pouch barns in twenty-two states. At the height of barn advertising, many companies paid farmers to use their barns as roadside advertisement. By the early 1990s, Mail Pouch Tobacco stopped using barns to advertise its product.

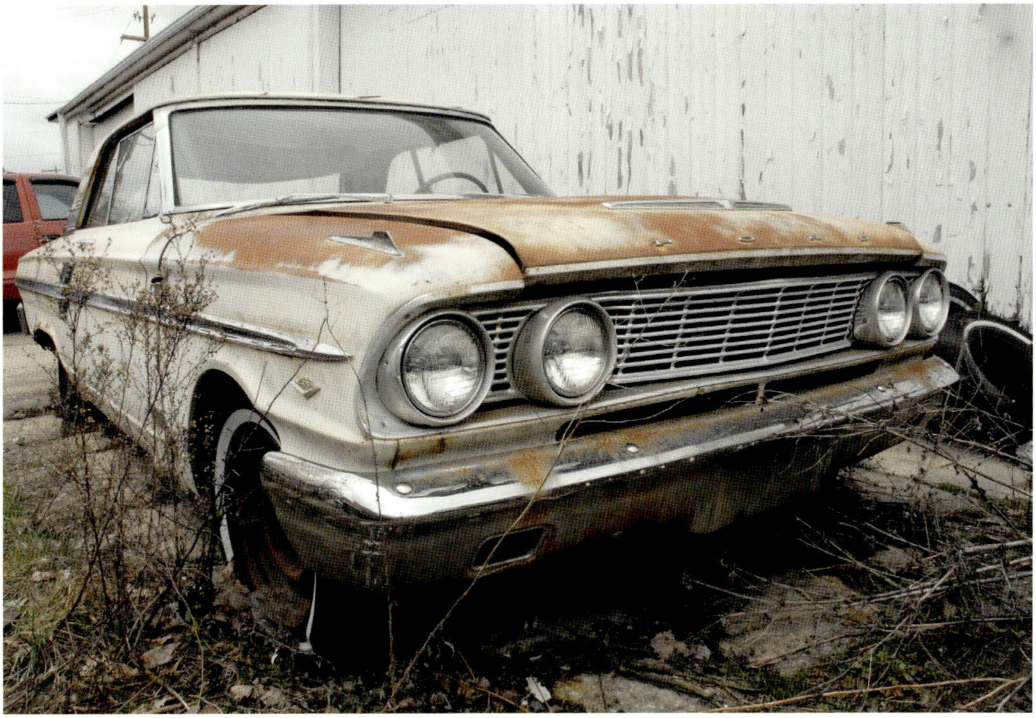

A Ford Fairlane Sports Coupe sits on the outskirts of Farmland near State Road 32. The Ford Fairlane was produced by Ford Motors from 1955-1970.

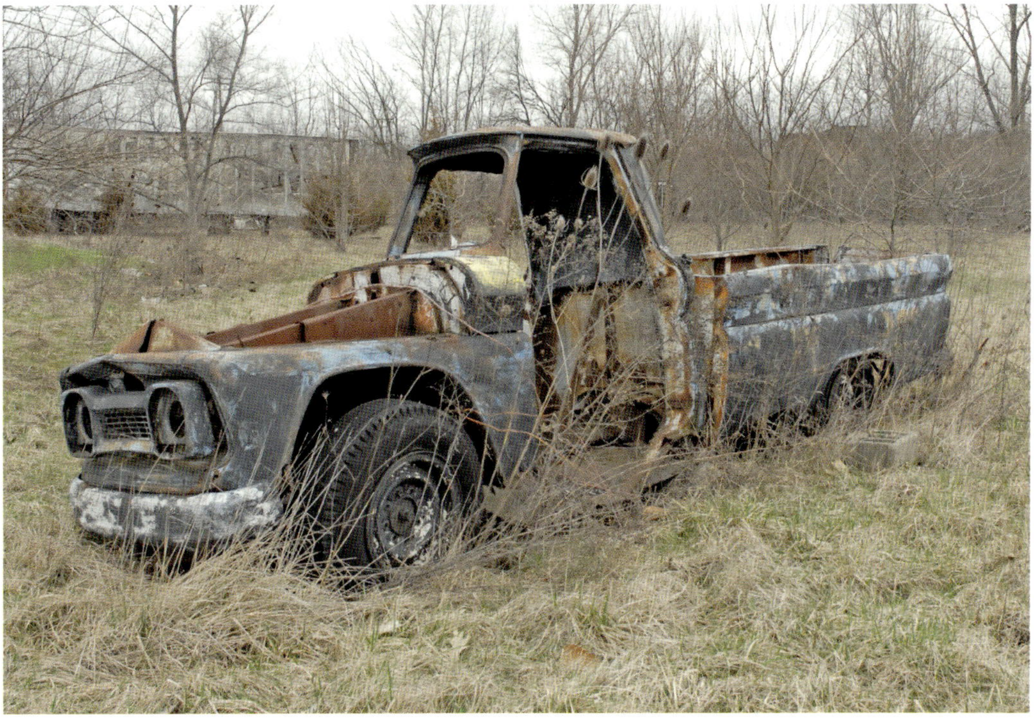

All that remains of this old pick truck is its frame and tires.

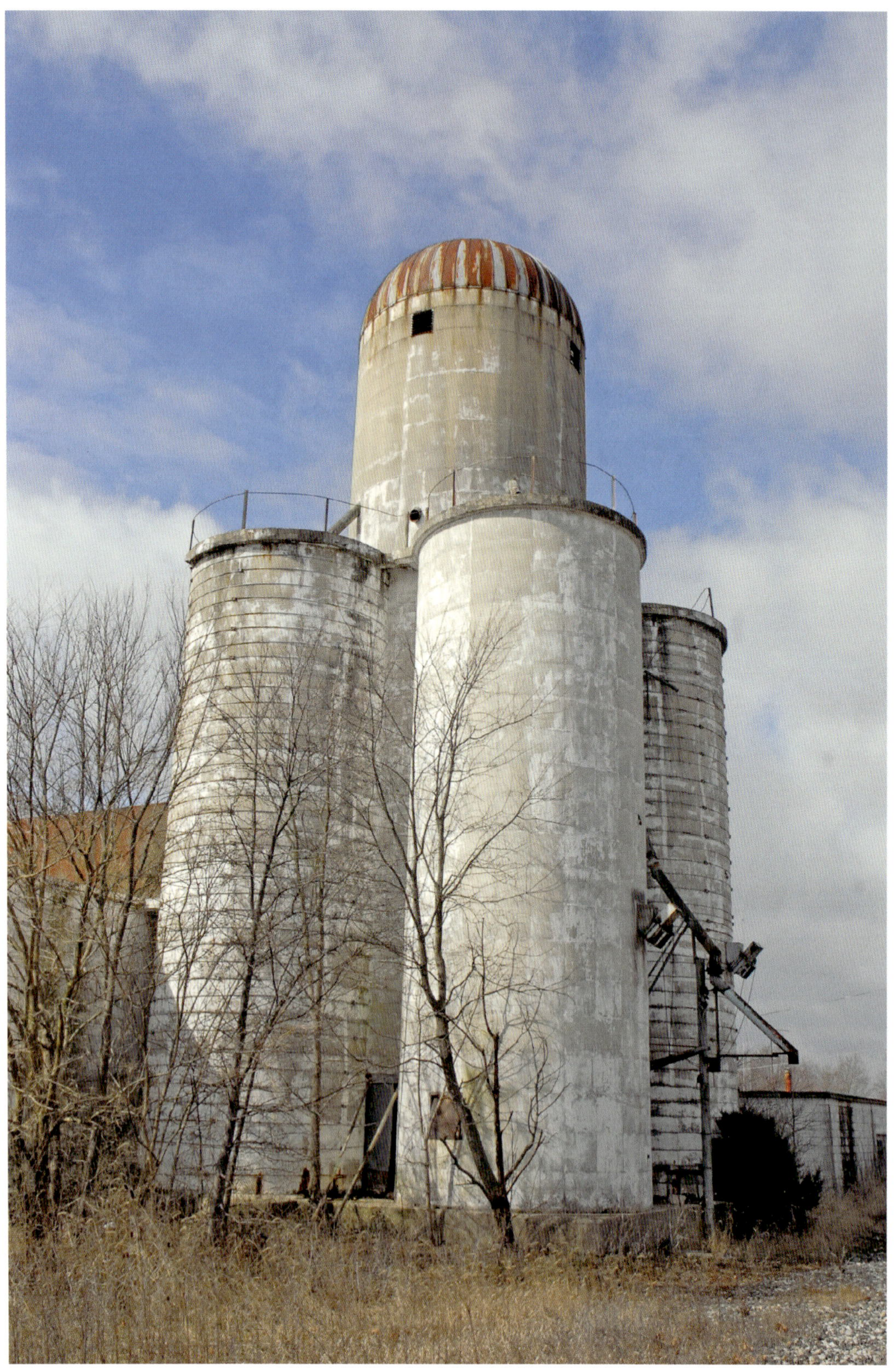

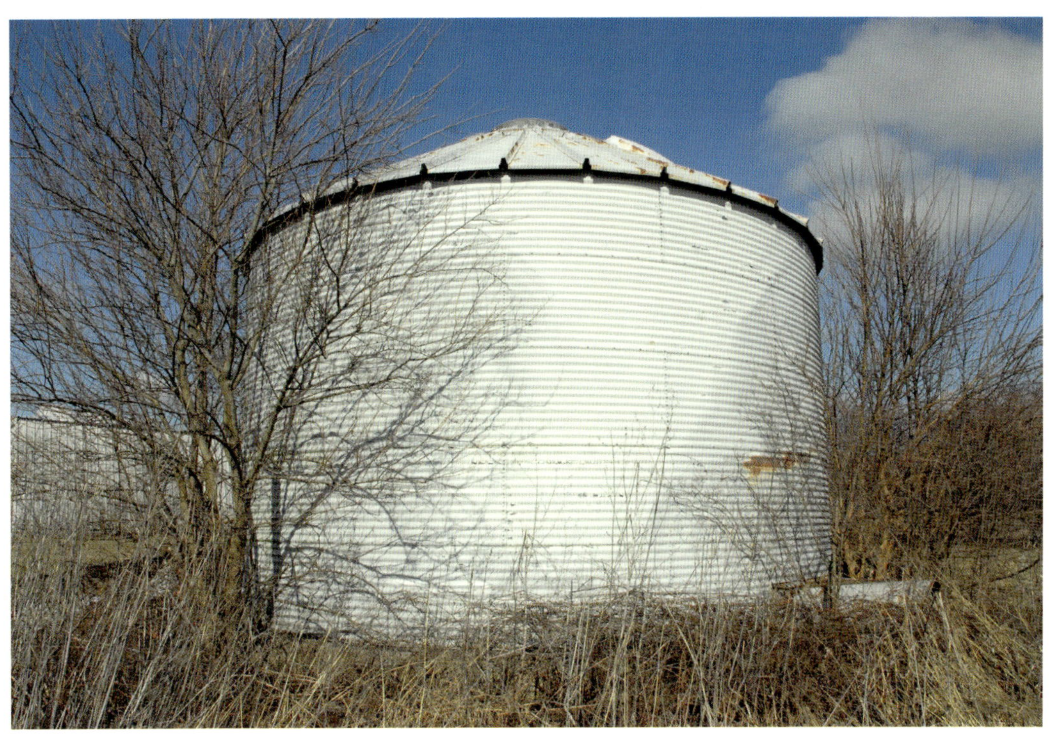

Above and opposite: Variations of abandoned silos photographed in the Selma countryside in Delaware County.

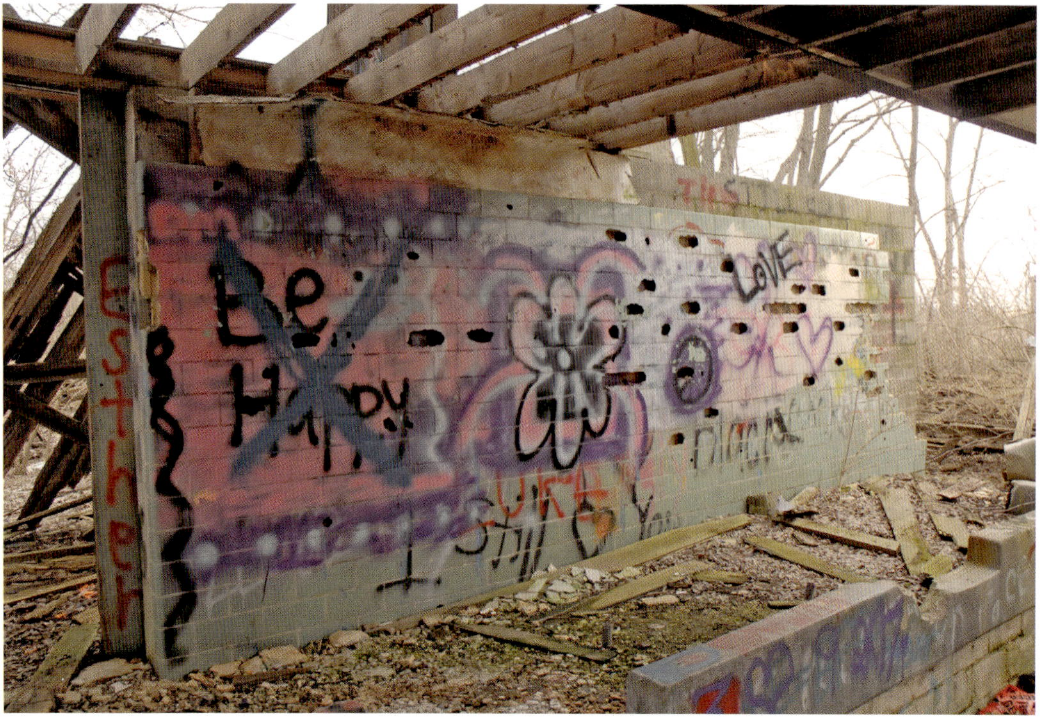

Spray painted graffiti on what remains of a razed house in Hamilton County.

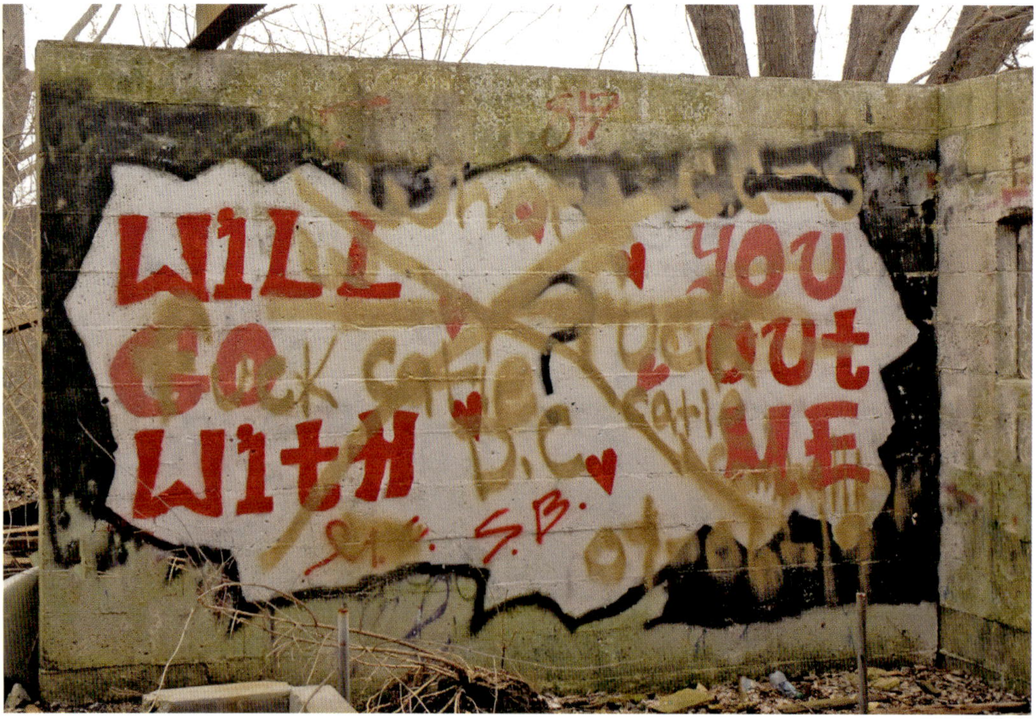

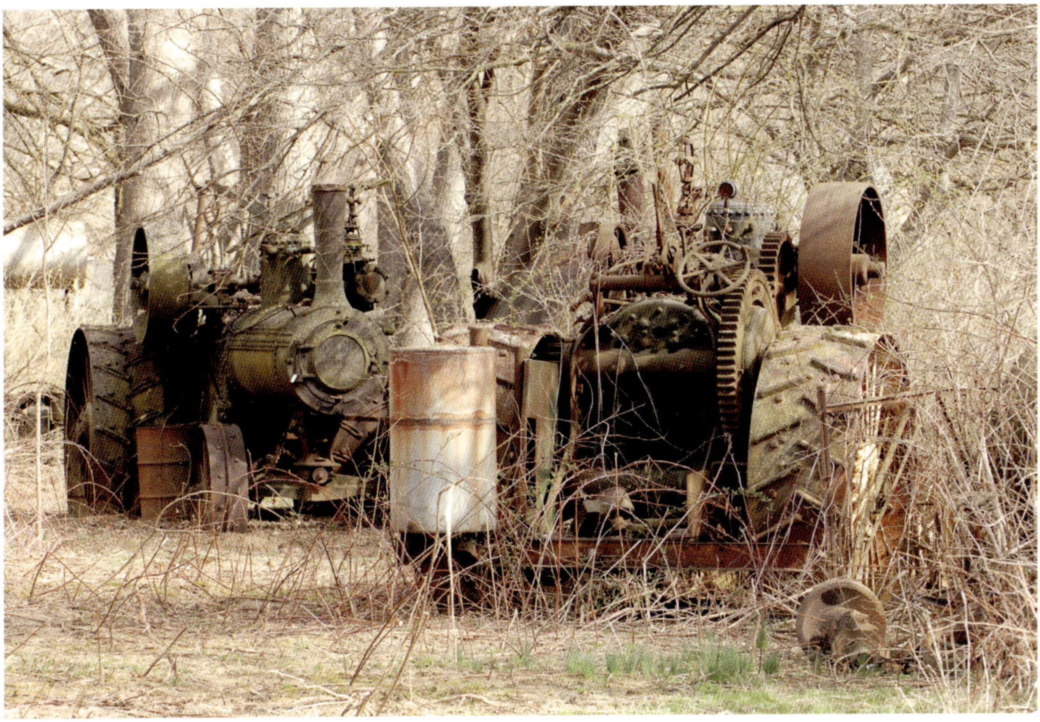

Rusted farm machinery in a weed infested field near Henry County.

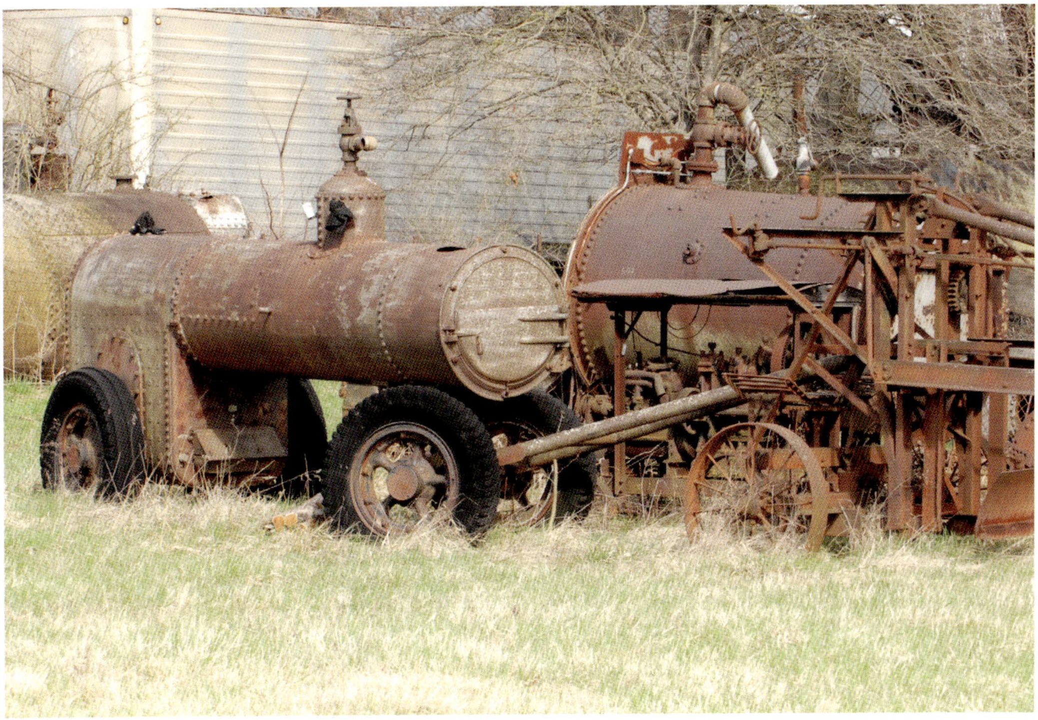

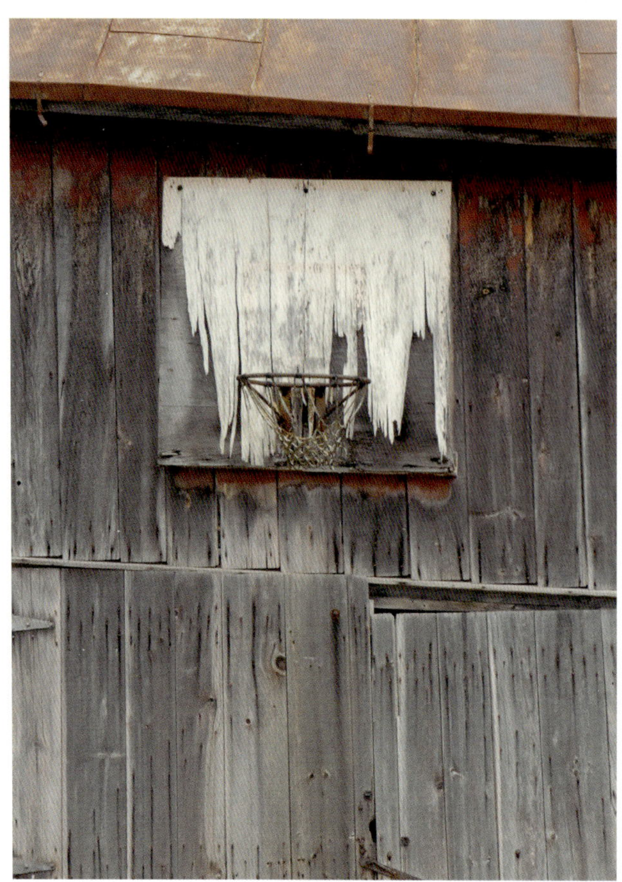

Left: Hundreds upon hundreds of Hoosiers learned to play basketball courtesy of a backboard and goal affixed to the side of a barn.

Below: Thornhaven Manor sits isolated and abandoned in a field off Indiana 3 near New Castle. Simon T. Powell, one of the richest and most influential men in Indiana, built the biggest house in Henry County in 1845. Thornhaven Manor is popular with ghost hunters, who have investigated reports of paranormal activity at the house.

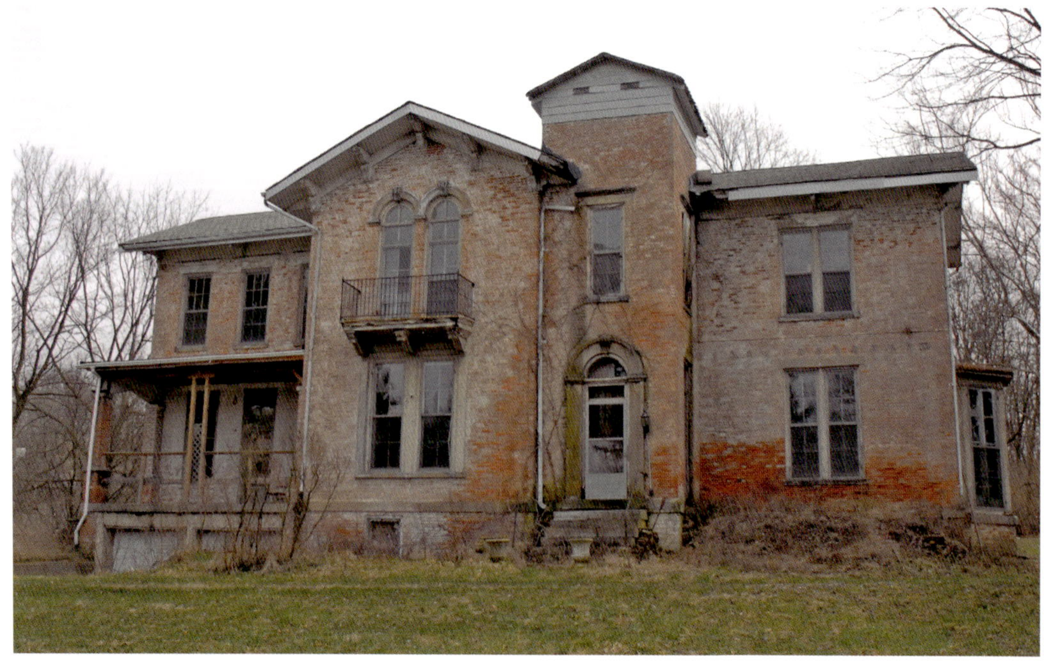

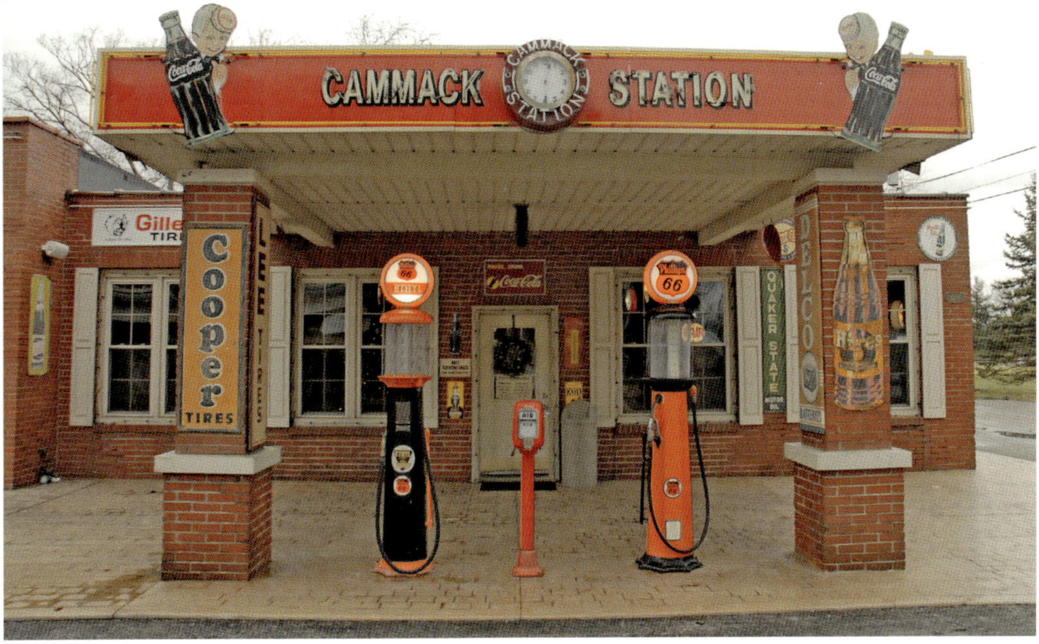

Cammack Station suits anyone who is nostalgic and loves good food, milk shakes, and ice cream. The old-fashioned restaurant is located at Old Mill Street and West Jackson Street in the town of Cammack, just west of Muncie. The historic building was built in 1931, and formerly used as grocery stores and gas stations. Cammack Station owner Dick Howe purchased the property and converted it into a restaurant in 2007. Cammack Station is proof that old historic buildings can be renovated and given a new purpose.

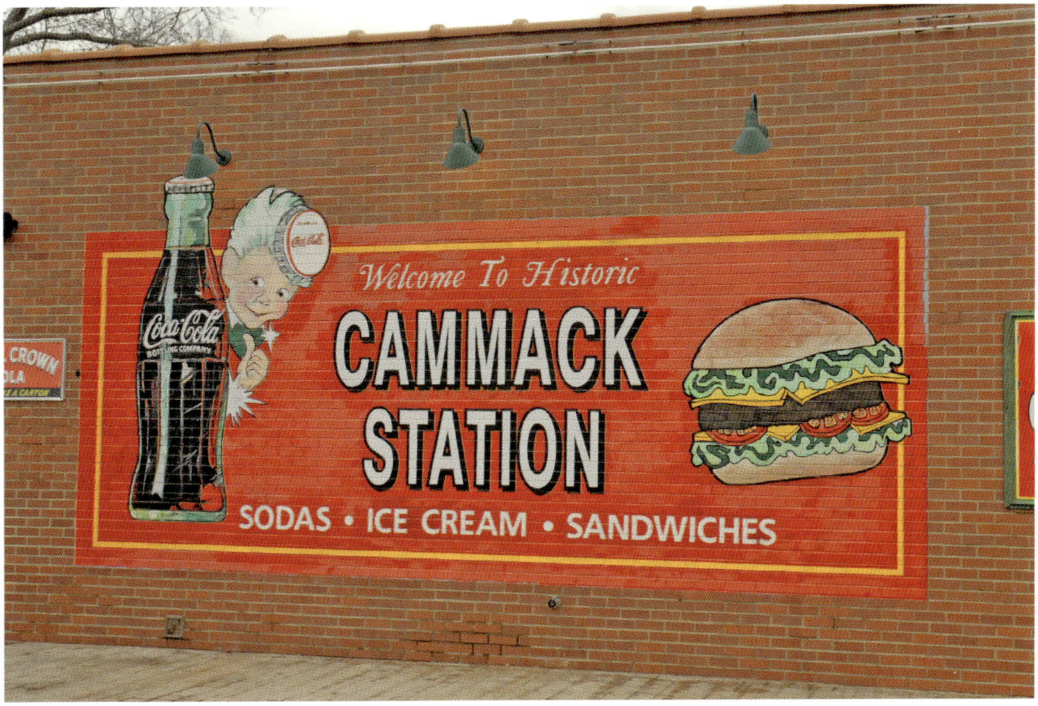

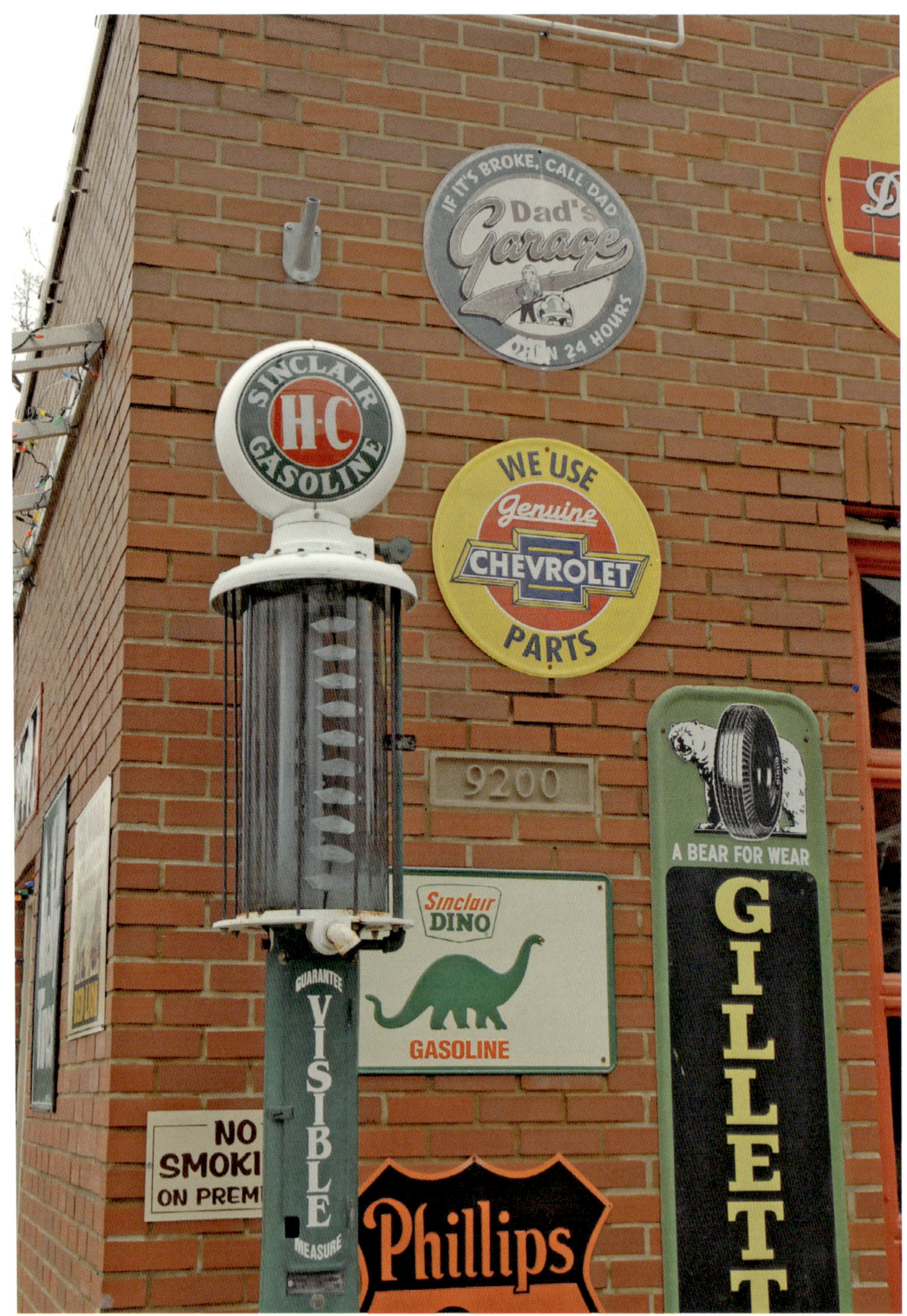

A Sinclair visible gas pump on display outside Cammack Station. Visible gas pumps were first introduced in 1918 and are in big demand with today's collectors.

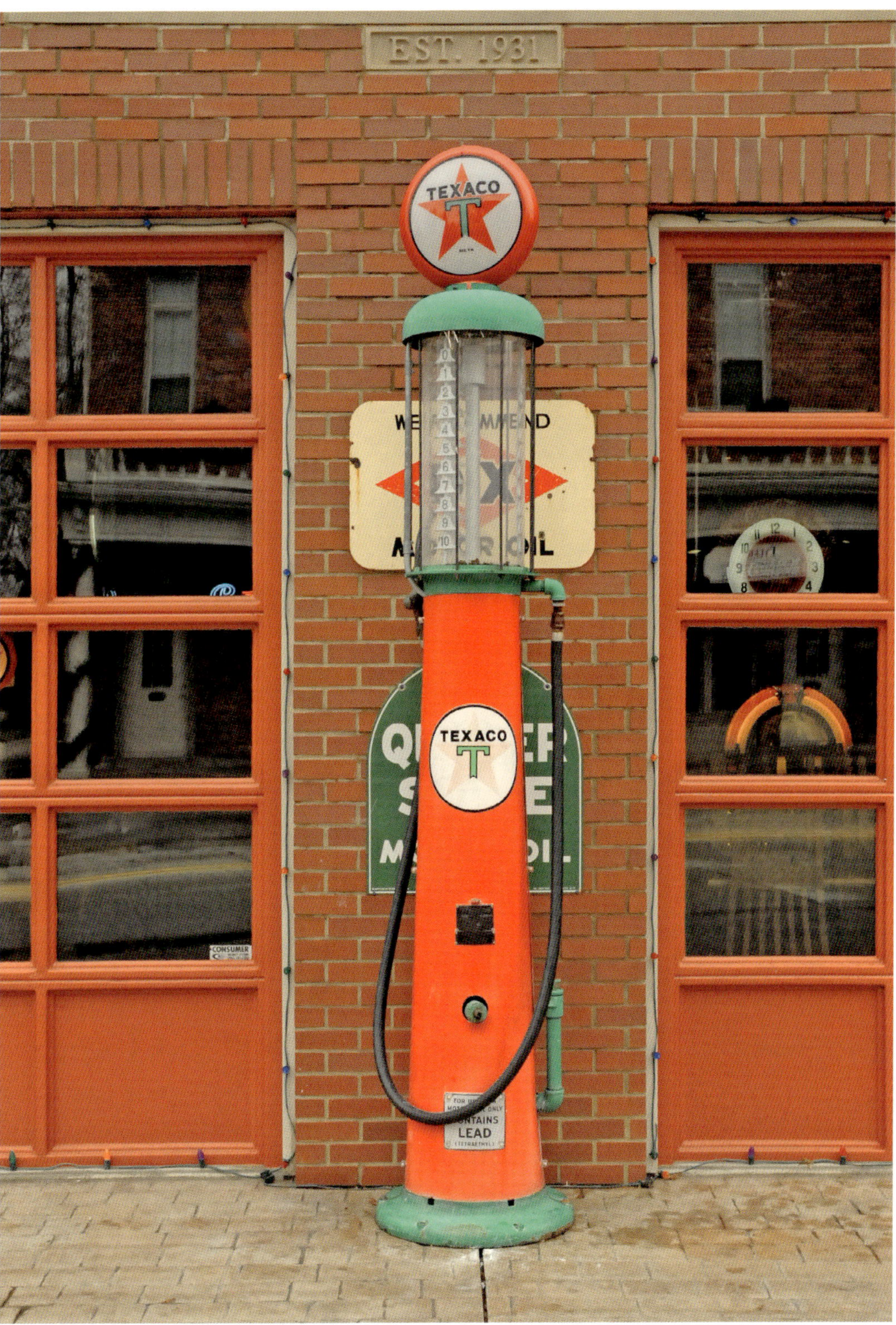

A Texaco gas pump.

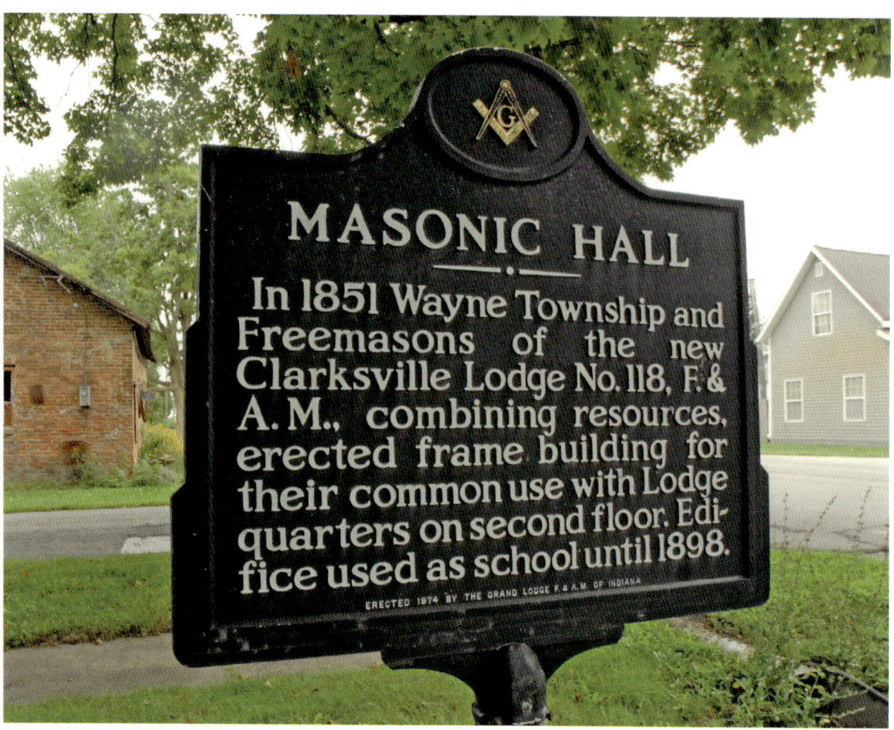

In 1974, the Grand Lodge of Free and Accepted Masons of Indiana, erected this historical marker on the grounds of the Masonic Hall in Clarksville. The Clarksville Masonic Hall is located off State Road 38 and Mason Street in the Hamilton County town.

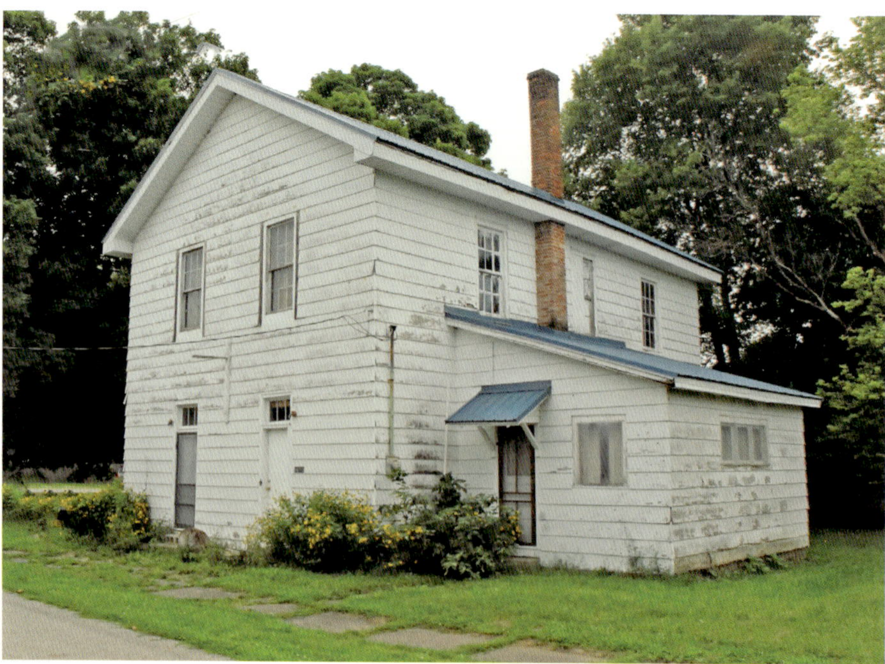

The Clarksville Lodge #118 was a two-story frame building built in 1850 at a cost of $1,600. In 1999, the Clarksville Lodge merged with Noblesville Lodge 57, just one year short of its 150th anniversary.

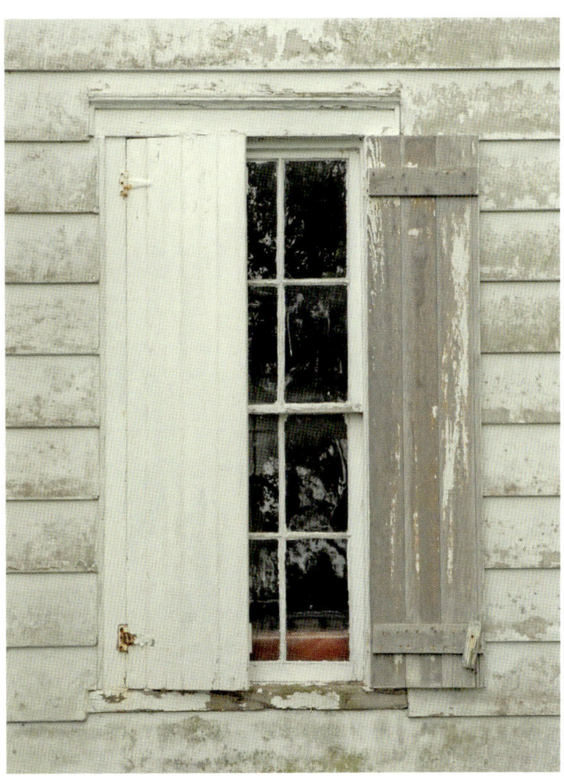

An open shudder on the south window of the Clarksville Lodge.

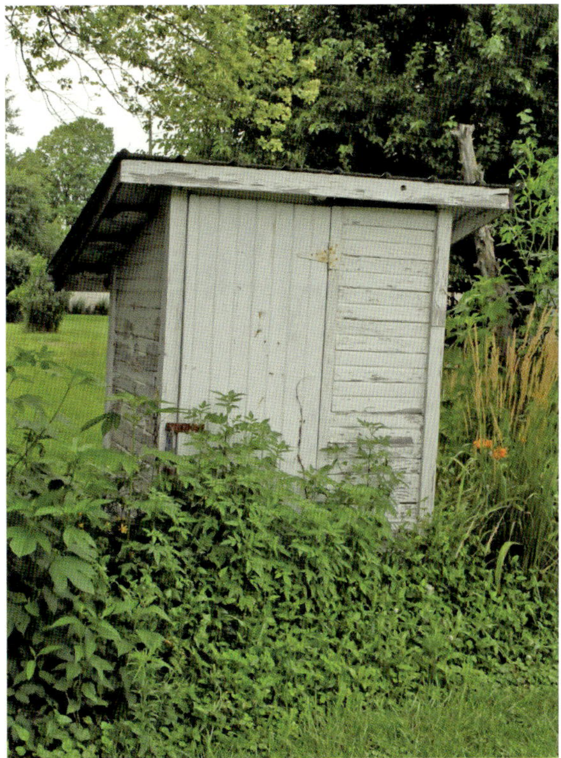

Sitting on the grounds of the Clarksville Lodge is this outhouse, also known as a "privy."

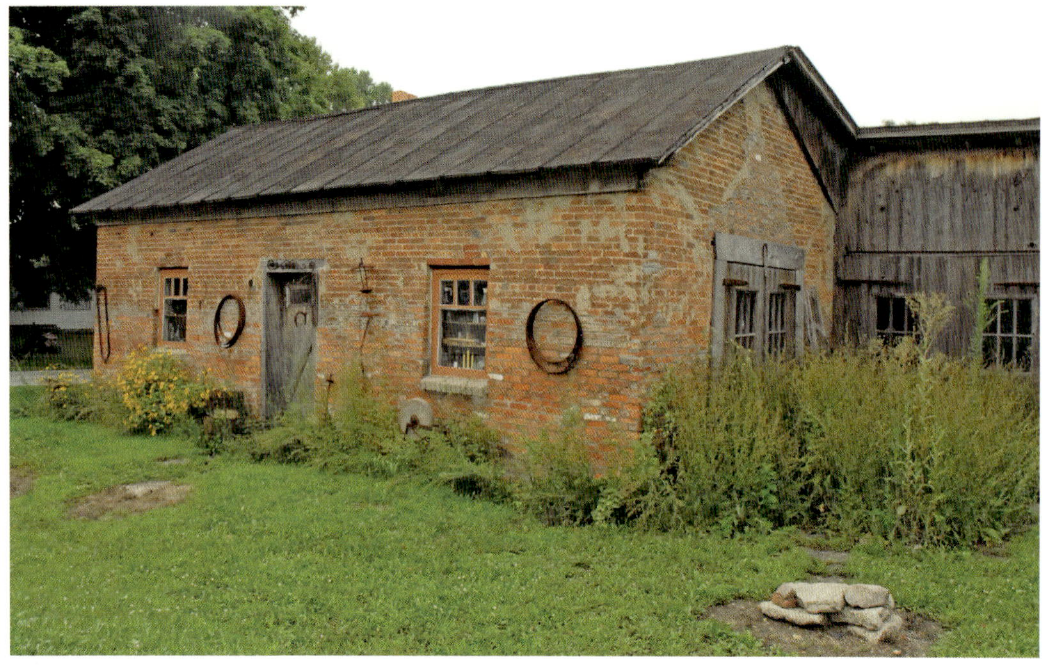

In 1880, the McCarty and Shawcross blacksmith shop began operation in this building. Located on the north side of State Road 38 in Clarksville, the brick structure is the oldest known building in the small Hamilton County town.

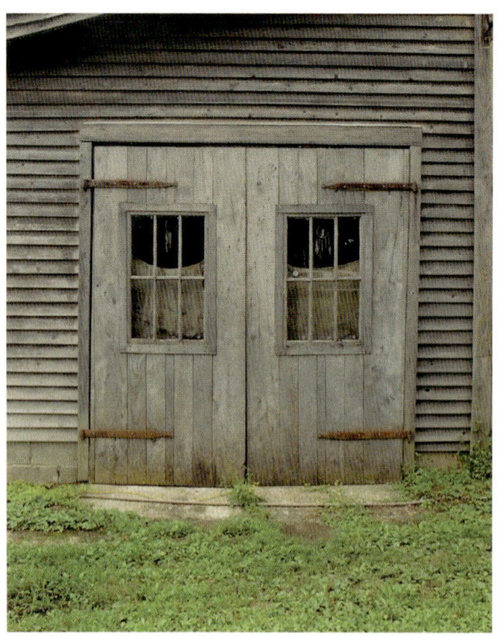

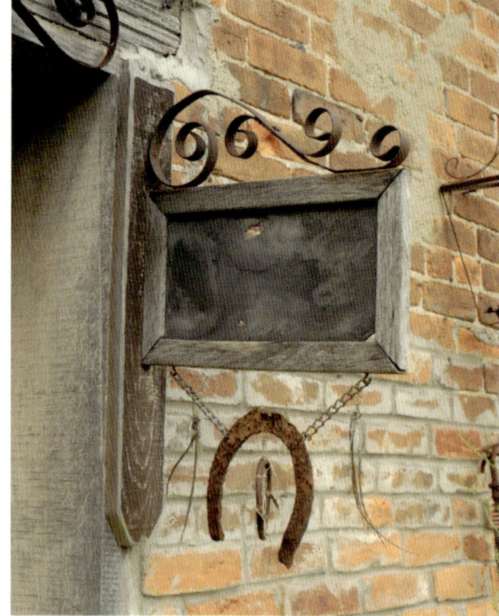

Above left: Doors leading to the section of the blacksmith shop constructed with wood.

Above right: A lucky horseshoe hangs near the entrance of the blacksmith shop. In the early 1900s, Charlie McDonald owned the blacksmith shop and was considered a master of the trade. Farmers in eastern Hamilton County relied on McDonald since he was an expert in iron work. McDonald died at the age of sixty-four in 1944 and is buried at Prairie Baptist Cemetery near Noblesville.

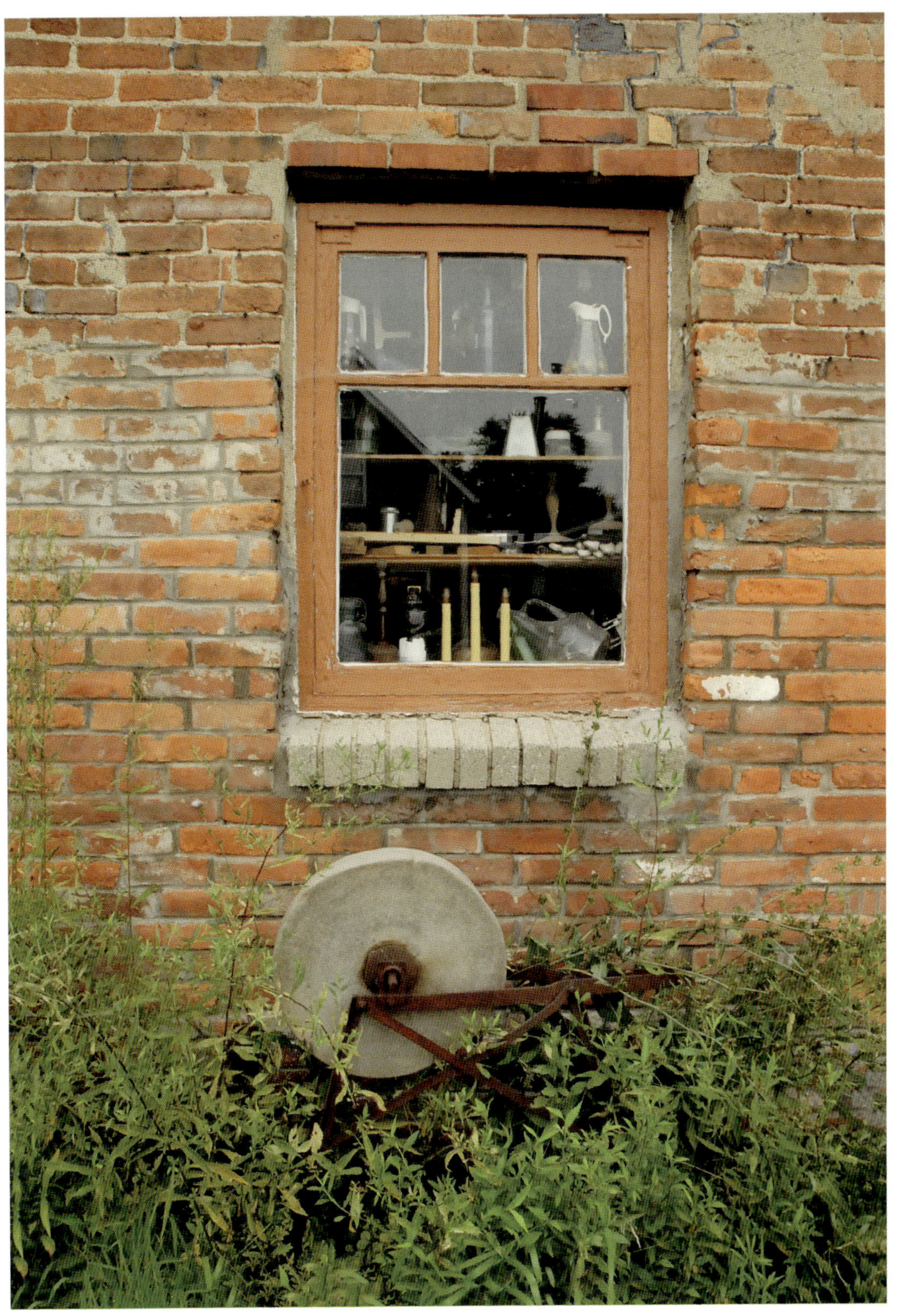

A grindstone sits beneath a window at the old blacksmith shop. Grindstones were used to sharpen, polish, and grind metal objects.

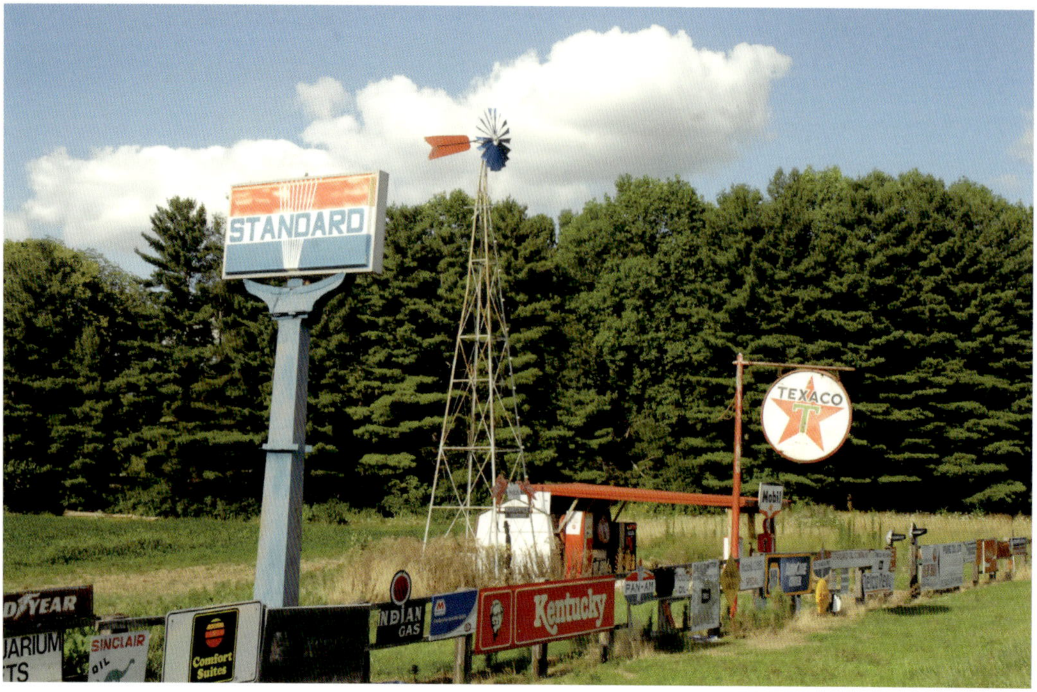

Nostalgia is alive and well on this stretch of Mounds Road in Anderson. Vintage signs of all kinds line the road making the area a picker's dream.

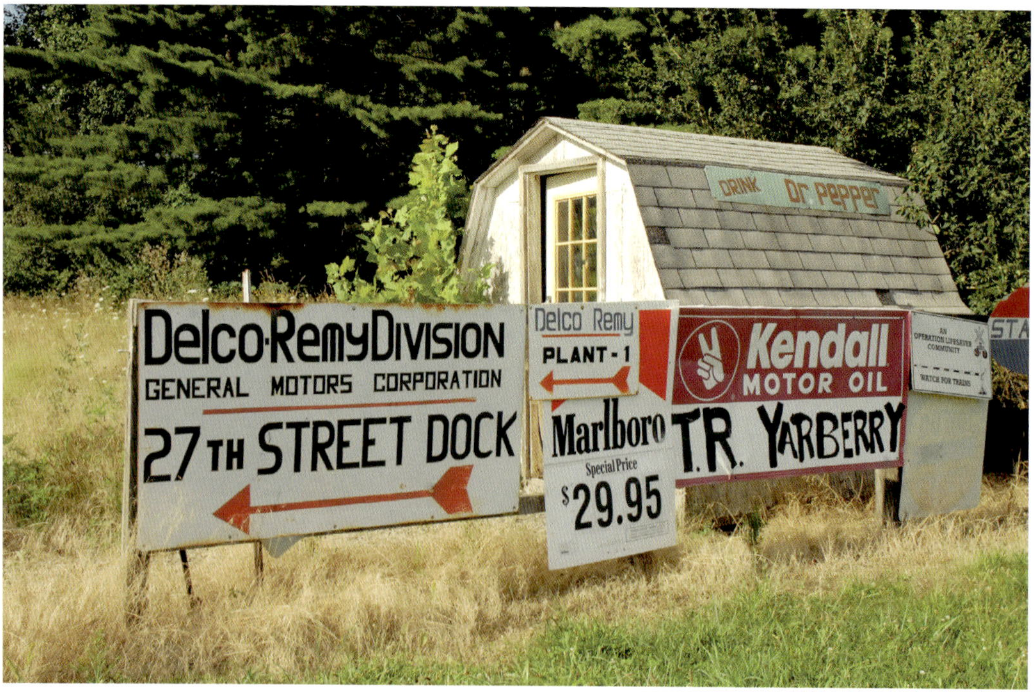

An arrow on this sign points the way to the Delco Remy dock on 27th Street in Anderson. Delco Remy had several factories on the east side of the city including one on 29th and Pearl streets.

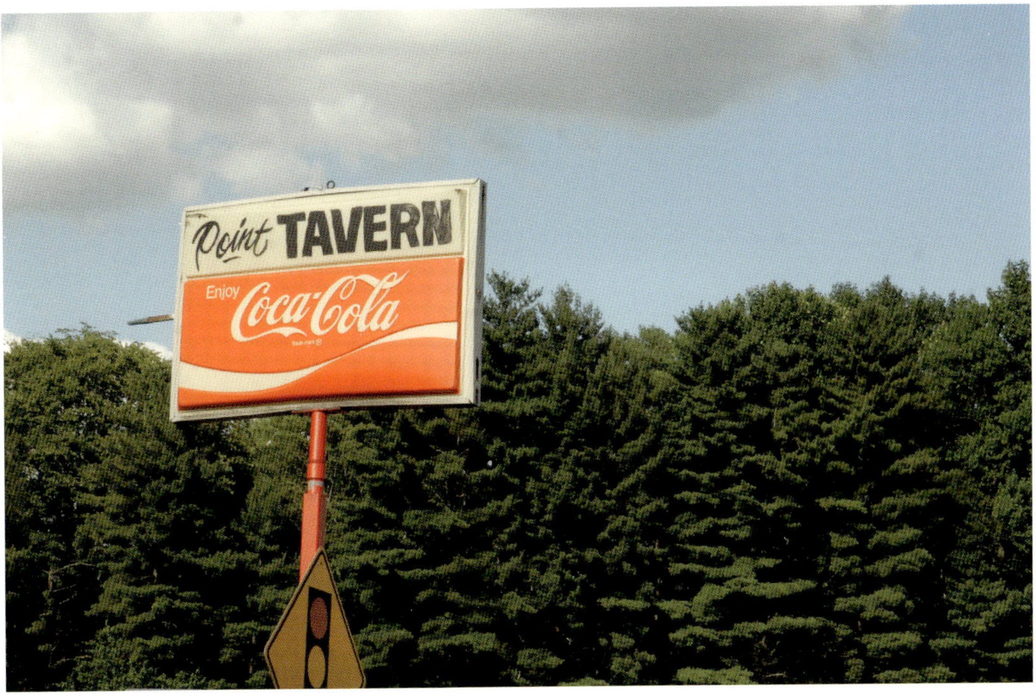

The now defunct Point Tavern was located off State Road 67 and 53rd Street on the south side of Anderson. At one time, "The Point" had a restaurant on the second floor and a bar on the ground floor. During the 1980s on Wednesday nights, "The Point" offered Lowenbrau beer at 5 cents per mug.

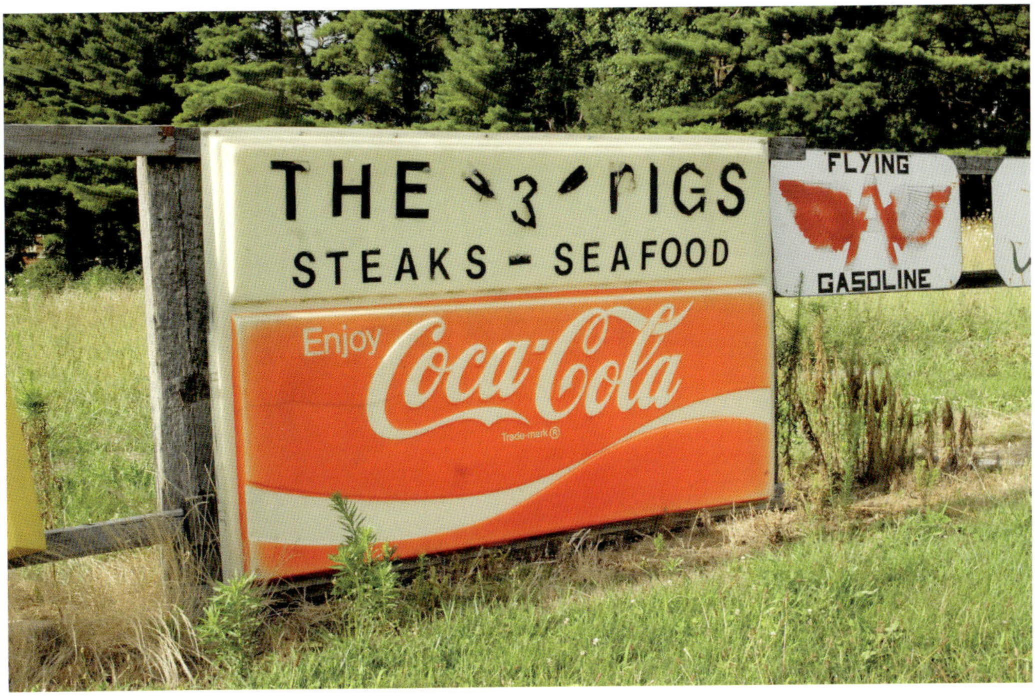

Vintage sign for the Three Pigs Restaurant once located on East 29th Street in Anderson. Before the restaurant closed, "The Pigs" was a hangout for Delco Remy employees, who worked at the nearby plant.

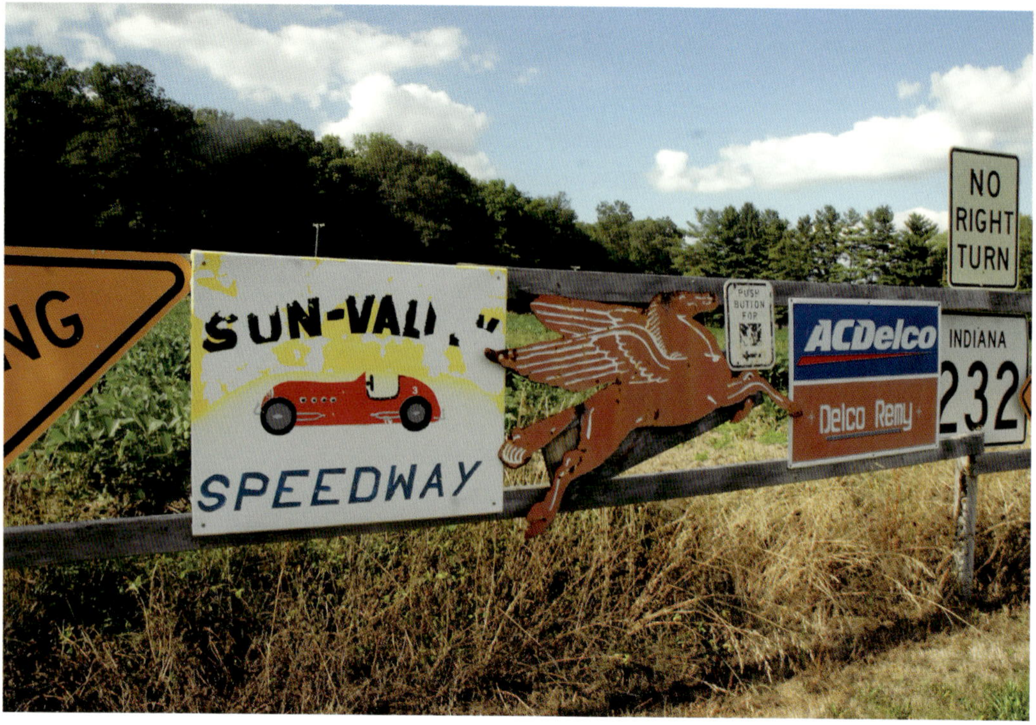

Above: A sign for the once popular Sun Valley Speedway in Anderson, home to the Little 500 race. Sun Valley is currently known as the Anderson Speedway.

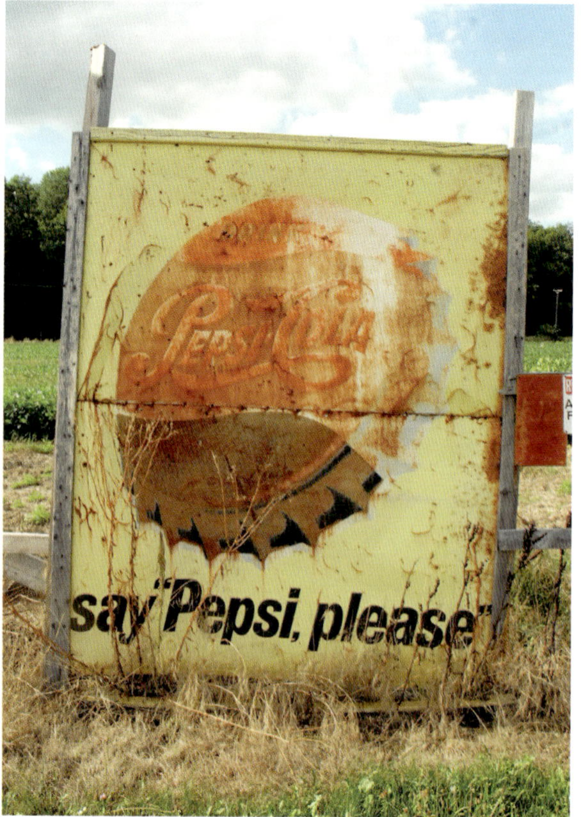

Left: Rusted "say, Pepsi please" sign mounted to a fence along Mounds Road.

4

FACTORY

At one time, industry dominated much of the American Midwest. Post-World War II prosperity and industrialization led to many cities becoming manufacturing powerhouses. Alas, times have changed, and the states that once held these booming industries now lie in the Rust Belt—the area stretching from the Northeast, across the shores of the Great Lakes, and down through the Midwest.

Like many cities, Muncie, Indiana, was once a bustling hub of industry. Today, while run down and full of decaying factories, the city fares better than many others. Muncie is home to Ball State University, alma mater of entertainment greats David Letterman and Jim Davis. The steady stream of college students moving in and out means that a youthful energy is constantly breathed into the city; it could hardly be described as "stagnant." On the north side of town, McGalliard Road is home to dozens of thriving businesses. However, echoes of the past remain. In less spruced up and renovated areas, the remains of former factories lie dormant, overgrown with weeds and smattered with graffiti.

While their heydays are long gone, these rusty ghosts haunt the skyline of this city and countless others.

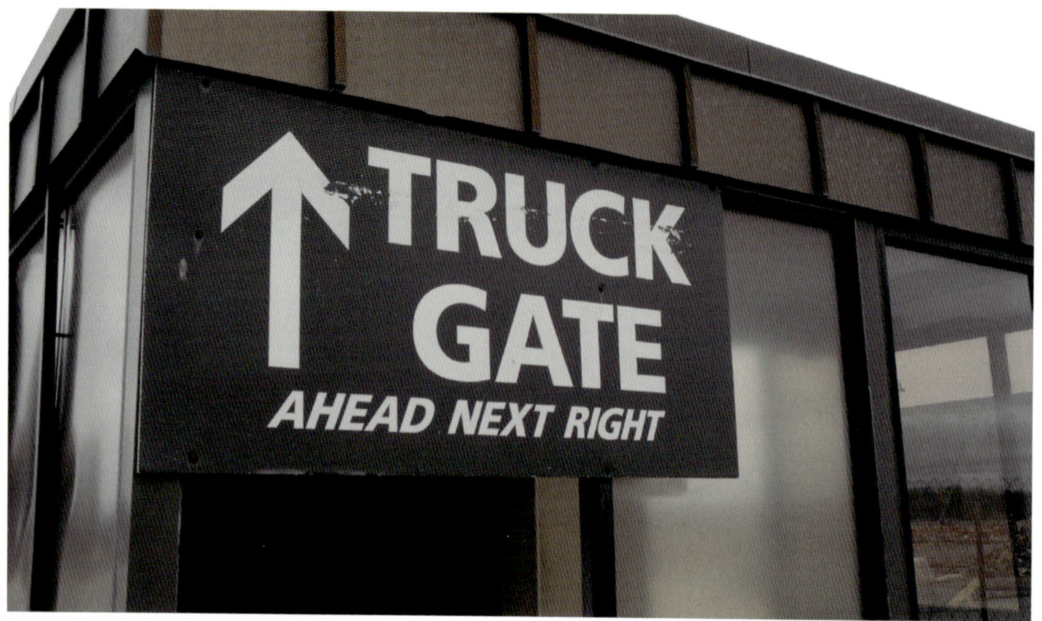

After sitting empty since 2009, demolition of the BorgWarner factory in Muncie began in 2017. The sprawling auto transmissions factory covered more than 1 million feet in workspace and was one-half mile in length. Pictured here is the truck gate entrance to the factory.

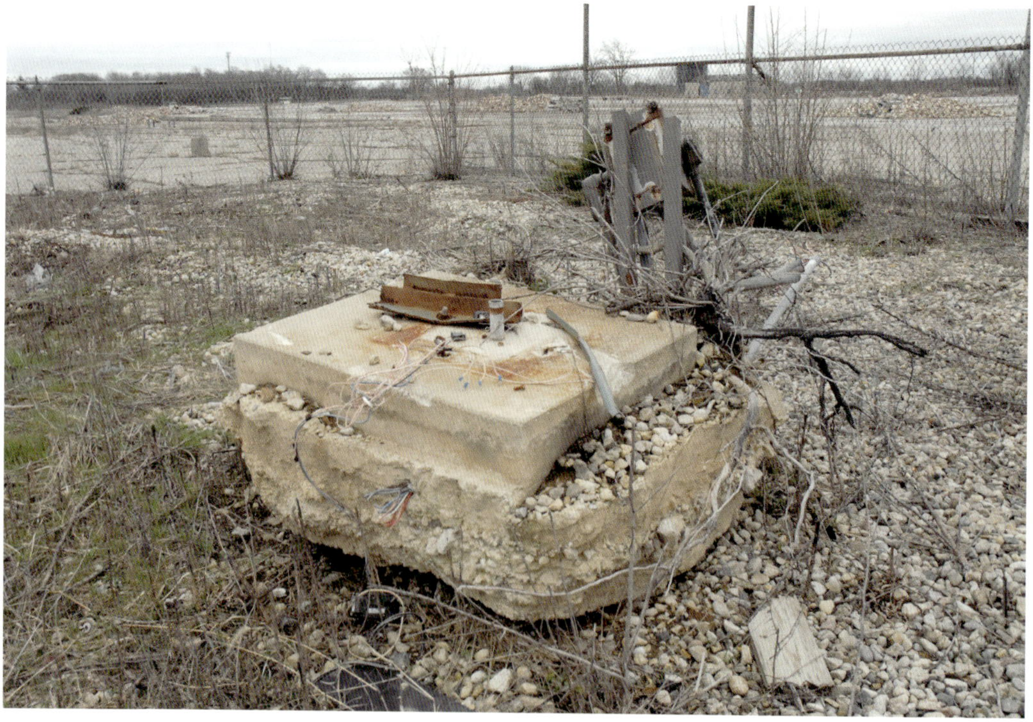

This concrete slab appears to be the base of a utility pole found in the parking lot of the demolished BorgWarner plant.

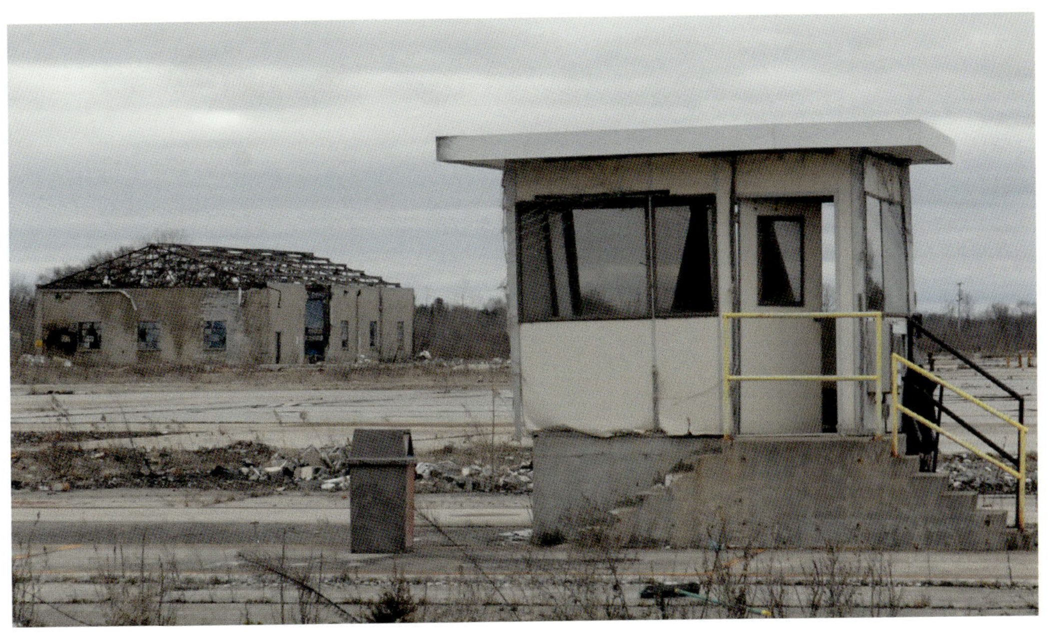

During the 1950s more than 5,000 people worked at Muncie's BorgWarner factory.

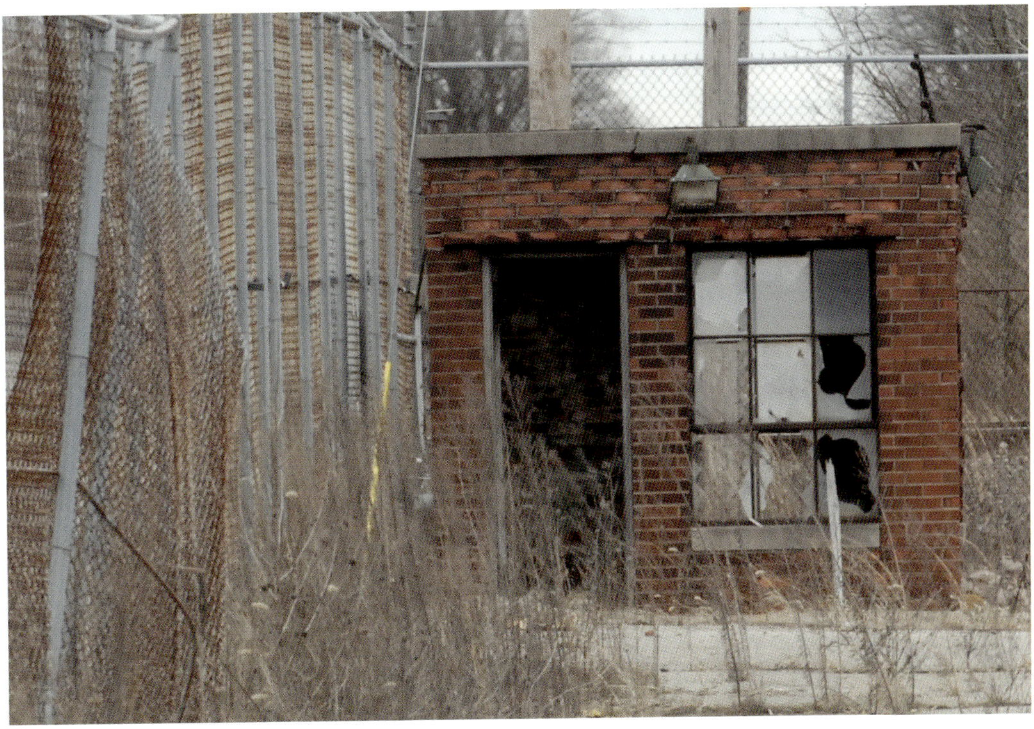

"Quality is remembered long after price if forgotten" was a slogan used by the company in 1913. The factory was called Warner Gear until 1985 when its name was changed to BorgWarner.

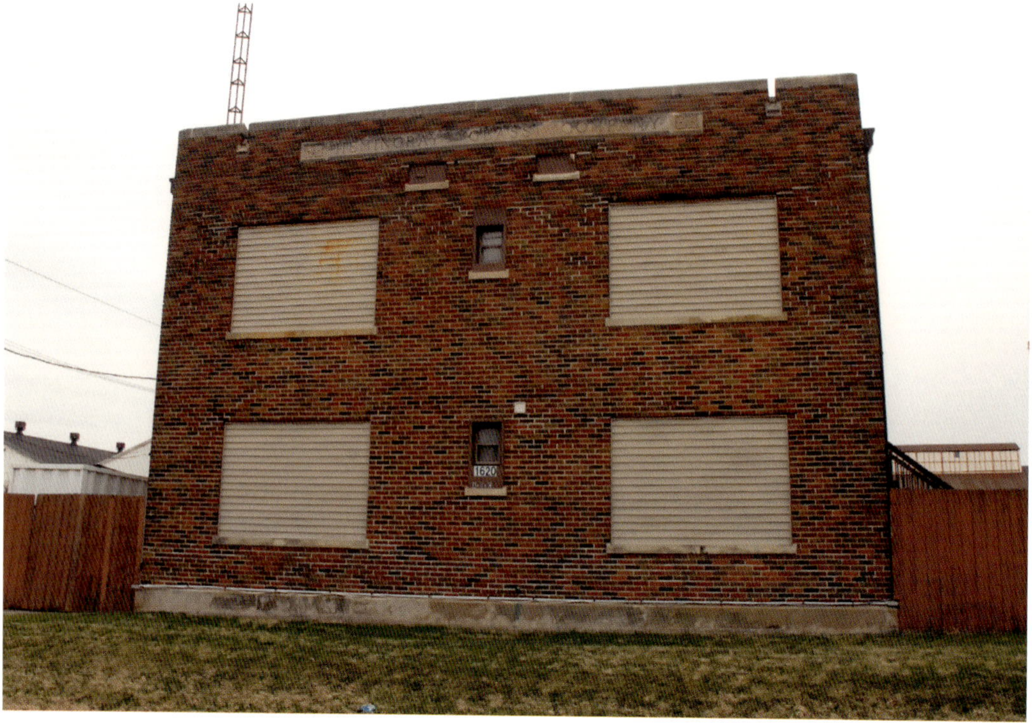

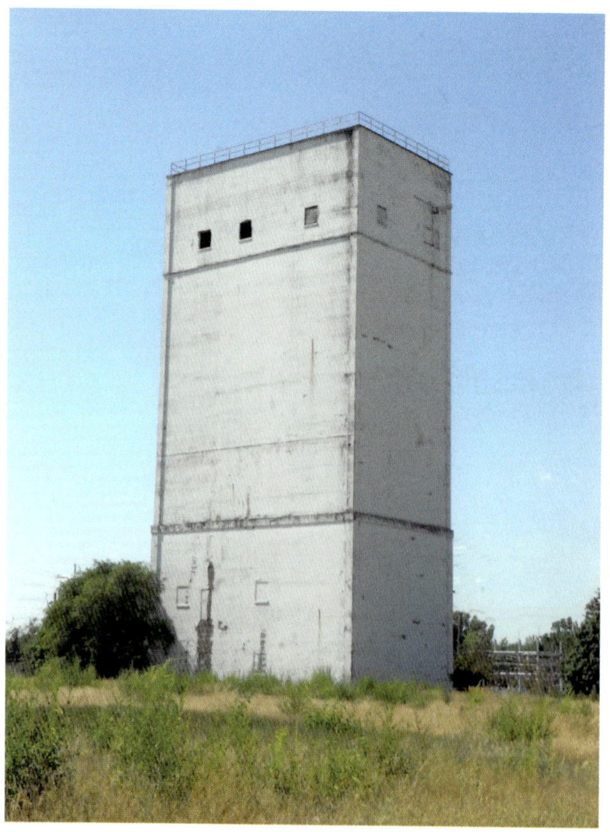

Above: Production at the Hemingray Glass Company in Muncie commenced on September 4, 1888. By the turn of the twentieth century, Hemingray had become a world leader of glass insulator manufacturing, that remained a major product until 1967. The company also produced fishbowls, fruit jars, tableware, and syrup pitchers. The Hemingray Glass Company was located on Macedonia Avenue and closed in 1972.

Left: One of the last remaining structures for the Ball Brothers factory is the old Batch Tower. The Ball Brothers plant produced thirty glass jars per minute and the glass brand became a household name. In the mid-1930s, over 2,500 people worked at the Muncie headquarters. In 1962, the Ball Brothers plant shut down.

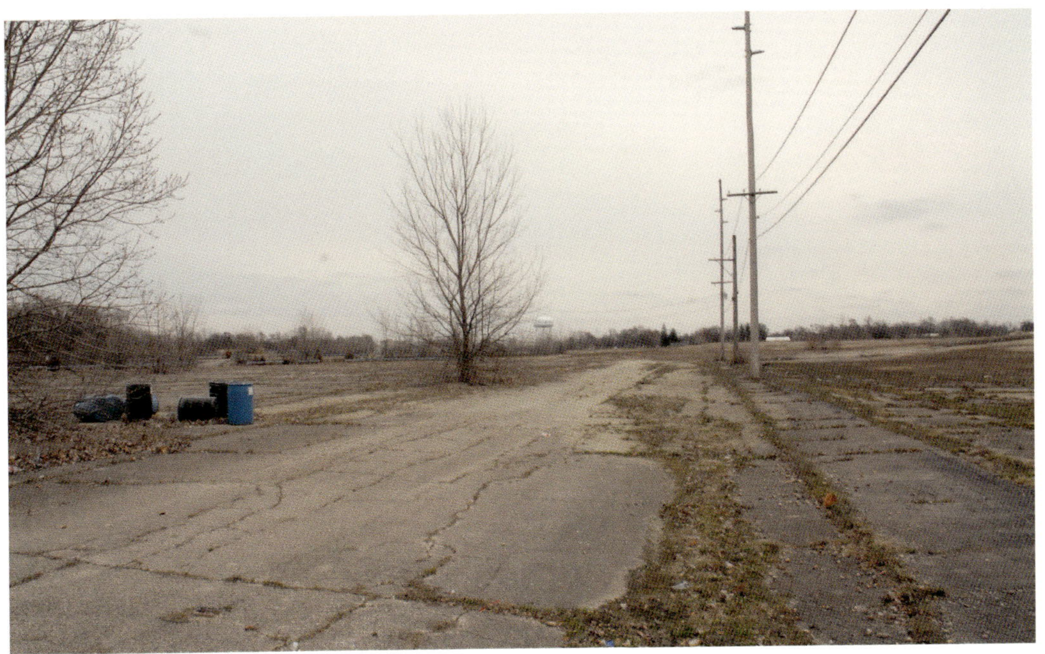

Site of the former Chevrolet auto plant in Muncie. The plant began to manufacture automatic transmissions for passenger cars and trucks in 1935. During the 1950s and 1960s, new and larger facilities were built to house the growing assembly lines. By the 1970s and 1980s, Chevrolet began the process of closing facilities and laying off workers. The Chevrolet auto plant in Muncie closed in March of 2006.

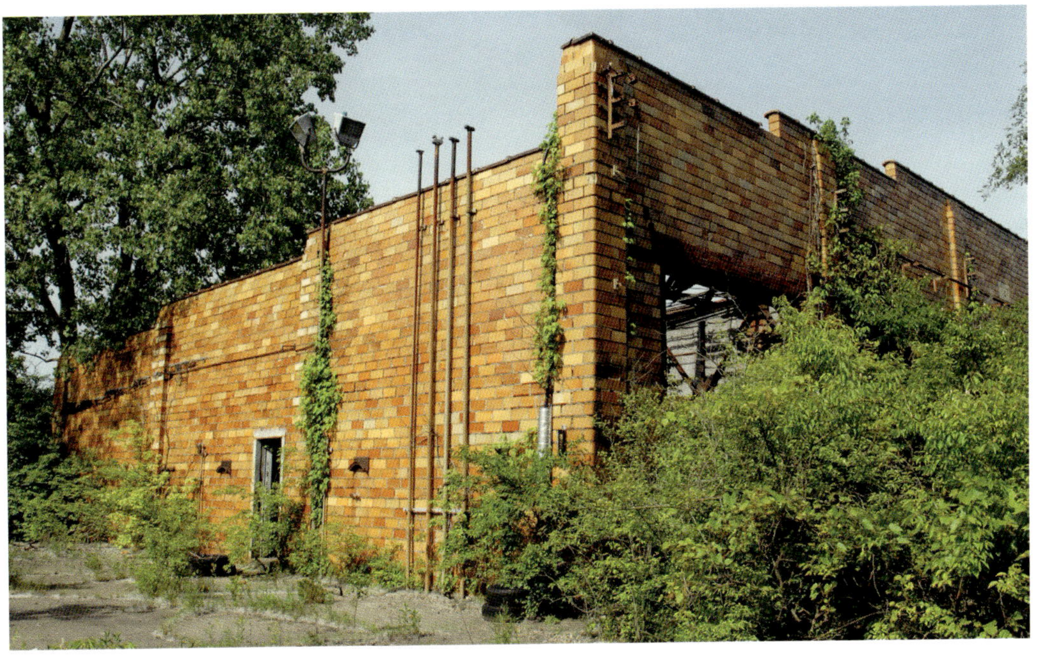

Muncie's Marhoefer Packing Company started as the Kuhner Packing Co. in 1901. Incorporated in 1911, Kuhner Packing Co. was acquired by the Marhoefer family in 1945. For the next eight years, the corporation was known as the Marhoefer Division of the Kuhner Packing Company. The Kuhner name was dropped in 1952, and the business became the Marhoefer Packing Company.

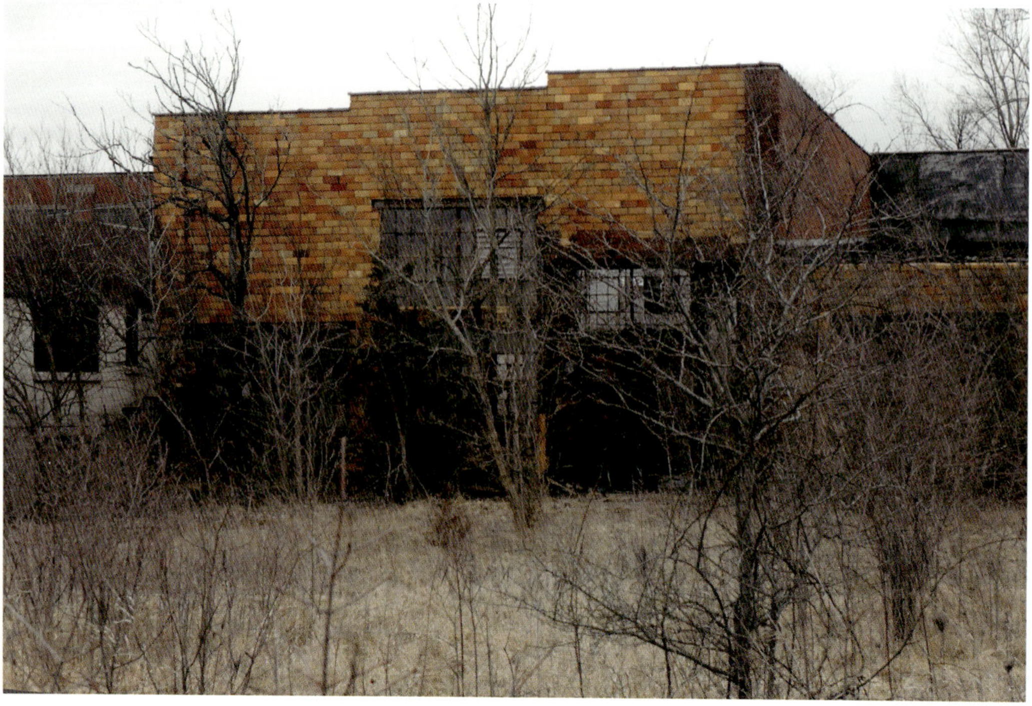

John Marhoefer and his family operated a profitable business for over thirty years. In 1978, Marhoefer Packing Company filed for bankruptcy, forcing the business to close.

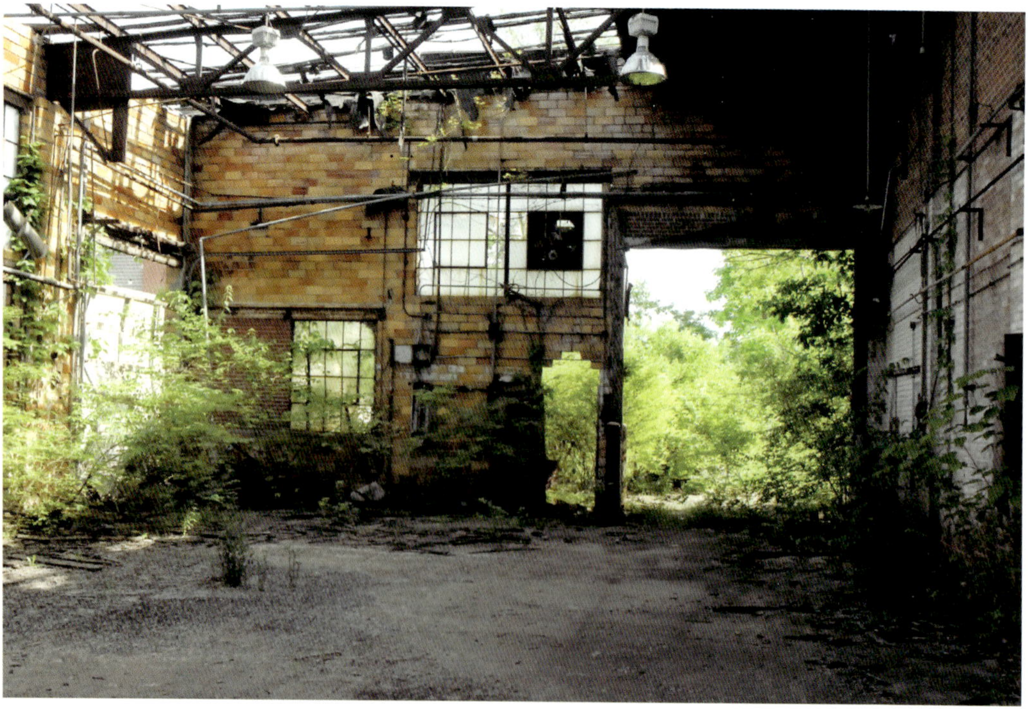

Marhoefer Packing Company had over twelve buildings during its height of production with over 380,000 feet of floor space.

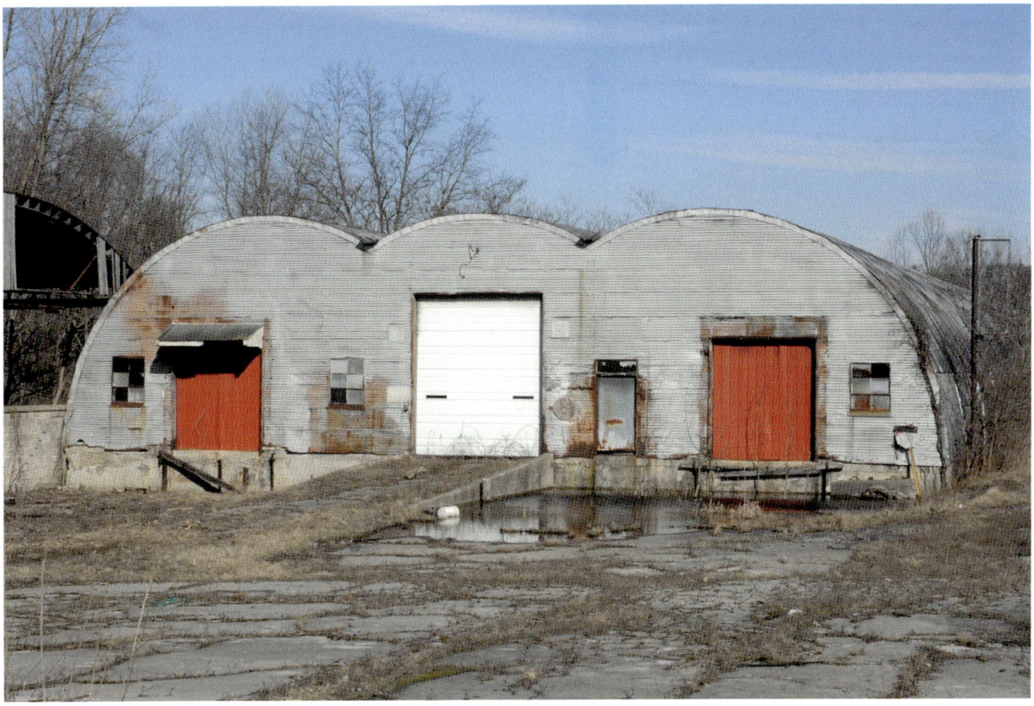

The Marhofer plant on Granville Avenue in Muncie covered 45 acres of land.

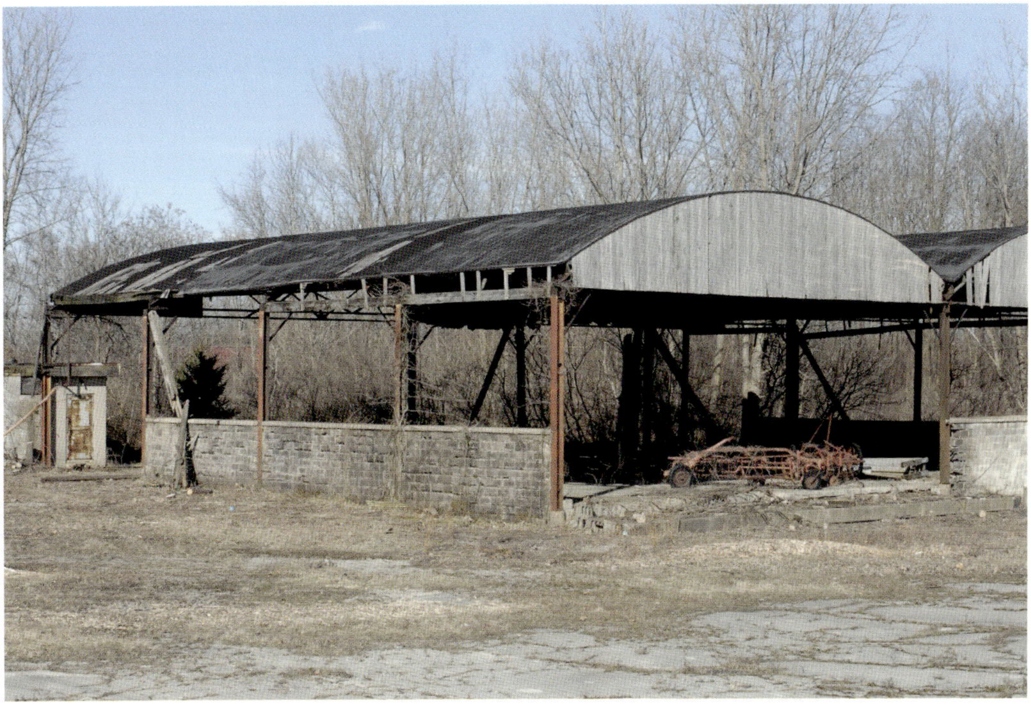

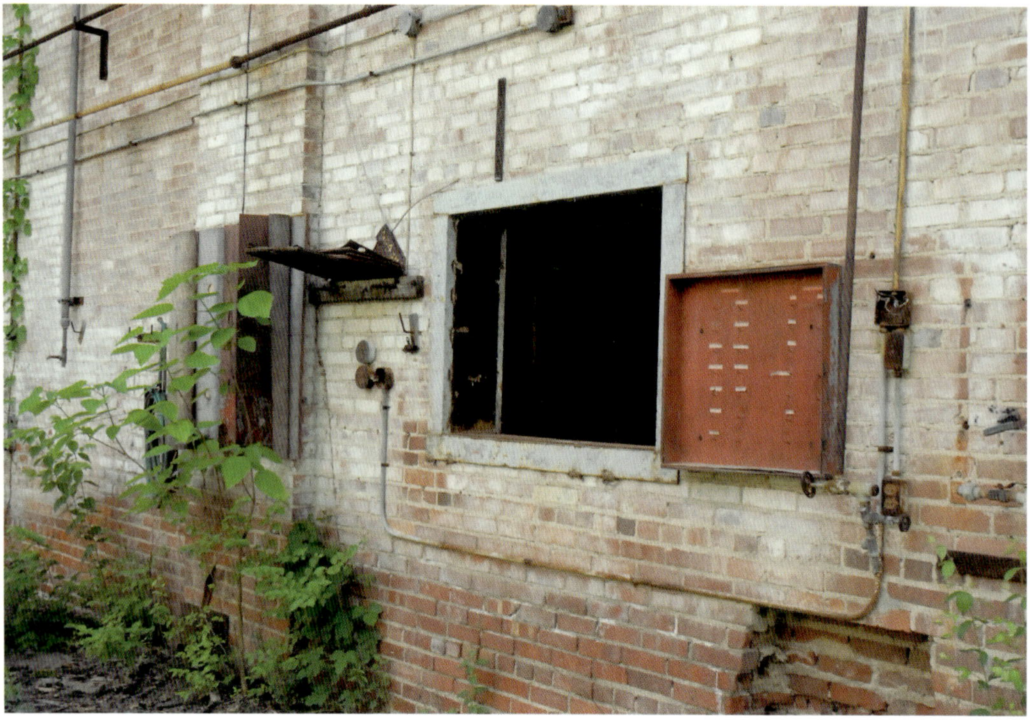

Interior shot of one of the production sites of Marhoefer Packing Company.

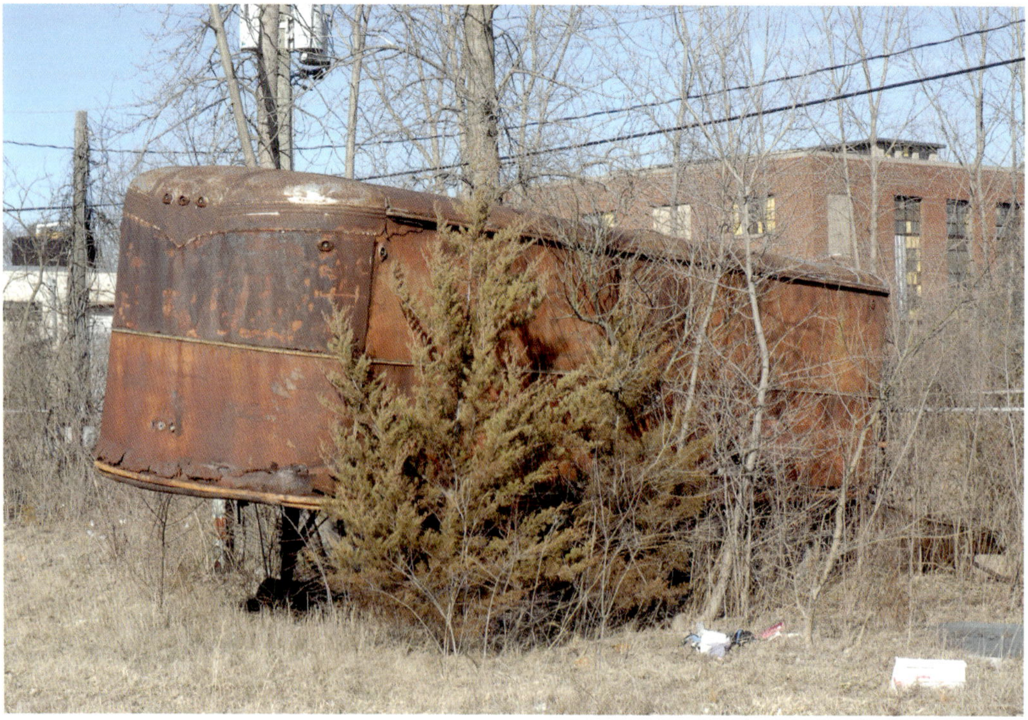

Weeds grow over and around a rusted Marhoefer delivery truck.

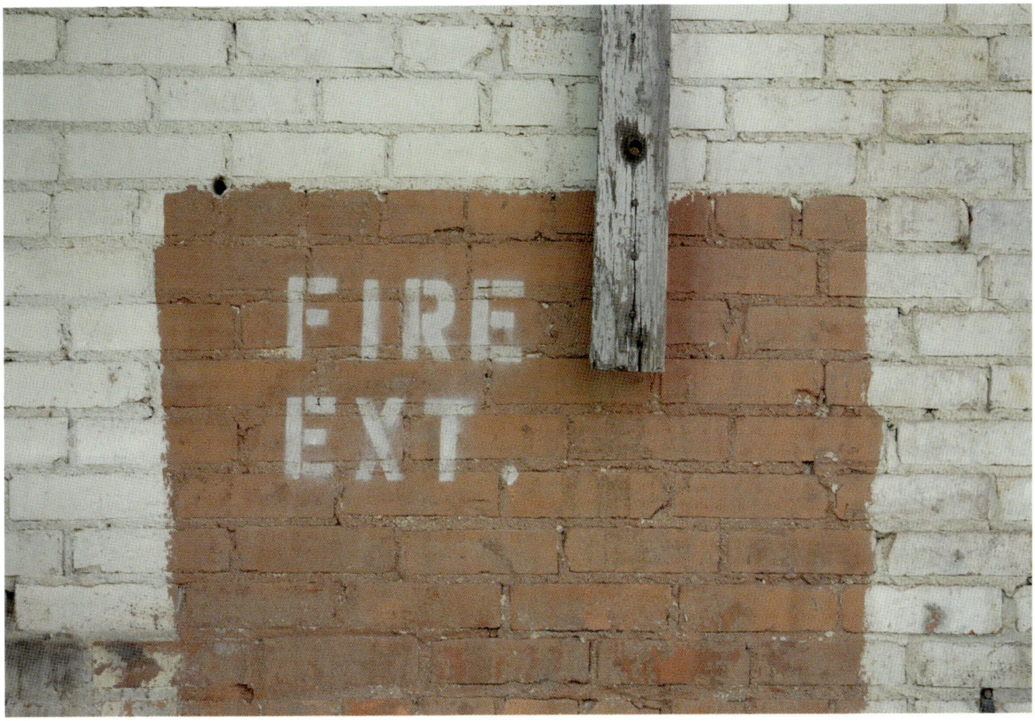

Above: Stenciled words signifying where a fire extinguisher was located inside the Marhoefer plant.

Right: A circuit breaker in one of the abandoned Marhoefer buildings.

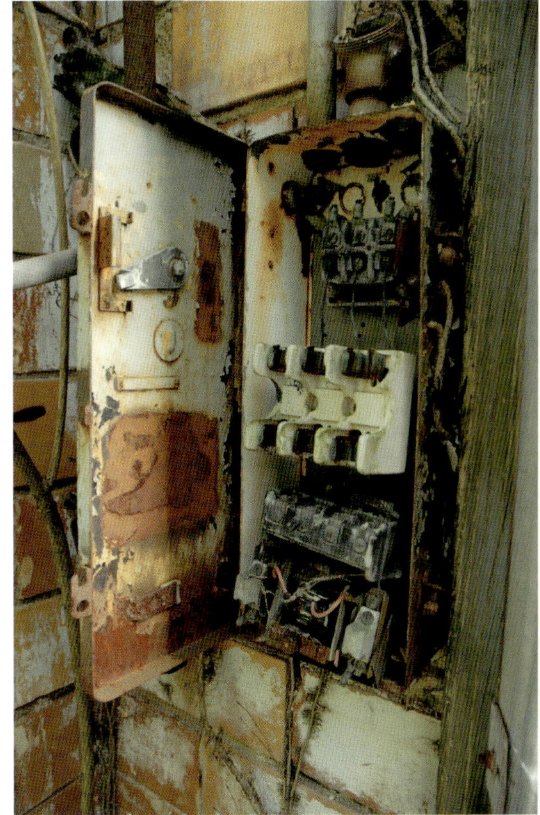

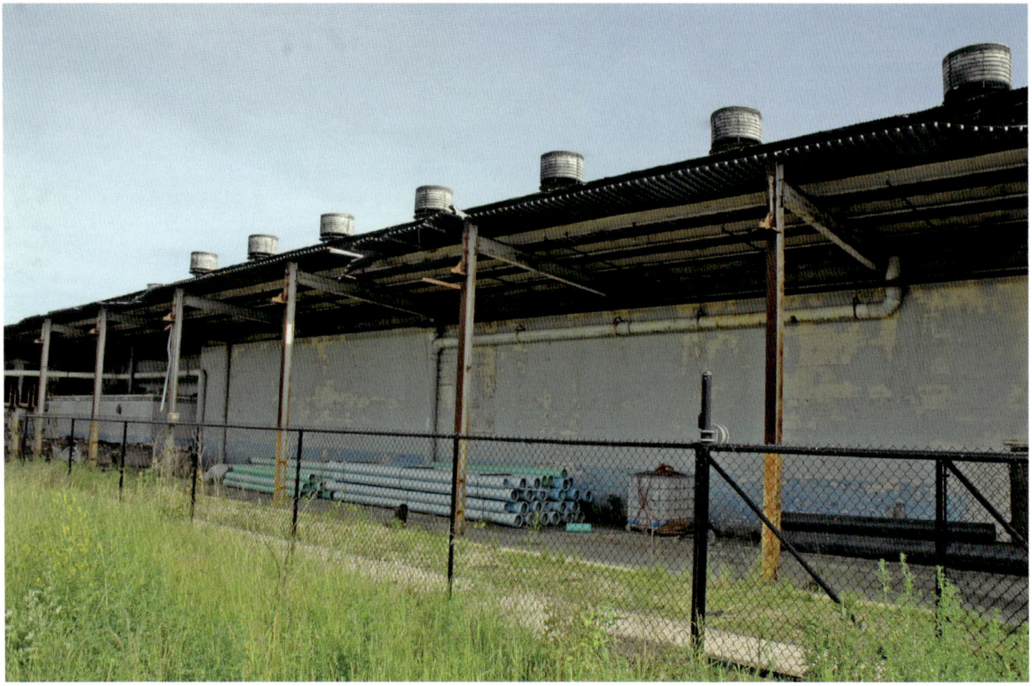

The Indiana Steel and Wire Company in Muncie was founded by the Kitselman brothers in 1904. The company manufactured galvanized steel wire, wire products, and telegraph wire for foreign and domestic sales. By the late 1950s, the company employed nearly 1,000 people at the Muncie location. Indiana Wire and Steel ceased operations in 2002. Today, the building serves the city as an environmental field office with two employees.

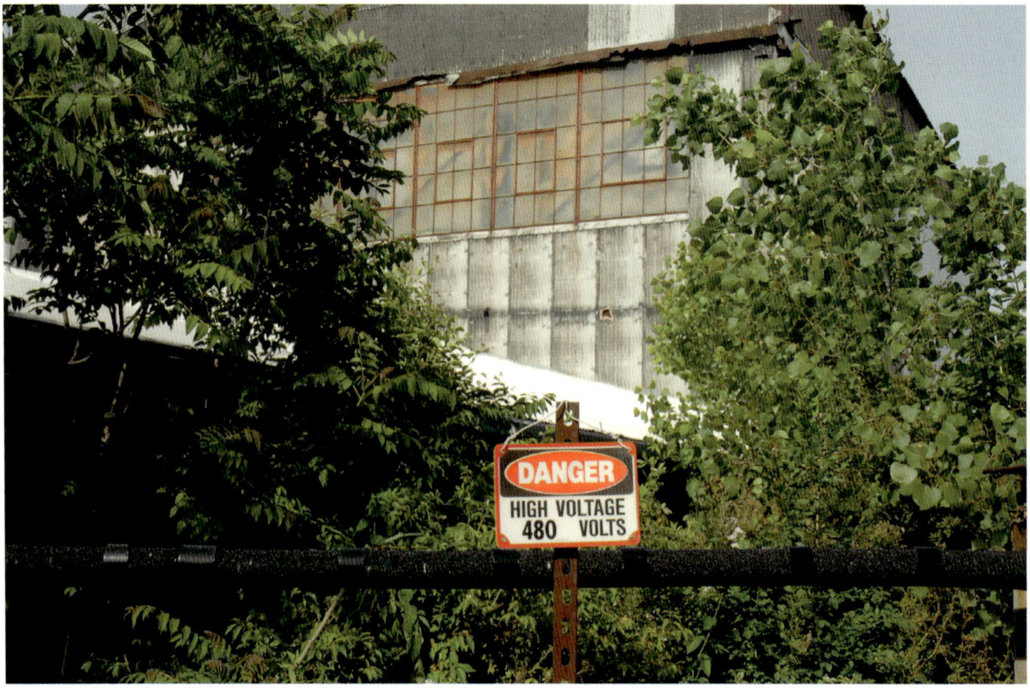

The Indiana Steel & Wire property covered several dozen acres and contained two landfills and a sludge pond.

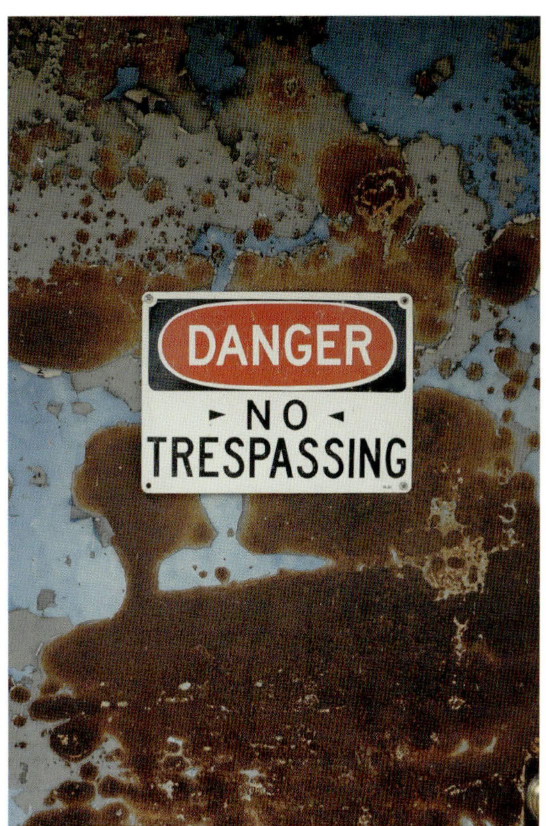

Right: "No Trespassing" sign on a rusted door at the closed Indiana Steel and Wire Company in Muncie.

Below: Loading dock at the old Indiana Steel and Wire Company.

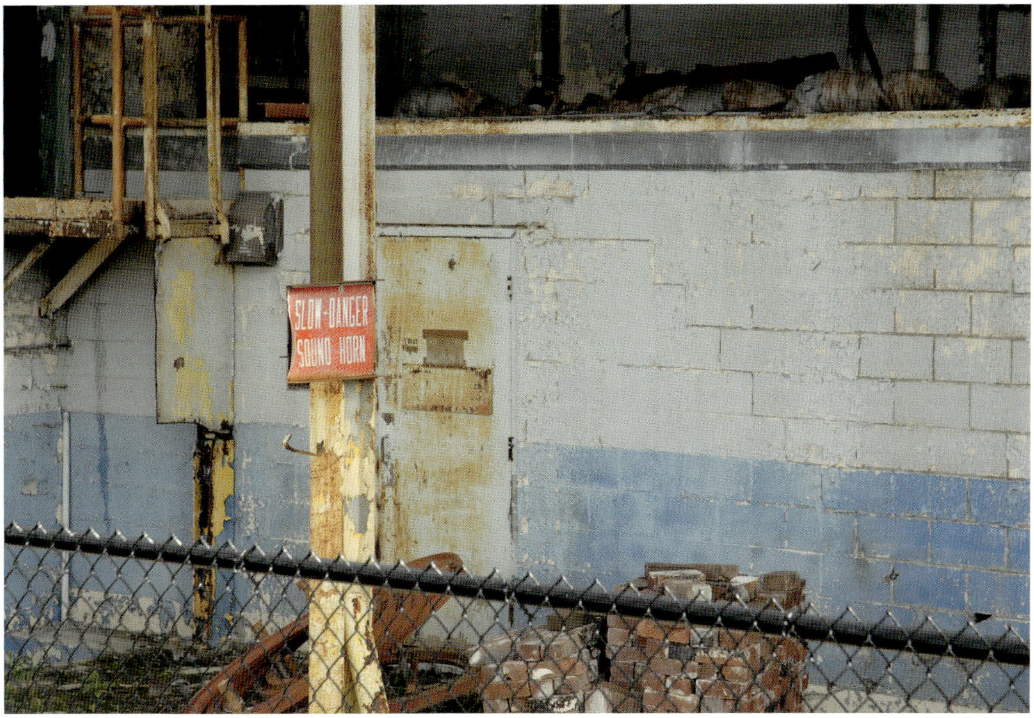

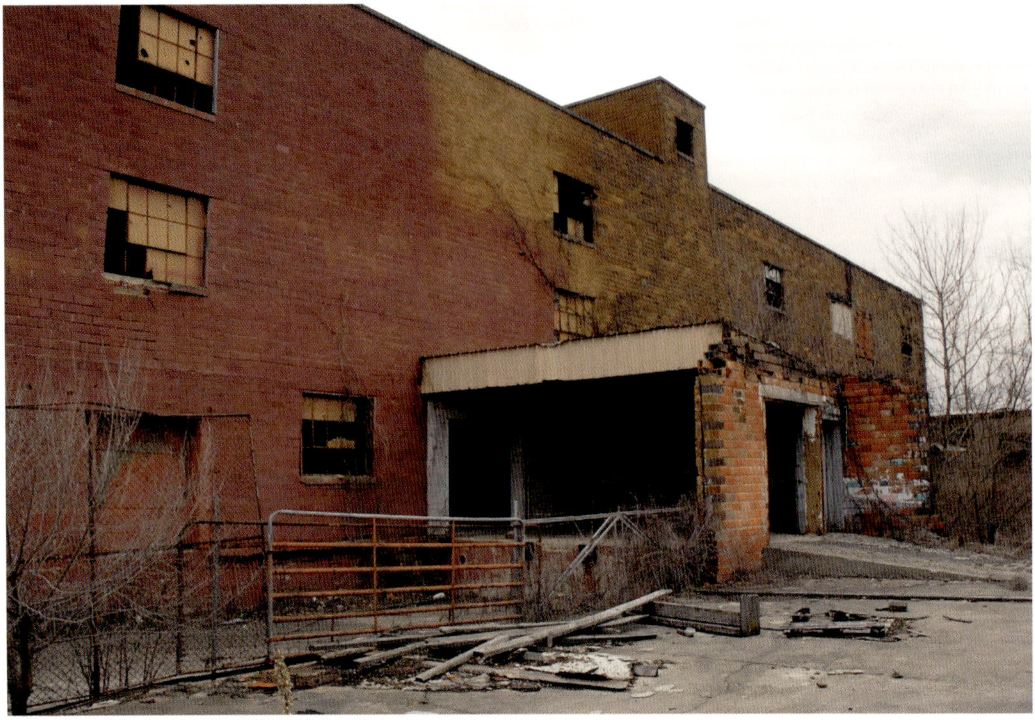

In the early 1900s, this abandoned building in Tipton served as a piano factory. Oakes Manufacturing purchased the building in 1909 and manufactured agricultural related products. Oakes Manufacturing remained in Tipton for fifty-seven years before consolidating with FMC Corporation, who manufactured fire trucks. FMC went out of business in 1986, and the building has remained empty since its closing.

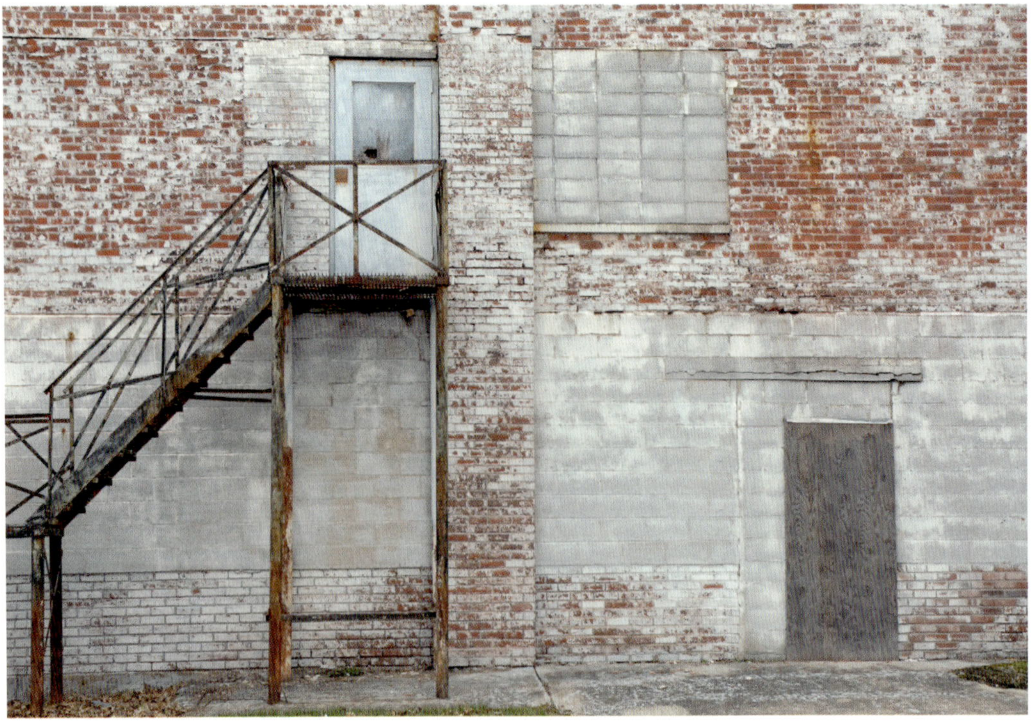

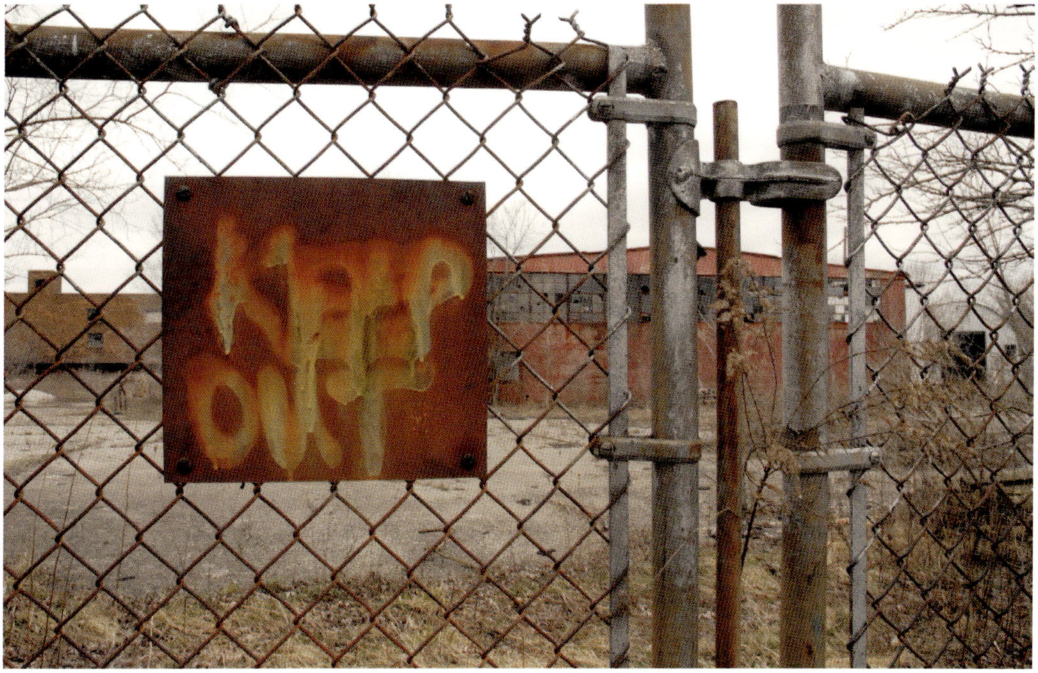

A rusted "Keep Out" sign on a locked gate outside the old Tipton piano factory.

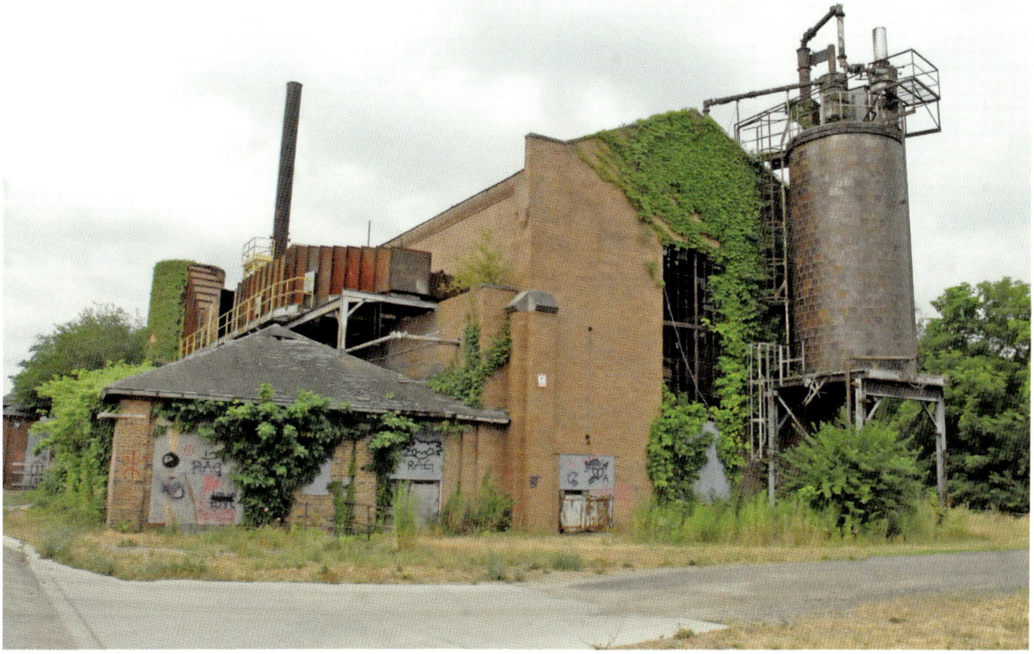

The abandoned power plant is the last remaining building on the grounds of the old Central State Hospital. Built in 1886, the building supplied electricity for the 148-acre campus, originally known as the Indiana Hospital for the Insane. Located on the west side of Indianapolis, Central State Hospital closed in 1994. A decade later, the city acquired the property.

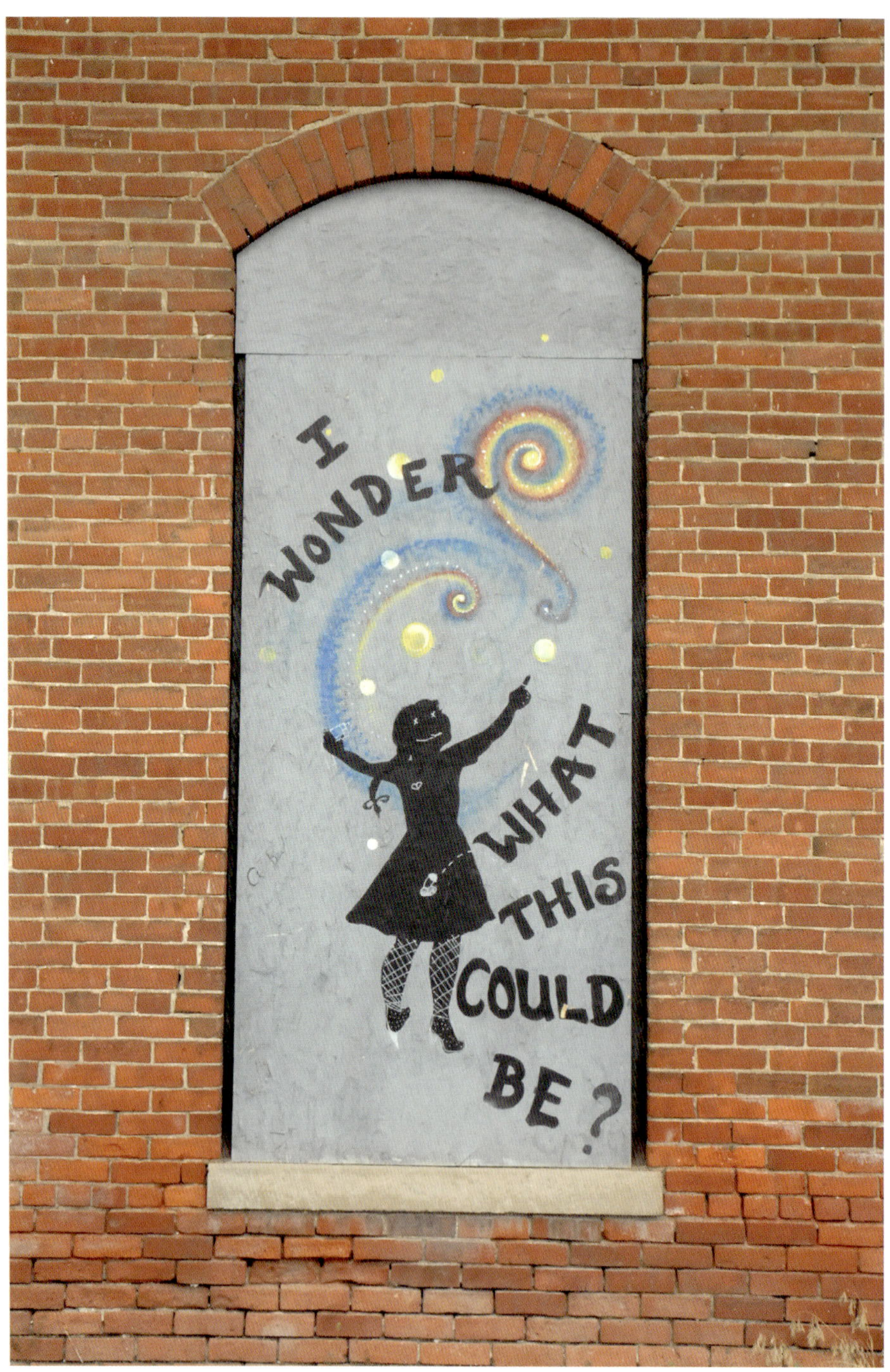

Spray painted graffiti and stenciled art cover the boarded-up windows of the dilapidated power building on the grounds of the former Central State Hospital.

5

THE FORGOTTEN

The topic of insane asylums conjures haunting imagery of barbaric facilities and horrifically mistreated patients. It is a sad fact that the proper understanding of and sympathy for mental disorders is a relatively recent revelation. Disorders such as schizophrenia, depression, psychosis, and stress-related issues are commonplace, and our society is fortunate to have real care and compassion for those who suffer. In the past, however, these people were all lumped together in one category: insane. The unfortunate people who were locked away in these hospitals were subject to confinement in straitjackets, electroshock therapy, and the highly controversial lobotomy surgery.

The Central State Hospital (formerly the Central Indiana Hospital for the Insane) is a defunct psychiatric hospital located on the northwest side of Indianapolis, Indiana. Founded in 1848, the hospital remained in operation for nearly a century and a half, being shut down in 1994 amid allegations of patient abuse. On the facility grounds lay an unkempt field surrounded by a chain link fence. This field is home to nearly 200 unmarked graves of deceased patients from the. hospital. While their identities may be lost to time, we must not forget their struggles nor our tragic history of insane asylums.

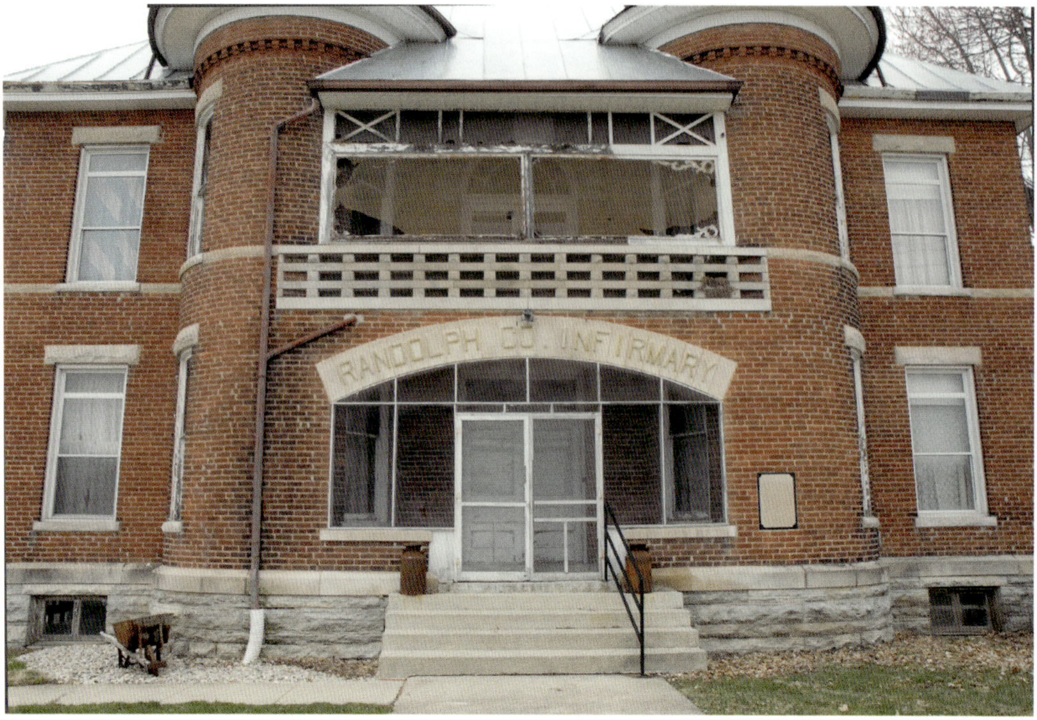

The Randolph County Infirmary is located off Highway 3, in Winchester. The original asylum was built in 1852 and held 16 patients. In 1854, a fire swept through the wooden structure, killing at least fifty people. The current Randolph County Infirmary was built in 1898, that included private rooms, six large wards, a laundry room, kitchen, and dining rooms. On the property was a barn, pump house, chicken house, and machine shed. The Randolph County Infirmary closed in 2008. During the years that the infirmary housed patients, about 200 people passed away.

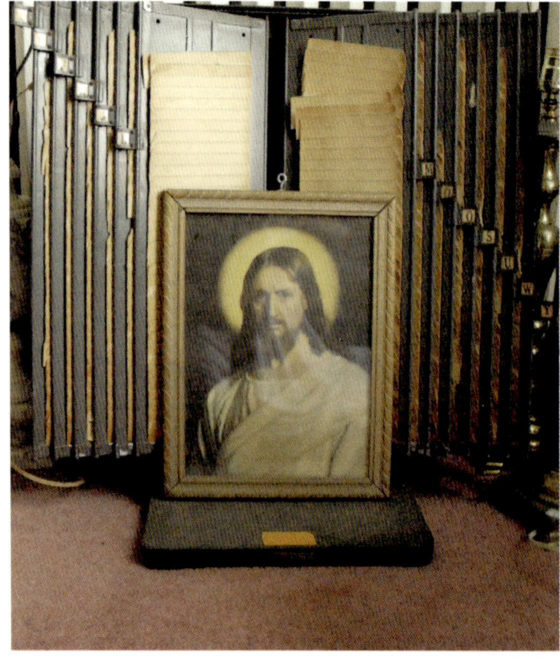

A painting of Jesus sits on the floor of a room near the entrance of the building.

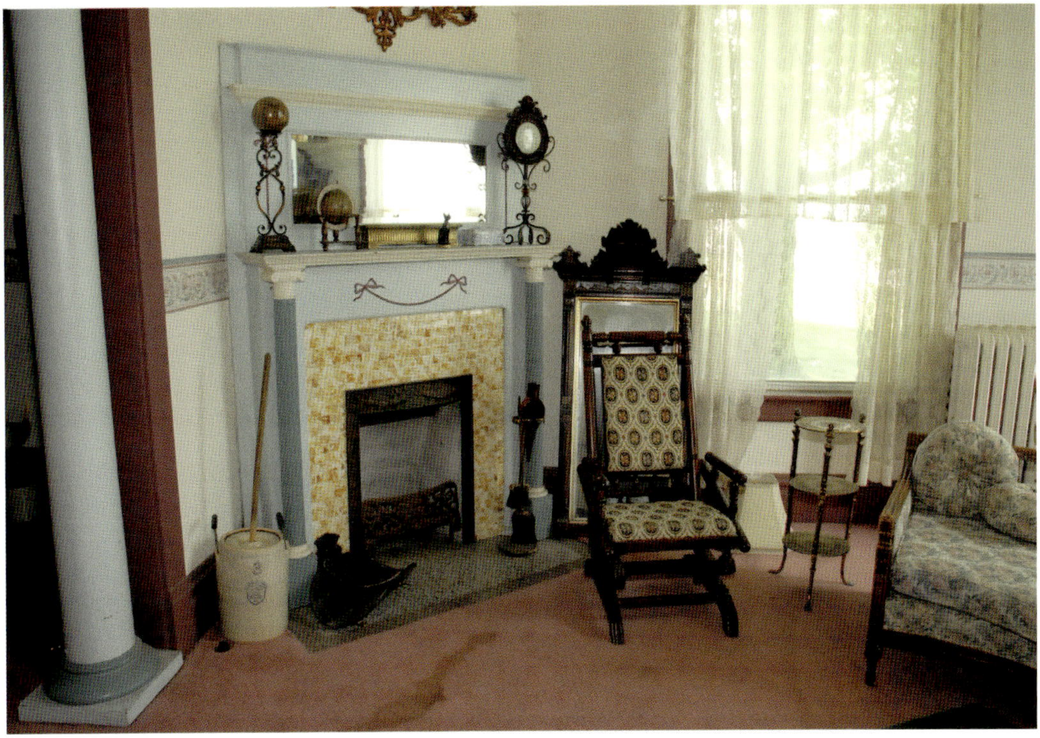

A parlor with a fireplace, rocking chair, and assorted furniture.

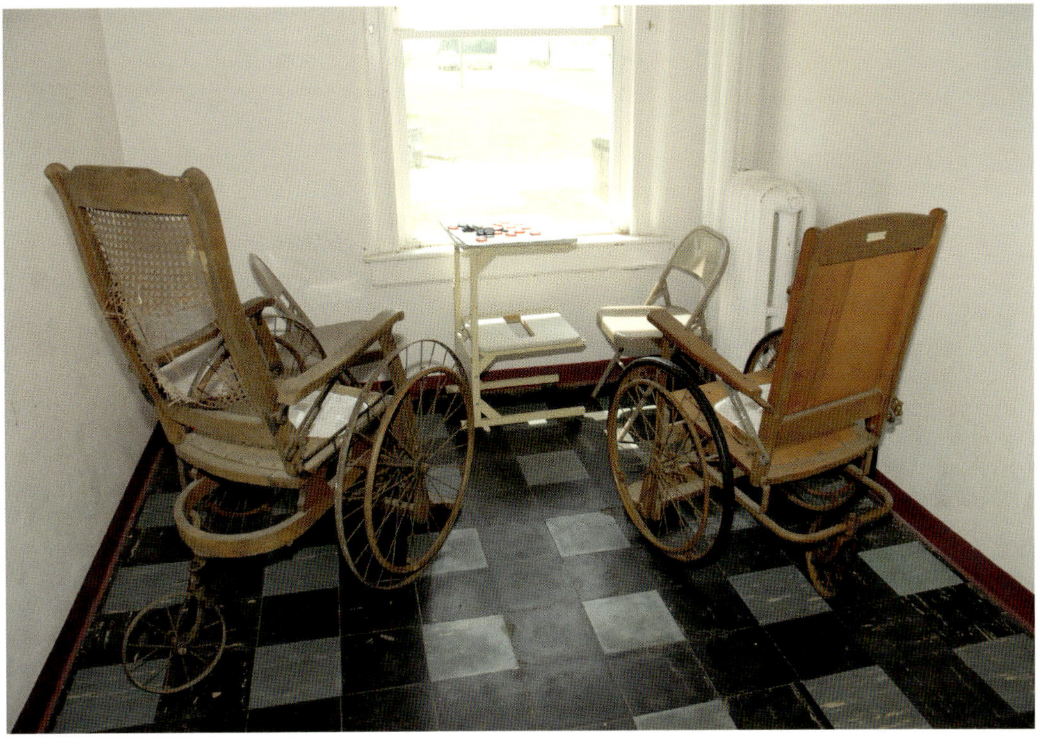

Two wheelchairs sit near an open window where patients played checkers.

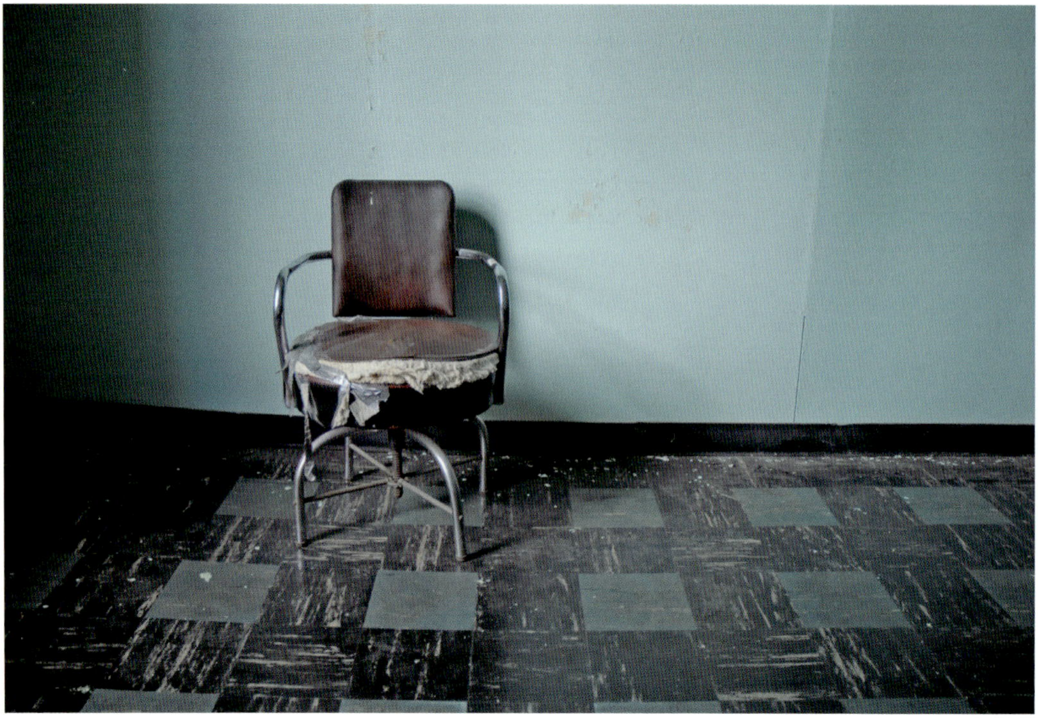

A chair sits in a darkened room on the second floor of the infirmary. Many patients in the infirmary died from suicide, hanging, and illness.

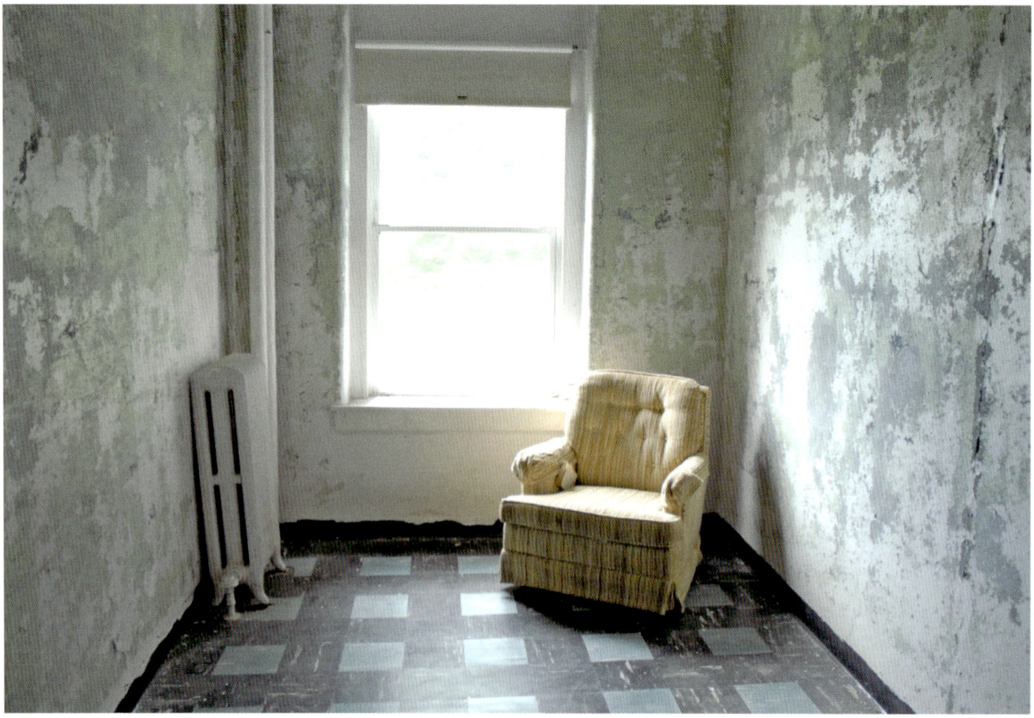

This covered rocking chair in an empty room signifies the loneliness that many patients endured at the infirmary.

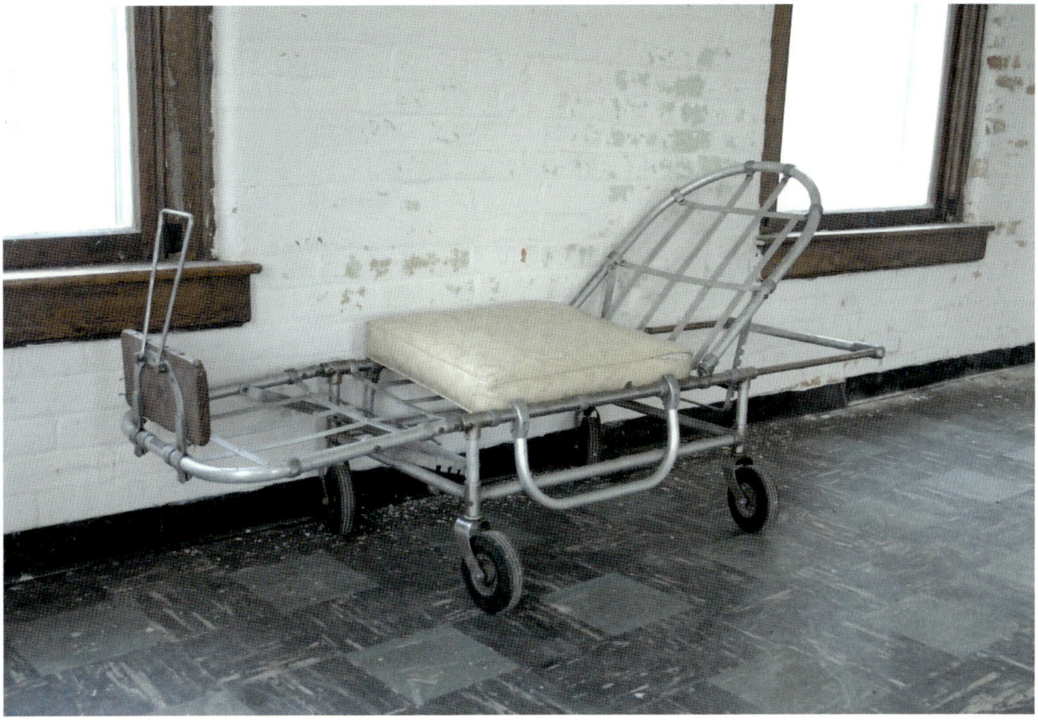

Gurneys with restraint straps are a common site at the infirmary. One patient tried to commit suicide by driving a penknife blade into his head with a flat iron.

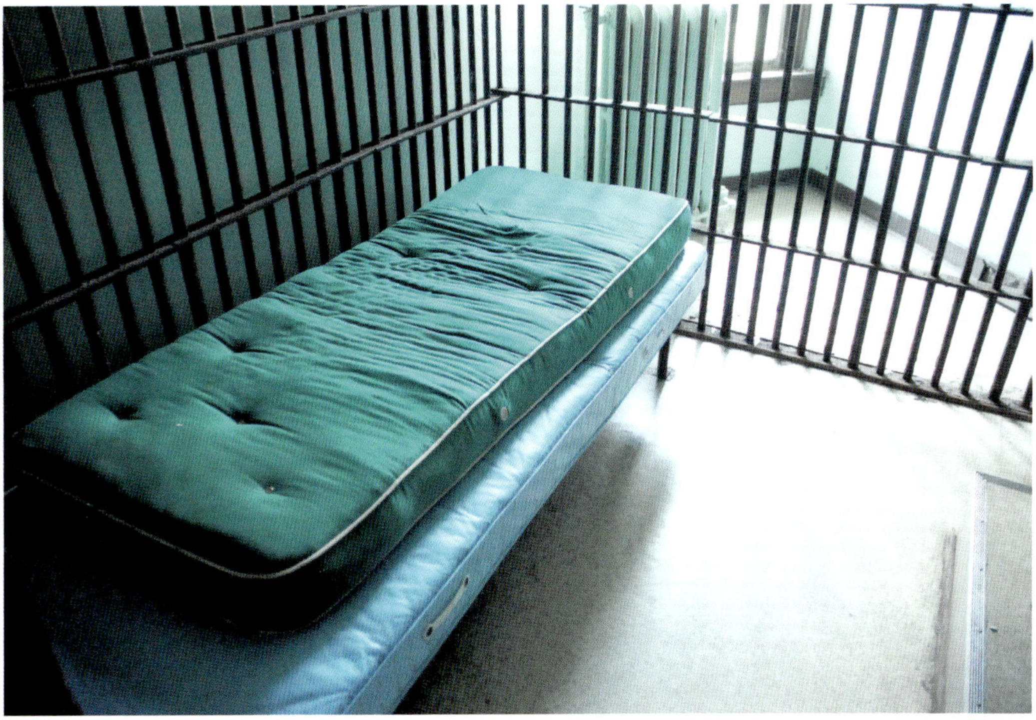

A cot sits in a cell with bars on the first floor of the infirmary.

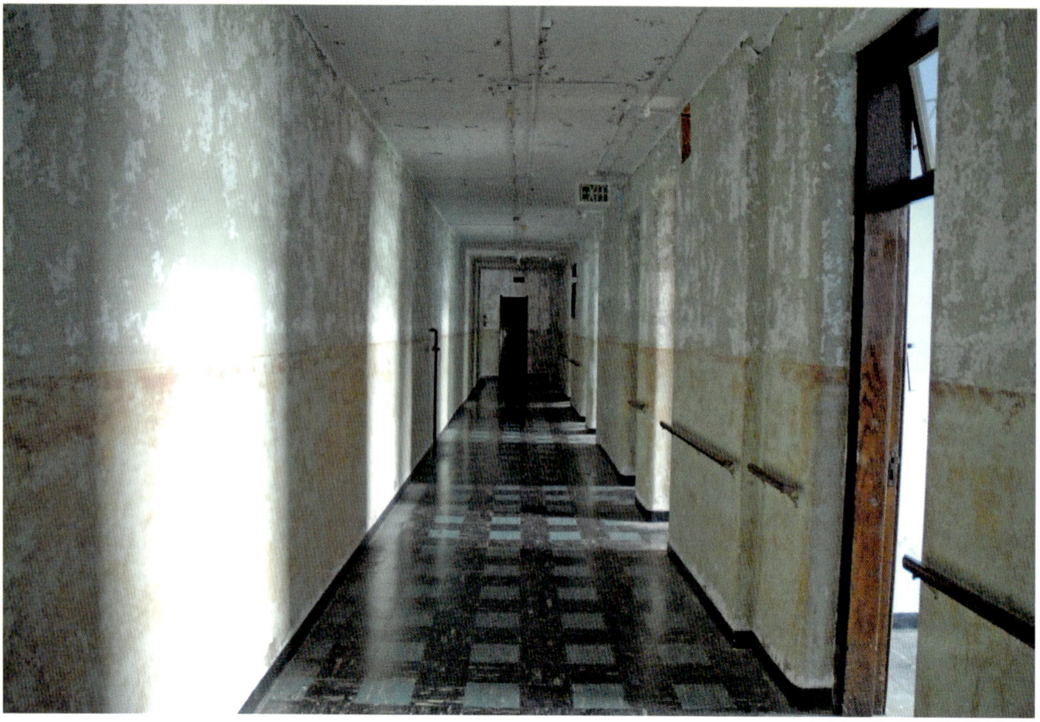

Afternoon sunlight casts shadows and reflections on the wall, with rooms visible on the right side of the hallway.

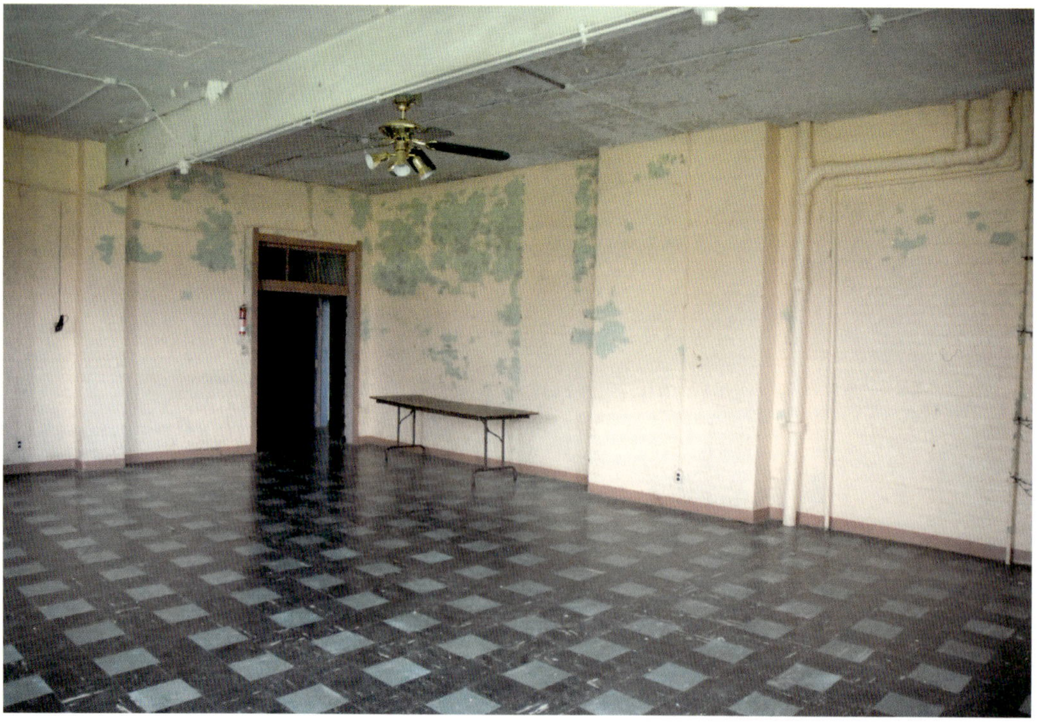

An empty room where patients went to seek solace from the harsh realities of the infirmary.

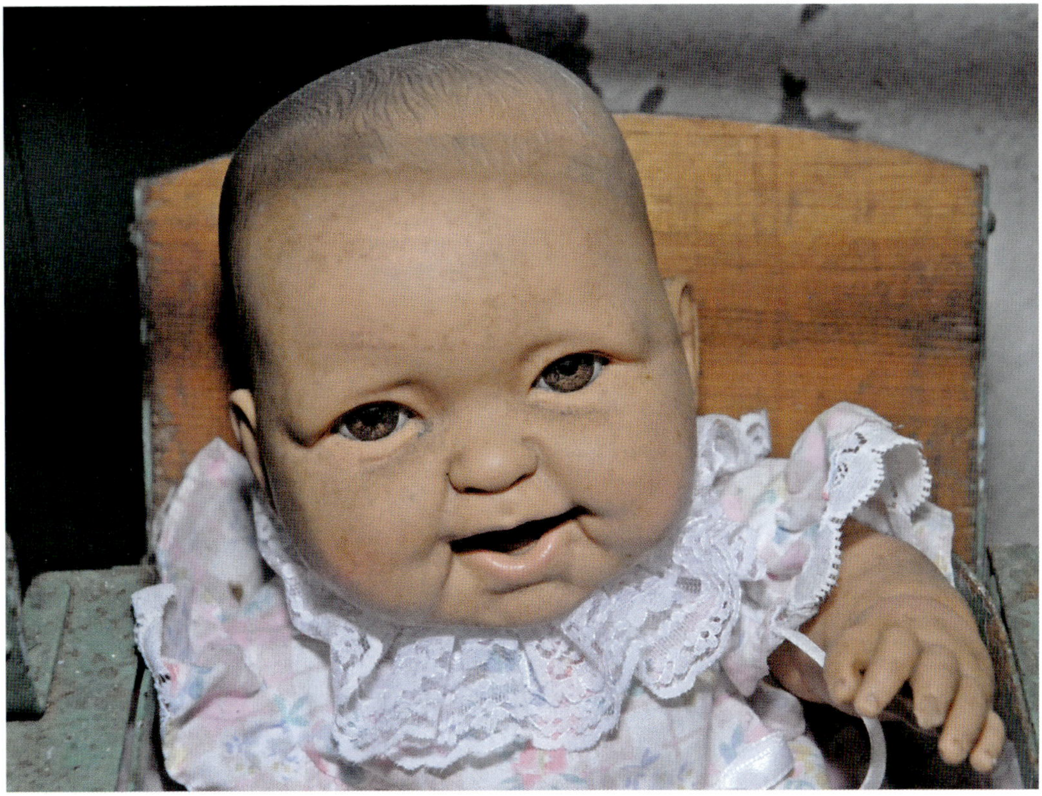

On the second floor of the Randolph County Infirmary is a collection of dolls that once belonged to patients.

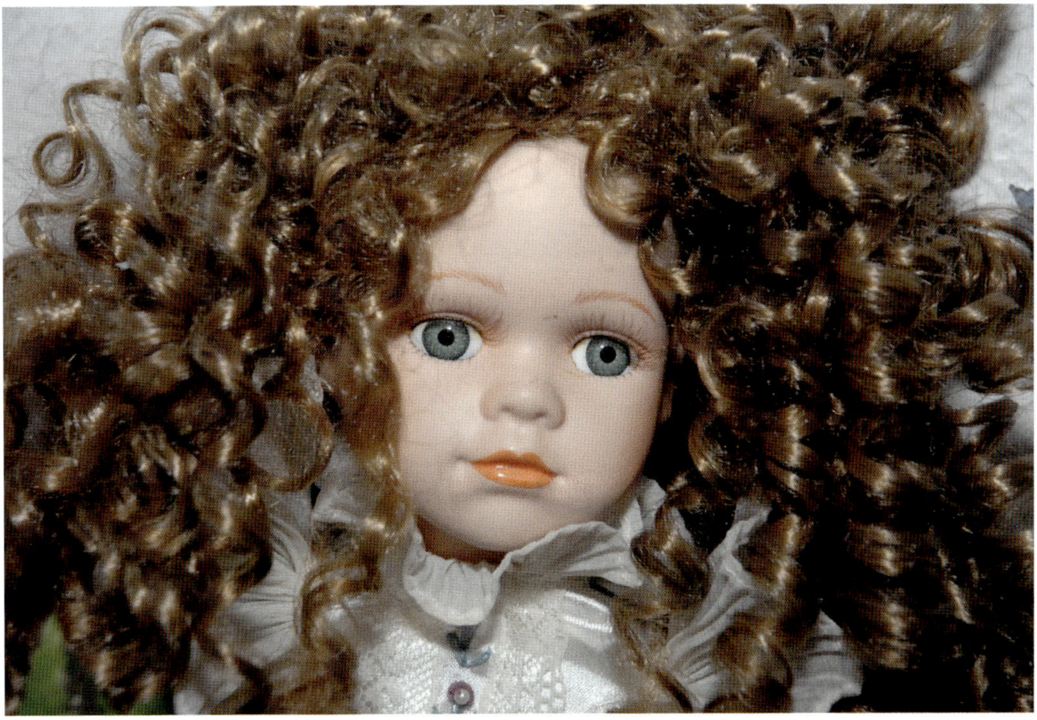

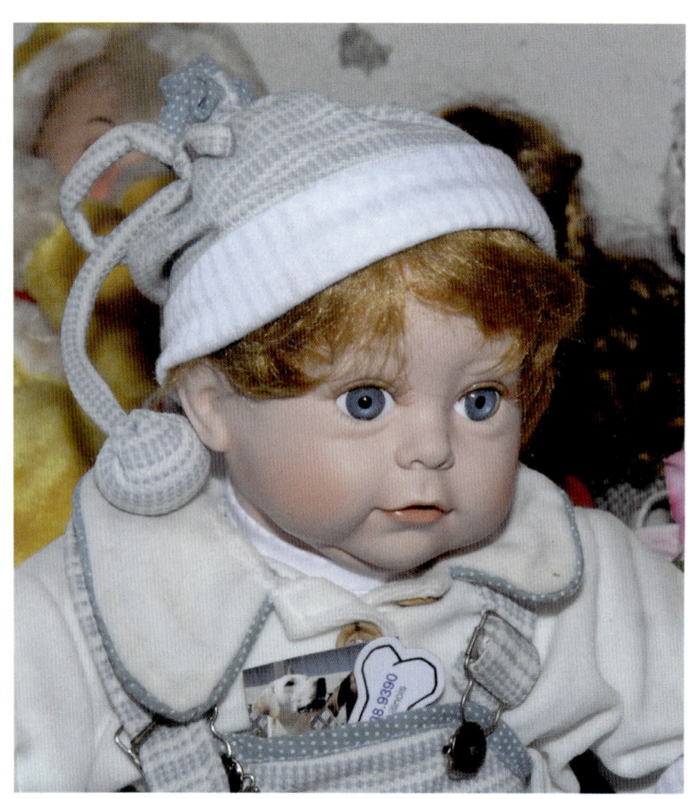

The dolls have remained untouched since the infirmary closed in 2008.

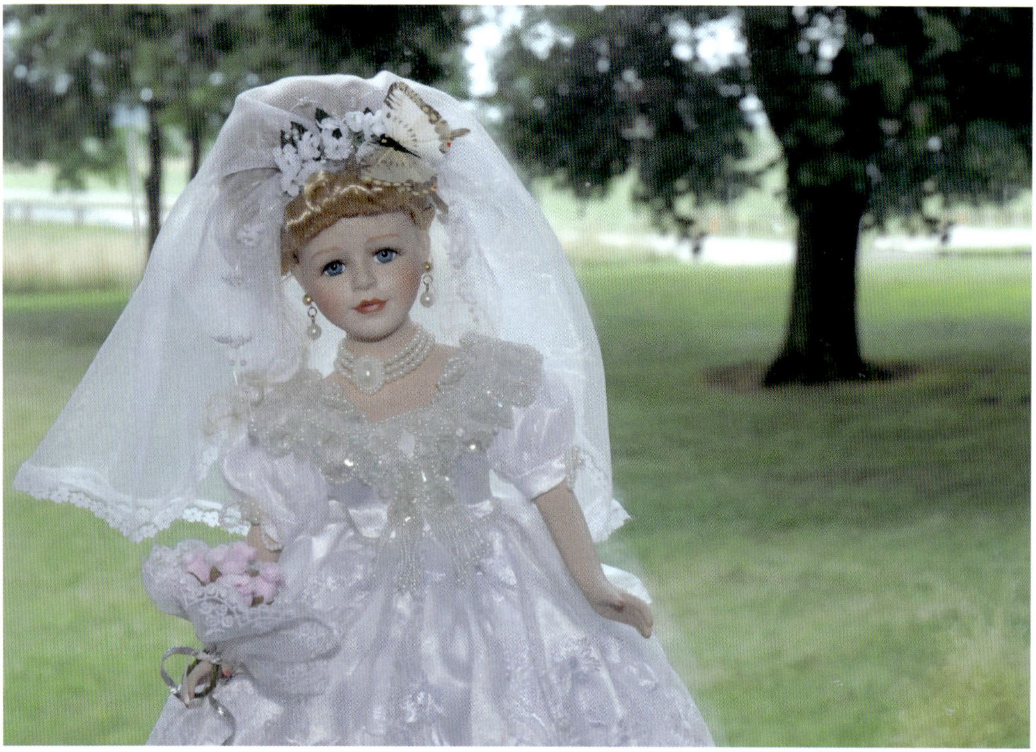